Beginning Modern Unix

Learn to Live Comfortably in a Modern Unix Environment

Manish Jain

Apress®

Beginning Modern Unix

Manish Jain
Jaipur, Rajasthan, India

ISBN-13 (pbk): 978-1-4842-3527-0   ISBN-13 (electronic): 978-1-4842-3528-7
https://doi.org/10.1007/978-1-4842-3528-7

Library of Congress Control Number: 2018950445

Managing Director, Apress Media LLC: Welmoed Spahr
Acquisitions Editor: Louise Corrigan
Development Editor: James Markham
Coordinating Editor: Nancy Chen

Cover designed by eStudioCalamar

Cover image designed by Freepik (www.freepik.com)

Distributed to the book trade worldwide by Springer Science+Business Media New York, 233 Spring Street, 6th Floor, New York, NY 10013. Phone 1-800-SPRINGER, fax (201) 348-4505, e-mail orders-ny@springer-sbm.com, or visit www.springeronline.com. Apress Media, LLC is a California LLC and the sole member (owner) is Springer Science + Business Media Finance Inc (SSBM Finance Inc). SSBM Finance Inc is a **Delaware** corporation.

For information on translations, please e-mail rights@apress.com, or visit http://www.apress.com/rights-permissions.

Apress titles may be purchased in bulk for academic, corporate, or promotional use. eBook versions and licenses are also available for most titles. For more information, reference our Print and eBook Bulk Sales web page at http://www.apress.com/bulk-sales.

Any source code or other supplementary material referenced by the author in this book is available to readers on GitHub via the book's product page, located at www.apress.com/9781484235270. For more detailed information, please visit http://www.apress.com/source-code.

Printed on acid-free paper

This book is dedicated very humbly to the Regents of the University of California, Berkeley.

Table of Contents

About the Author

Manish Jain studied Mechanical Engineering at the Indian Institute of Technology, Kharagpur, graduating in 1992. In 1998, he switched to computer programming of his own volition, and of his own education.

Following an intense period of learning, during which Manish acquired expertise in Unix and C/C++, he went on to work as a software programmer for some illustrious organizations: IBM, Pitney Bowes, and Cognizant. This was between 2002 and 2014.

Medical issues, some dating back to his childhood, then forced Manish to stay at home and do the other thing he loves: write. Between 2015 and 2017, he wrote for a variety of outlets on a freelance basis.

Beginning Modern Unix is Manish Jain's first book.

About the Technical Reviewer

 **Massimo Nardone** has more than 23 years of experience in security, web/mobile development, and cloud and IT architecture. His true IT passions are security and Android.

He has been programming and teaching others how to program with Android, Perl, PHP, Java, VB, Python, C/C++, and MySQL for more than 20 years.

He holds a Master of Science degree in Computing Science from the University of Salerno, Italy.

He has worked as a project manager, software engineer, research engineer, chief security architect, information security manager, PCI/SCADA auditor, and senior lead IT security/cloud/SCADA architect for many years.

His technical skills include security, Android, cloud, Java, MySQL, Drupal, Cobol, Perl, Web and Mobile development, MongoDB, D3, Joomla, Couchbase, C/C++, WebGL, Python, Pro Rails, Django CMS, Jekyll, Scratch, etc.

He worked as a visiting lecturer and supervisor for exercises at the Networking Laboratory of the Helsinki University of Technology (Aalto University). He holds four international patents (in the PKI, SIP, SAML, and Proxy areas).

He currently works as the Chief Information Security Office (CISO) for Cargotec Oyj and is member of ISACA Finland Chapter Board.

Massimo has reviewed more than 40 IT books for different publishing companies and is the coauthor of *Pro Android Games* (Apress, 2015).

Preface

What is Unix? It's an evolving question that is as old as the Unix operating system itself. In the beginning, there was a clear answer—Unix was what AT&T, its creator, shipped to customers and developers beginning around 1970. Its chief architects then were Ken Thompson and Dennis Ritchie.

One of the participating developers was the University of California, Berkeley. Early into its Unix journey, UCB introduced a number of fundamental improvements, which were made available open source to the rest of the world as BSD (Berkeley Software Distribution) Unix.

The AT&T line is now defunct. BSD Unix lives on as FreeBSD, and the question, "What is Unix?", lives on in its original form with not-so-clear answers.

The answer *de jure* is an operating system that meets two criteria:

- Largely complies in its behavior with the standards mandated by POSIX, an overseer committee

- Has paid the POSIX committee for Unix certification

While the first stipulation is readily agreeable, the second one is not. Linux, quite rightly as well as righteously, refused to pay the token US$1 solicited by POSIX for formal certification. I am of the humble (but well-considered) opinion that the second norm must be this and this only:

An operating system, the base (kernel and essential binaries shipped by the operating system's maker) of which is fully open source.

Note that this norm permits vendors to provide closed-source drivers, which is what happens, for instance, with nVidia graphics cards and many Epson printers. If the operating system installer prepackages any such closed-source drivers, this must be transparent to the end user.

There are two principal operating systems today that are POSIX-compliant as well as open source at the base level:

- Linux, which belongs to the GNU family.

- FreeBSD, primarily a part of the BSD family, and secondarily of the GNU family. (The BSD family has more players: OpenBSD/NetBSD/DragonFly.)

So this is what Unix is per the definition this book considers relevant for the day: GNU/Linux and BSD/FreeBSD. Any POSIX-compliant system, Apple's MacOS X for instance, that is not open source in its base qualifies as Unix-like.

Once you begin to agree with the proposed definition of Unix, you can readily appreciate why this book has been given its pithy title: *Beginning Modern Unix*. I do hope the book does justice to its title.

If you have any comments or suggestions for the book's improvement, feel free to email me. I have an email address that no one else has.

—Manish Jain
bourne.identity@hotmail.com

QOTD (Question Of The Day):

GNU = GNU's **N**ot **U**nix ✓
LINUX = **L**inux **I**s **N**ot **U**ni**X** ?

PART 1

Preparing for Part I

This book has deliberately been structured to begin with a section (Part I that follows) that does not require Unix installation. The structure is intended to make things simple for Windows users planning to migrate to FreeBSD/Linux. If you already are on a FreeBSD/Linux box, you can skip this foreword and proceed directly to Chapter 1. From this point on, this foreword assumes you are on a Windows box.

Windows users can flag off their Unix essay while remaining within Windows. This is possible because of Cygwin, a Unix-emulation suite for Windows that works remarkably well. You can use Cygwin to bone up on text-editing and Unix command-line skills. By the time you finish with Part I, you will have sufficient acumen to work with a full-fledged Unix system, which happens in Part II.

You should have at least 1GB free disk space to host a midsized Cygwin installation. Windows 7 and Windows 10 users can download the 64-bit Cygwin installer (about 1MB) using the URL: `http://www.cygwin.com/setup-x86_64.exe`.

Run the installer and select a mirror to download Cygwin packages. When you reach the `Select Packages` page, set the `View` (top-left) option to `Category`.

The only packages pre-selected by default are those under `Base`. Use the following guidelines to select a few more:

1. Click the circle between of the category `Admin` and its installation mode, `Default`, a few times, until its installation mode changes to `Install`. This will install everything under the `Admin` category: equivalent to `Admin/*`.

2. The two packages you must toggle on are Editors/vim and Editors/joe—just click the circle to the left of Skip for each to set the installation mode to Install.

3. Another couple of important packages are under the Web category: Web/wget and Web/wput. Toggle those on too.

This is a fairly lean-and-mean set of packages. If there is any other package that interests you, toggle it on too. You can try the list of add-ons underneath: Archive/zip, Archive/unzip, Archive/xz, Devel/gcc-g++, Devel/git, Devel/vala, Interpreters/dialog, Mail/email, Net/ncftp, and System/e2fsprogs.

When your selection is made, click Next to begin the download and installation process. Go through and finish the rest of the installation.

At this point, you have the Cygwin emulator in your system, which can be accessed from the Start menu or from its desktop icon. If you double-click the Cygwin icon, you will be face-to-face with the Cywgin terminal using Bash as the login shell, with a large chunk of the Unix arsenal on tap.

If you later want to add more packages to your Cygwin installation, just re-run setup, select additional packages, and go through the installation regimen again.

For Windows XP users, I suggest not using mainstream Cygwin (which no longer supports Windows XP). You can instead use the Cygwin fork Babun, available for download at the URL http://projects.reficio.org/babun/download.

Babun is an all-in-one package. Unzip the download and open a command prompt window. Use cd to set your path to the unzipped directory and run install.bat.

Babun uses Zsh (not Bash) as the default login shell. Adding a package to Babun is as simple as running the command 'pact install <package>'.

Note   The stage is now set for us to wade in to Unix. There is one term that you must first understand, *process*. A process is an instance of a running program (an executable).

Let's open C:\cygwin64\etc in Windows Explorer. Then follow these steps:

1. Right-click the plain text file fstab and open it with Notepad.

2. Right-click the plain text file shells and open it with Notepad too.

    You now have two editor (Notepad) processes running.

3. Close both the Notepad windows.

4. It is possible for a single editor process to open up both files. Open a shell (Cygwin Bash or Babun Zsh).

5. Use the shell to run the command 'vim /etc/hosts'.

6. Inside the vim window, issue the following vim command
    :split /etc/shells.

    You now have one single editor (vim) process looking into two files.

7. Close the vim session with the vim command :qa

Every time a new process is launched, the operating system has to set aside quite a few dedicated resources for the process. At the very least, it sets aside a thread (corridor for instructions to be fed to the CPU), memory, file handles, and a process ID.

## CHAPTER 1

Editing Text with Vim and Joe

In the world of Unix, there is—quite happily for everyone—just one type of document: plain text.

It makes sense that any Unix quest should begin with acquisition of skills for editing text. While graphical text editors (of which there is an entire slew) make very good scratchpads when X is around, expertise with console-mode text editing is what gives you the ability to ease into Unix.

This is such an important aspect that I opine that one should acquire text editing skills first and any Unix-specific skills later—not the other way round. It does not help if you are working with an operating system (Unix in particular) under which you have no idea how to insert or delete a line of text in a plain-text file. Before you can get to the web browser to Google how to use the text editor, you will likely need to get into the text editor itself—possibly with no graphical environment around yet.

I therefore begin this book with this particular chapter, which you can use to leverage editing skills under Windows very easily as well. Both Vim and Joe, the venerable Unix text editors that I discuss, are available as Windows applications.

1.1 A Brief History of Unix Text Editors

In retrospect, it is hard to believe that when AT&T first shipped Unix circa 1970, for all its might and goods, it did not have a text editor. The only "editor" that shipped with Unix in those days was the ed command, which was so supremely unfriendly—designed as it was for a pure teletype interface—that it contributed a good deal to the "Unix is difficult" impression that goes around to this day.

© Manish Jain 2018
M. Jain, *Beginning Modern Unix*, https://doi.org/10.1007/978-1-4842-3528-7_1

It fell to the mantle of the University of California, Berkeley (where BSD Unix—now known as FreeBSD—was born) to set Unix right. UCB pioneered three major components that revolutionized Unix and computing:

- *The C shell*: A significant improvement over the Bourne shell in terms of user interaction (but not in terms as a scripting environment).

- *Berkeley sockets*: These are the sockets that everyone uses for networking all over the world (Microsoft® Windows® included).

- *The vi editor*: This was the first full-screen Unix text editor.

The vi editor, created by the cheery-named Bill Joy—a graduate student at UCB—was a major step. vi, short for *visual*, permitted users to visually edit text files. Although still not particularly user-friendly by modern-day standards, it permitted users something in the nature of a WYSIWYG (what you see is what you get) experience when editing text files (and their family members: source code).

The vi editor still exists in its original form in FreeBSD. If there is no other editor around, the good, old vi command would still be there.

Whether you are working with the pristine vi or with the latest generation of editors, there are a few terms common to all editors that you need to understand.

1.2 Important Terms

1.2.1 Line

I'll make this absolutely clear once and then you must always remember this: a line is not a line, and what is not a line is a line. I hope that's clear.

Since I suspect there would be a few grumbles in the backbenches, I will try to shed some light on this delicate matter.

For an example, this is a pretty well-recognized statement you would have seen sometime or the other:

```
<<<
THIS SOFTWARE IS PROVIDED BY THE AUTHOR AND CONTRIBUTORS AS IS AND
ANY EXPRESS OR IMPLIED WARRANTIES ARE DISCLAIMED. IN NO EVENT SHALL
THE CONTRIBUTORS BE LIABLE FOR ANY DAMAGES.
>>>
```

Question of the day: How many lines can you count between the opening <<< and the closing >>>? (The <<< and >>> are placeholders for carriage return/linefeed generated with the ⎡Enter⎤ button, of which there are none in the main body of the text.)

Unless you are poor at counting, you would be able to make out that the text wraps around two times, stopping roughly three-quarters to the end in its last track.

So the answer is a simple one: 2.5+ (almost three).

That answer is wrong. Those of the linguistic bend would immediately spot that the period after DISCLAIMED splits the text in the middle—so there are not 2.5+ lines, but precisely two.

The fight between the mathematically gifted and the linguistic experts is not an easy one. Particularly when both are wrong.

In the world of text editing, there is just one line in that text, spread over two sentences and three rows. What counts as a line in text is all that goes between two consecutive newlines: carriage-returns (CR) and/or linefeeds (LF). While editing text, a newline is what you get when you press ⎡Enter⎤.

The opening line of a text file is an exception. That line has no leading CR/LF, but does have a trailing one.

The closing line of a text file is *not* an exception. That has a leading CR/LF, and must have a trailing one too. If you forget to append the trailing newline, most editors will save the day for you by appending one automatically. If the editor does not, the last line is technically orphaned. If you pass the file to a line-count algorithm (wc, for instance), the algorithm will likely miss the last line.

DOS (and consequently Windows) uses CR (ASCII code 13) and LF (ASCII code 10) to denote a newline, while Unix uses LF only. There are a few tools, like unix2dos and flip, that can do conversion between the two formats.

We now have one rudimentary idea in the bag. The next idea is not rudimentary, but is crucial for your bag, so that you can work smart with the editor and the Unix shell.

1.2.2 Regular Expressions: What You Need To Know Right Now

Quite frankly, I would have liked to skip the discussion of regular expressions until a later point in this book. But, after due consideration, there really is no way I can elucidate console-mode text editing without first making sure you understand regular expressions.

We'll initiate the understanding with a fundamental truth about Tinkerbell, my cat:

```
"i love TinkerbeLL 24*7"
```

If you ignore the enclosing double quotes, you will agree:

- The text starts with a lowercase letter (`i`)
- The text has one punctuation character (`*`) followed by a closing digit (`7`)

With this agreement in place, you might wonder whether there is a computing engine that can spot such easy-to-spot patterns in text?

The answer is yes. That engine is called regular expressions and is implemented by `grep` (pattern searcher) as well as by every single text editor available in Unix.

This might sound like a good, cool deal—and it is. Let's try to match our example text for regular expressions with `grep`, one match for each of the two patterns we agreed upon:

```
echo "i love TinkerbeLL 24*7" | grep '^[[:lower:]]'
```

The vertical bar (the *pipe*) in the middle says, "Let the side on the right use the output (result) of the left side". And on the left side, we have the `echo` command, which just prints whatever it is given.

The pattern to be matched here by the `grep` command asks (under single quotes) for a couple of tokens:

`^` is the token that matches the beginning of a line.

`[[:lower:]]` asks for a lowercase alphabetic character.

We could have relaxed things a bit by using `[[:alpha:]]` in place of `[[:lower:]]`. That would not have affected the outcome because `[[:alpha:]]` just means an alphabetic character, with both `[[:upper:]]` (uppercase) and `[[:lower:]]` (lowercase) permitted.

Since both conditions have been met, `grep` will echo the string `"i love TinkerbeLL 24*7"` on your output device (monitor), which is confirmation that the pattern matched.

```
echo "i love TinkerbeLL 24*7" | grep '[[:punct:]][[:digit:]]$'
```

This pattern says three things need to be matched:

- Any punctuation character
- A numeric character

- The dollar sign at the end demands that the combination of the punctuation and numeric characters is needed at the end of the line

Since every requirement is again met, `grep` will again print the string `"i love TinkerbeLL 24*7"` on your display.

While we looked at a few character classes (a deserved nomenclature for those `[[:XYZ:]]` creatures), one has missed our attention, and that's the `[[:space:]]` class. Anything that is whitespace (space or tab) qualifies as `[[:space:]]`. Note that a single tab character can also be denoted with the regular expression `\t`.

There are a few RE (regular expression) builders that you need to know at this stage.

- The `.` character lets you search for exactly one character as a fill-in.

```
echo "i love TinkerbeLL 24*7" | grep 'T.n'
# This asks "Is there exactly one character between 'T' and 'n'" => SUCCESS
```

Note   Since any character matches for `.` (the period character), you match for a literal period using `\.`. Use of backslash to match a character literal is called an escape sequence. As you might have already induced, to match a literal backslash, one can use `\\`

- The `*` character lets you ask for zero or more occurrences of the previous character's class (not necessarily the same character, just its type).

```
echo "i love TinkerbeLL 24*7" | grep 'T..*n'
# This asks "Is there at least one character between 'T' and 'n'" => SUCCESS
```

Matching for a specific number of occurrences is facilitated by the syntax `\{N\}` - as illustrated in this next example:

```
echo "i love TinkerbeLL 24*7" | grep 'T.\{2\}n'
# Are there exactly two characters between T and n ? => FAILURE
```

When `grep` fails to match the requested pattern, there is no output. This is different from an error condition: if `grep` were to run into an error condition parsing your RE, it would throw a fit at the console - quite legitimately too.

If you are now beginning to get the hang of regular expressions, let's next try to find out whether any character in our text is repeated (i.e., occurs twice in succession).

This is made possible by back-references. You can store a token for reference later by using the technology \(TOKEN\), and then refer to it later as \1 (which means get a TOKEN here too).

```
echo "i love TinkerbeLL 24*7" | grep '\(.\)\(\1\)'
```

Since there are two consecutive L characters in the string, this pattern matches too.

You will often need to match for words. For instance, our example text has the string "Tinker", but not as a word. The law of word boundaries states that a word must have whitespace (or special characters) on both sides. Since "Tinker" is followed by a regular character (b), it does not qualify as a word. Of course, "TinkerbeLL" does.

We can confirm this hypothesis with a few quick examples that illustrate two different (and equivalent) ways to check for word boundaries:

```
echo "i love TinkerbeLL 24*7" | grep -w 'Tinker'
# This asks "Is Tinker a word in the text" => FAILURE

echo "i love TinkerbeLL 24*7" | grep '\<TinkerbeLL\>'
# This asks "Is TinkerbeLL a word in the text" => SUCCESS
```

You can make the match case-insensitive with the -i option:

```
echo "i love TinkerbeLL 24*7" | grep -i '\<tinkerbell\>'
# This asks "Is tinkerbell a case-insensitive word in the text" => SUCCESS
```

The question now is not whether I love Tinkerbell, but whether are you are falling in love with regular expressions. If your answer is no, you are perhaps reading the wrong book at the wrong time. Otherwise, here's a small exercise for you (with no Googling permitted; using grep --help and man grep are permitted though).

Using the grep command, print the portion of our example text ("i love TinkerbeLL 24*7") that is purely a sequence of numeric or punctuation characters. Stated another way, get the 24*7 part, and nothing else.

Hints:

- The -o option of grep lets you print only the matching portion.

- The double square brackets of the character class notation [[:XYZ:]] exist for a reason. Multiple character classes can be clubbed as [[:class1:][:class2:]], with any of the club being character literals.

Here's an example:

```
^[aeiou[:upper:]]
```

This asks for any text that begins with a lowercase vowel or an uppercase letter. Both "i am" and "He is" would match, but "we are" won't.

If you are alive and kicking in our RE discourse, you'll get the answer—it might get printed one character per line or in a single line, either of which is acceptable.

We now quickly discuss the other terms of immediate interest in editing jargon.

1.2.3 Remaining Terms of Endearment

One term in text editing lingo is *buffer*, which denotes the working copy (hosted in memory) of a file. This is what the text editor uses as a playground for text manipulation, and it holds your current goods - which can be vastly different from what lies in the disk file. When you save the file, the buffer gets mirrored to storage. The contents of the buffer and file are then exactly the same, until you make the next change in the buffer.

Another term is *window*. That means the portion of the buffer that is currently being displayed by the editor. If the buffer holds 1000 lines, don't expect all of them to show up on the display device. Only the portion that can fit in the editor's current view is deemed the window's text, and this will dynamically change as you scroll the text.

Occasionally, all this can get a mite confusing. If so, just tag the context.

We are now ready to invade the world of text editors. Both the sections that follow (Vim and Joe) have installation notes tucked in at the end.

1.3 Vi IMproved (Vim)

In the world of text editors, Vim is God, even if you are an atheist. Created by Bram Moolenaar, a Dutch gentleman devoted to charities for Uganda, Vim builds on the vi editor by adding a whole lot of user-friendliness, as well as bells and whistles that vi lacks. The bells and whistles in Vim derive not from vi, but from a wagonload of libraries (81 on my system, compared to just three that vi links to).

Vim is what is called a *modal editor*. This means that when it's opened, it is ready not for text input, but for you to execute commands, much like a shell. That mode is called Command (or Normal) mode.

If you are using Vim for the first time, you probably want to get into Insert (or input) mode to put something in a file. The command for Insert/Input mode is i.

When you're done inserting text, you need to save it, which is a two-step operation:

1.   Press the Escape key Esc to return to Command mode.

2.   Use :w <file_name> to save the text as <file_name>.

If you would like to exit Vim, use the :q command.

At this stage, I suggest that you put the following in your ~/.vimrc configuration file:

```
set laststatus=2
set ruler
set showmode
```

Here are the commands to do that:

```
echo "set laststatus=2" >> ~/.vimrc
echo "set ruler" >> ~/.vimrc
echo "set showmode" >> ~/.vimrc
```

That configuration renders a nifty status line near the bottom of Vim's window, which:

- Gets you the best of late-breaking news (name of file, cursor position, and current operational mode)

- Yields a split between the text zone and the command entry section at the bottom

While you now know the first steps in Vim, you'll do yourself an immense favor by invoking the vimtutor command, which does an excellent job of explaining text editing under Vim. While Unix and Cygwin have the vimtutor command if Vim is installed, installing gvim (graphical Vim) under Windows (via its setup executable) lends you access to the tutor through the Start menu also.

Before you proceed to the material, be sure you have gone through the graduation accorded by vimtutor at least once, perhaps a couple of times, hopefully thrice. I'll confirm your tryst with the tutor with a few questions. Each time you fail to answer, you must go through the tutor exercise again. No other help is permitted.

A few points that may not be covered in `vimtutor` but are needed for our quiz are mentioned here:

- When operating on words with actions like copy (y) and delete (d), a denotes the start-of-word, while e denotes the end-of-word.

- Edit operations that act on (or to the right of) the cursor position can often be made to go left using the command's uppercase. So P pastes to the cursor's left, and X deletes a character to the left.

- fx searches the current line in the forward direction for the character x, while Fx searches backward.

Figure 1-1 holds the sentences for our Vim quiz. You need to work with the primary sentence (until prompted to use the secondary sentence too).

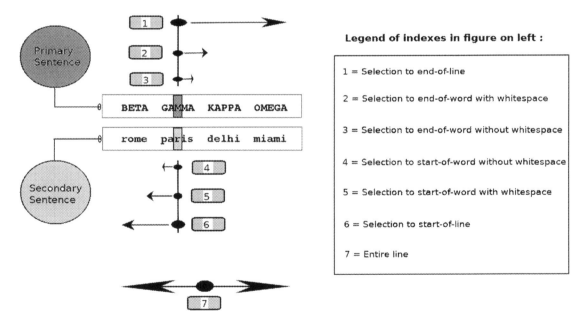

Figure 1-1. *Vim quiz sentences*

If you want to copy sentences to your Vim buffer, use the following:

```
BETA GAMMA KAPPA OMEGA
rome paris delhi miami
```

Copy the text (which is space-separated), press i in Vim, right-click, and choose paste. Move the cursor until the current character is the first M of GAMMA.

13

Note   Instructions to follow each time you carry out a command:

1.   Undo the last change (if any). If you are wondering how to undo the last change, run the command `vimtutor`.

2.   Return (if needed) to command mode, with the cursor placed on the first M of GAMMA again.

Tip to remember for the quiz that follows: a vowel can be matched as a regular expression using the character group `[aAeEiIoOuU]`.

I will now start the Vim quiz, with questions you will need to answer right until the end of this section. Each such question I call a "step".

Enter Command (Normal) mode and then follow these steps:

1.   Move the cursor to the beginning of the next word.

2.   Move the cursor to the end of the line.

3.   Delete the current character (which should be the first M of GAMMA).

4.   Delete the current character along with one on its left and the one on its right.

5.   Replace the current character with m.

6.   Change the case of the current character without using r in your command.

7.   Delete the current word (from cursor position to end-of-word) without touching the trailing whitespace.

8.   Paste the current word (from cursor position to end-of-word) at the beginning of the next word.

9.   Delete the current word from start-of-word to end-of-word (along with trailing whitespace).

10.   Insert the contents of the /etc/fstab file between the two lines.

11.   Change all the text to start-of-line to 1234.

12.   Change all the text to end-of-line to 789.

13.   Change the entire line to 567.

14.   Move the current (entire) line one line below (i.e., delete the current line and paste it underneath itself).

15.   Change three characters forward (current character and the next two) to 1234 (on-screen character counting not permitted).

16.   Change three characters backward (current character and the previous two) to 1234 (on-screen character counting not permitted).

17.   Insert 1234 at the beginning of the line.

18.   Append 789 at the end of the line.

19.   Replace all M characters in the line with n.

20.   Item 20 in first enumeration removed to make way for new item# 2 in second enumeration.

21.   Insert the output of the ls command between the two lines.

You will now need to use the secondary sentence as well:

1.   Delete both lines using d in your command a maximum of twice.

2.   Copy and paste both lines at the bottom of the buffer.

3.   Change all the vowels in the two lines to h using a single s command.

4.   Move the cursor to the start of the first line and then traverse (jump through) all the A characters in the line without using /.

5.   Move the cursor to the end of the second line and then traverse (jump through) all the vowels from end-of-second-line to start-of-first-line.

If you scored 25/25, continue reading.

There are a few points that you might have already grasped, but I do not like to leave it to wishful thinking:

- You can use ˆ to move the cursor to the first non-blank character in the current line, or 0 to move to the first character in the line.

- The . command in Vim repeats the last change.

- In Vim, <motion> means the amount of text being manipulated.

Here are a few `<motion>` entities and their meanings:

ˆ	To the beginning of line
e	To the end-of-word without whitespace
w	To the end-of-word with whitespace
b	To the start-of-word without whitespace
$	To the end of line

We'll continue with material and steps as needed, with self-monitoring only from now on.

1.3.1 Moving Around in the Buffer

Moving the cursor in the Vim buffer is easy:

h   `Left` : Moves left one character
j   `Down`: Moves one character south
k   `Up` : Moves one character north
l   `Right` : Moves one character right

You can make larger jumps with `Page Up` or `Ctrl`+`B`, and `Page Down` or `Ctrl`+`F`.

While keyboard shortcuts are set up with Vim with no extra effort, you should still remember the hjkl navigation toolbox mentioned here. When nothing else works (while, for example, recording a Vim macro), those keys still will.

There are other ways to obtain big jumps. A couple of often-needed jumps are to the buffer's first and last lines.

The nG command moves the cursor to the buffer's line number n. G by itself moves to the the last line, whereas gg moves to the first line.

There is an alternative way to move to top and bottom of the buffer:

```
:1    # move to the first line
:$    # move to the last line
```

If you want to move the cursor around in the window, there are window-specific commands too:

```
H     # move the cursor to the top line in the window
L     # move the cursor to the bottom line in the window
zt    # make the current line the top line in the window
zb    # make the current line the bottom line in the window
```

1.3.2 Registers and Clipboard Integration

While it is very easy to yank (copy) text with (y<motion>) to and paste (p) it from Vim's own scratchpad (an anonymous register), this is not the only Vim facility for yanking text around.

Vim has named registers too—26 of them, one for each letter of the English alphabet. Not surprisingly, those registers are named a through z.

To yank the current line into register a, you can tell Vim this:

```
"ayy      # that is a double-quote followed by ayy
```

To paste the contents of register a, you can later issue "ap

One masterful idea in Vim is the process of appending to the registers. If you yank something into register A (the uppercase of a), Vim will append the yanked text to the existing contents of register a. If the user then pastes the text residing in the register, (s)he will collect the original yank plus the appendage.

Vim integrates nicely with the system's clipboard too, which permits text exchange with other applications (and, of course, itself as well).

Vim denotes the clipboard as a register with the + character. So to copy text to the clipboard, you use:

```
"+y<motion>
```

To paste the contents of the clipboard, you use:

```
"+p
```

Here are a couple of steps for you:

1. Copy the first line (primary sentence in Figure 1-1) to the system's clipboard.

2. Paste the contents of the system's clipboard below the first line.

Note   To paste clipboard contents inside a Vim buffer using a mouse, right-click and then press i in Vim (to get yourself into Insert mode) before pasting.

1.3.3 Marks

One cool way to navigate text in your file's buffer is with Vim marks, which simulate bookmarks.

The mq command places the mark q on the current line.

To get to this position from anywhere in the file, you use 'q

The '' command (that's two single quotes) lets you jump between marks (as well as previously recorded locations).

Here are a few very easy steps to ensure you remember marks:

1. Place mark x in the primary sentence and mark y in secondary sentence.

2. Use the marks to jump between the sentences.

3. Repeat the jumps by using ''.

1.3.4 Find and Replace

By now, I suppose you are aware that the Normal command fq searches ahead in the current line for character q, whereas Fq searches backward.

Searching forward for the text xyz is done with /xyz

To search backward, use ?xyz

You can repeat a search in the same direction with n (or in the reverse direction with N).

One particularly handy search is the * command, which searches for the word under the cursor in the forward direction. The # command searches backward.

Substitution operations work with the s command, which supports ranges.

Use the :[range]s/abc/xyz/[modifiers] command to substitute the string abc with xyz. A few often-used modifiers include:

i: Ignore case-sensitivity

g: Substitute for each occurrence; not just the first one in the line

e: Do not treat it as error if no substitution was made

c: Prompt for confirmation with each substitution being made

If no [range] is specified, substitutions will take place on the current line only. When you're specifying [range], you need to give two line numbers separated by a comma (,):

1   represents the number of the first line in the file

.   represents the current line number

$ represents the number of the last line in the file

The % character represents all the lines in the file - a short form for 1,$

This is the nuts and bolts of find and replace. But the one feature you are bound to start using as you work with Vim (or any other Unix text editor) is using regular expressions for find and replace.

This feature is a very welcome one. We are dealing with just two sentences. But see how easy it makes life if you decide to replace all the whitespace sequences with one tab each:

```
:%s/[[:space:]][[:space:]]*/\t/g
```

You can imagine what it would be like to manually make those changes in a file that is one million lines!

So here's one of those steps to get your Vim and RE world zooming. This is a tough one, but if you have been picking up my regular expression wisdoms, you'll get it:

1. Using regular expression-based find and replace, remove the hearts in the eight words in our two sentences, meaning:

    ```
    BETA => BA; GAMMA => GA; KAPPA => KA; OMEGA => OA
    rome => re; paris => ps; delhi => di; miami => mi
    ```

A solution is available in the appendix, but you should try it on your own first.

1.3.5 Visual Selection Modes

Visual selection, briefly touched on in `vimtutor`, is one of the most powerful features in Vim. While not a distinct mode by itself, it exists as a sub-mode of Normal mode and lets you move the cursor around to make a selection bigger or smaller, getting visual feedback in real-time about the text you are playing with.

There are three distinct ways you can enter Visual selection:

v for character-based selection
V for line-based selection
[Ctrl] + [v] for block-based selection

You will need to use these commands by yourself in your buffer to get familiar with how the selection expands and contracts with keystrokes.

Once you are familiar, continue with these steps:

1. Delete both lines using d in your command just once.

2. With the cursor placed on the first A of GAMMA, delete the hearts of GAMMA (leaving GA) and paris (leaving ps) with a single command. Leave all the other words untouched.

19

Visual selection makes indenting a range of lines very easy:

- To indent a range of lines, use V to define your range, and then press >

- To un-indent a range of lines, use V to define your range, and then press <

Commenting a range is a mite trickier, but still a walk in the park. I should mention at this point what constitutes a comment sequence is environment-defined:

- C and Vala use //

- Shell scripts use #

- Latex uses %

Interestingly, Vim's own configuration file (`~/.vimrc`) uses ".
(That's one double-quote character).
It's a mad world, but let's use the # commenting character.
To comment a range of lines, place your cursor on the top-left character, and then follow these steps:

1. Press `Ctrl` + `v` and travel south to define your range.

2. Press I (must be uppercase).

3. Insert #.

4. Escape to Command mode.

Your commenting will magically pop up for the whole selected range.

Uncommenting follows a similar approach. To uncomment a range of lines, place your cursor on the top-left commenting character, and then

1. Press `Ctrl` + `v` and travel south/southeast to select the block that hosts the commenting characters.

2. Press `x` (or `d`; both are equally good).

3. Original manuscript error. Step 3 is entirely unneeded.

You would be mighty disappointed if find and replace didn't work in a Visual selection. Bram Moolenaar's brainchild leaves you nothing to fret about, with full-fledged support of regular expressions to boot.

Let's say you want to change all words ending with i in the secondary sentence to end with I.

There are multiple ways to do this. Here is a game plan that uses Visual selection.

Move down into the secondary sentence and press V to start line-based Visual selection. Then use the following command:

```
:'<,'>s/\<\(..*\)i\>/\1I/g
```

That converts delhi to delhI and miami to miamI.

You don't need to bother about the :'<,'> at the beginning of the command. Vim will fill that portion automatically when you press : with a Visual selection underway. '<,'> is Vim's way of referring to the selection made.

There are still more things you can do with Visual selections:

```
:'<,'>w <file>
Writes the selected range to <file>
```

```
:'<,'>w>> <file>
Appends the selected range to <file>, which must already exist
```

One final point shows how context-specific Vim commands can be. You might remember from your vimtutor wheeling and dealing that "u is for undo". That's true, but not across the board. With a Visual selection made, the u command changes the selection to lowercase (while U changes it to uppercase).

1.3.6 Recording and Playing Macros

Unix console-mode text editors try to stick close to the philosophy of "Do it once". If you need to do it again, let the system repeat "it" whenever and wherever needed.

Snuggled right in the heart of that tenet is the concept of macros. If you need to carry out a complex series of operations at multiple locations in a large file, do it carefully the first time and let Vim record your keystrokes. The next time around, don't operate; just tell Vim to replay the recording.

As an example of how powerful Vim macros are, we'll use a small trick up the publisher's alley, where the numerals 1-10 should be represented as words, but 11 and up are written as numbers: 1 should be one, 2 should be two, 3 should be three, but 11 is written as 11.

This is what we will play with (three newline-terminated sentences):

```
<<<
I have 2 bananas which I shall eat 1 by 1.
3 is company, but more than 3 is a crowd.
At times, 11 is a team.
>>>
```

This is what we want in the end:

```
<<<
I have two bananas which I shall eat one by one.
Three is company, but more than three is a crowd.
At times, 11 is a team.
>>>
```

To achieve the transformation, we can use a Vim macro, of which Vim permits 26 to the user, each one named as a letter of the English alphabet. We will record our macro as macro a.

To start the recording, we use the q command, qa, which starts the recording stored in register a. (Note the close connection between macros and registers.) When the recording starts, Vim will display the "recording @a" diagnostic message in the command entry window.

The following macro forces three substitutions in the top line:

```
:s/\<1\>/one/ge
:s/\<2\>/two/ge
:s/\<3\>/three/ge
```

We now stop the recording with the q command, and our macro at this stage looks like this:

```
:s/\<1\>/one/ge^M:s/\<2\>/two/ge^M:s/\<3\>/three/ge^M
```

The ^M in the macro stands for a carriage return, which can be simulated in plain text inside a Vim buffer with Ctrl + v followed by Ctrl + M.

Note that you need to be in Insert mode when you type in the sequence. Ctrl + v asks Vim to insert the next character literally, while Ctrl + M is the equivalent of a carriage return (ASCII 13).

If you want to see the contents of a macro, it is incredibly easy. If the macro name is z, just paste the contents of the register z somewhere, which essentially means use the Vim command "zp

We now cycle the cursor through each of the next two lines and issue the command @a, which means we are asking Vim to execute the macro named a on this line too. (Note the nifty @@ shortcut. It can be used to repeat the last macro executed. So you can execute @a on the middle line, and then @@ on the bottom line.)

By the time we finish these operations on the text, it looks like this:

```
I have two bananas which I shall eat one by one.
three is company, but more than three is a crowd.
At times, 11 is a team.
```

That's a pretty decent result, but we won't rest in peace until we capitalize the "three is company" line. So we hop on to the top line again and restart the recording, but this time we don't record in a new register. Instead we record in register A, which is a way saying, "Append this recording to the contents of register a". The command for this purpose would be qA.

```
:s/^\<one\>/One/e
:s/^\<two\>/Two/e
:s/^\<three\>/Three/e
```

The commands result in the following appended to register a:

```
:s/^\<one\>/One/e^M:s/^\<two\>/Two/e^M:s/^\<three\>/Three/e^M
```

That looks a bit scary, but all it is doing is asking for one/two/three to be capitalized if the string is at the beginning of a line.

When recording finishes, we can ask Vim to invoke @a upon each of the other two sentences, fetching us the transformed text.

You might not guess it, but one of the beauties of a Vim macro is that it may never actually be recorded, and yet be available for execution.

Let's return to the first of our macros:

```
:s/\<1\>/one/ge^M:s/\<2\>/two/ge^M:s/\<3\>/three/ge^M
```

If you copy the macro text to register b, you can treat b as a macro and execute it directly with @b. It goes without saying that, unless you are Bram Moolenaar, this is one practice you need not make a standard way of life.

1.3.7 Vim Utilities

Vim has a fair number of utilities built into it too.

We'll have a quick look at some important ones.

1) When editing a file, you might come across a character that's not part of the ASCII character set, although it might look like one. Funny things like those occur every once in a while.

    While there is no way the editor can block out "funny" characters, you can at your leisure check the contents of your file with the Vim command `ga`. That command displays the ASCII value of the character under the cursor.

    If the `ga` command (short for Get ASCII) of Vim prints a decimal value greater than 127 for any character in the file, it would suggest that this is not a good, plain ASCII text file.

2) The `gf` command (Goto File) is a quick way to open a file in an existing Vim session. If your cursor is placed on a file path that you need opened, you can use `gf` to look into that text file.

3) Vim has a built-in encryption facility. If you invoke Vim with the `-x` argument, it will prompt you for an encryption key, which then becomes the password needed to access the contents of the file. The user can return to unencrypted mode by using the Vim command:

    `:set key=`

    While Vim's encryption is weak, it is a good, easy way to keep out the casual sniffer and prowler. It will not deter the expert hacker with plenty of time to spare.

4) If you want to print the current file, use `:ha!` (short for hardcopy).

1.3.8 Vim Configuration

As you might expect, a supremely flexible and power-packed editor like Vim has a humongous range of configuration options. The following line in my Vim configuration file `~/.vimrc`, for instance, ensures that there is no visible bell each time I go past the top or bottom of the buffer:

```
set vb t_vb=
```

Settings can be conveyed to Vim as part of the configuration in `~/.vimrc`, or on a per-session basis by passing the setting in as a Normal mode command.

`set ruler` in `~/.vimrc` switches on the ruler that shows the cursor position. If, at runtime, you pass in the command `:set noruler` to Vim, the ruler disappears.

You can even query existing Vim settings, typically by using the ? character in place of = (and everything after it).

For instance, if you want to find out whether the option `showmode` is on, you can use this:

```
:set showmode?
```

If the setting is on, Vim will print `showmode` and if it is off, Vim will print `noshowmode`.

If you were to query for a numeric setting such as `laststatus`, Vim will print `laststatus=2`.

I won't delve into each Vim setting. I'll leave it you to look them up when the time is right. Here are a few settings you can get detailed online help about with the Vim command `:help <topic>`:

```
autoindent
nohlsearch
nonumber
ruler
linebreak
wrap
laststatus
tabstop
shiftwidth
noexpandtab
showmode
nocompatible
```

```
vb
syntax
ignorecase
textwidth
nomodeline
```

Many editors (including Vim) have the questionable habit of creating backups when writing to a file. This is not particularly heartening since it pollutes the filesystem with wanton backup files.

Luckily, putting the following in `~/.vimrc` takes care of the pollution:

```
set nobackup
set nowritebackup
set noundofile
```

With this configured, Vim will studiously work with the text file only, nothing else. (Vim will still create a hidden swap file, but that does not persist—when you exit Vim, the swap file gets deleted automatically.)

Since you can now start browsing `help` for common Vim settings, we'll move on to a nicety that is a little bit more than a setting to turn on/off: key mapping.

Vim permits keyboard keys to be mapped to functions.

If, for example, you are working with a mixture of DOS and Unix files, you might like to change every file to the same format. So you can set up a keyboard-mapped function in your `~/.vimrc`:

```
:map <F11> :set fileformat=unix<CR>:w<CR>
```

If you now press F11 while editing a file in Vim, the file will be converted to Unix format and saved as such.

`<CR>`, as you might have guessed, denotes a carriage return. Note that this mapping does not just convert the format, but also saves the converted file, right down to the second `<CR>`.

Of course, you can chain as many Vim commands in a key mapping as suits you. And you need not set up the map in `~/.vimrc`: you can do so on a per-session basis through Normal mode commands just as well.

I suggest a small exercise for the reader: map the F12 key to toggle on/off syntax highlighting.

1.3.9 Vim Abbreviations and Auto-Completion Framework

Vim caters to the stenographer inside you with a couple of distinct enterprises: abbreviations and auto-completion.

The editor supports abbreviations established via ~/.vimrc as well as Normal mode commands. If you want Vim to auto-complete #i as #include, try this in a Vim session:

```
:iab #i #include
```

When you start working, let's say, on some C source code in Vim, just type in #i followed by a space. Vim will expand it as #include.

Auto-completion is the programmer's dream, whereby long words are typed by the system itself, under the radar control of the user.

Let's say you are typing a document in Vim in which there is just one line: "As of today, most motherboards are manufactured in Taiwan".

If later in the document, you again start writing about motherboards, it might start itching and irking your ergonomic wholesomeness having to type in such a long word again and again. The solution is to type in a few lead characters and then press Control+P while still in Insert mode:

mot `Ctrl` + `P`

When you press Control+P, Vim will search backward for all words beginning with the lead "mot". Since "motherboards" is the only candidate, you can accept Vim's only suggestion for auto-completing the word.

Of course, you could have invoked the auto-completion framework with a smaller cue. If you type this:

mo `Ctrl` + `P`

Vim will find two words ("most" and "motherboards") that match the cue. In such case, Vim will present you with a menu of suggestions, and you can select one.

Just as Control+P makes Vim search backward, Control+N searches forward.

We now know Vim well enough to work comfortably with the editor. The foregoing discussion assumes you already have Vim installed. It might still be handy to have Vim installation commands for the various Unix and Unix-emulation platforms readily available for reference.

1.3.10 Installing Vim

Note that a graphical Vim (`gvim`) installation automatically installs a console version (`vim`) too.

1. In Windows:

   There are two distinct ways to install Vim under Windows. One is via its setup executable, which you can download at `http://www.vim.org/`.

   The other way is to install Vim is as part of Cygwin, which makes Vim available under the Editors category in its setup executable. If you are using the Cygwin fork Babun, Vim is likely there already as part of the base distribution. If it is missing, you can install it with:

   ```
   pact install vim
   ```

2. In Linux:

   Linux distributions provide a number of Vim packages. For Ubuntu-flavored distributions, you can get the graphical version of Vim with:

   ```
   % sudo apt-get install vim-gnome
   -OR-
   % sudo apt-get install vim-gtk3
   ```

   If you need just the console-mode Vim, use:

   ```
   % sudo apt-get install vim-nox
   ```

   Arch-based Linux distributions can use: `ROOT# pacman -S vim`

3. In FreeBSD:

   For console-mode Vim, use: `ROOT#    pkg install vim-lite`

   For graphical Vim, use: `ROOT#    pkg  install vim`

1.4 Joe's Own Editor (Joe)

The one editor Vim most often gets compared to is Joe's Own Editor (called Joe). It's perhaps the most user-friendly console-mode text editor ever made.

If you were to perform a statistical analysis of text editing jobs that consume most of your time with the editor, the tasks would be:

- Inserting new text

- Moving/copying existing text

- Deleting existing text

A bit further down the line would be stuff like finding/replacing, as well as complex, repetitive tasks that you would ideally want to do just once and let the editor perform the repetitions.

Given this scenario, you might like to ask if there is someone who can get this done with significantly less effort compared to Vi IMproved. Answers will vary depending on whom you ask, but my vote would be for Joe.

The creation of Joseph H. Allen, this funky little editor packs a fair punch that amounts to what I like to classify as 50% of Vim with 10% of the learning curve—if even that much.

Unlike Vim, Joe is a non-modal editor, which gets it a thumbs up from folks who dislike the idea of having to switch between operational modes. Joe starts off in text input mode and remains that way. If you need to carry out a command, you need to use the Control modifier key (or sometimes the Escape modifier) to feed your command to the editor.

Note that Joe uses ˆ to refer to the Control key, which is what we too will do for the remaining chapter.

While everything in Joe has been designed for ease of use, the standout feature that makes Joe very easy to work with is its online help system. *Online* here does not refer to any Internet-backed facility. Rather, it is a secondary window that Joe opens automatically when invoked with the -helpon argument. The extra window illustrated in Figure 1-2 lists the shortcut keys for every major editing operation available in Joe.

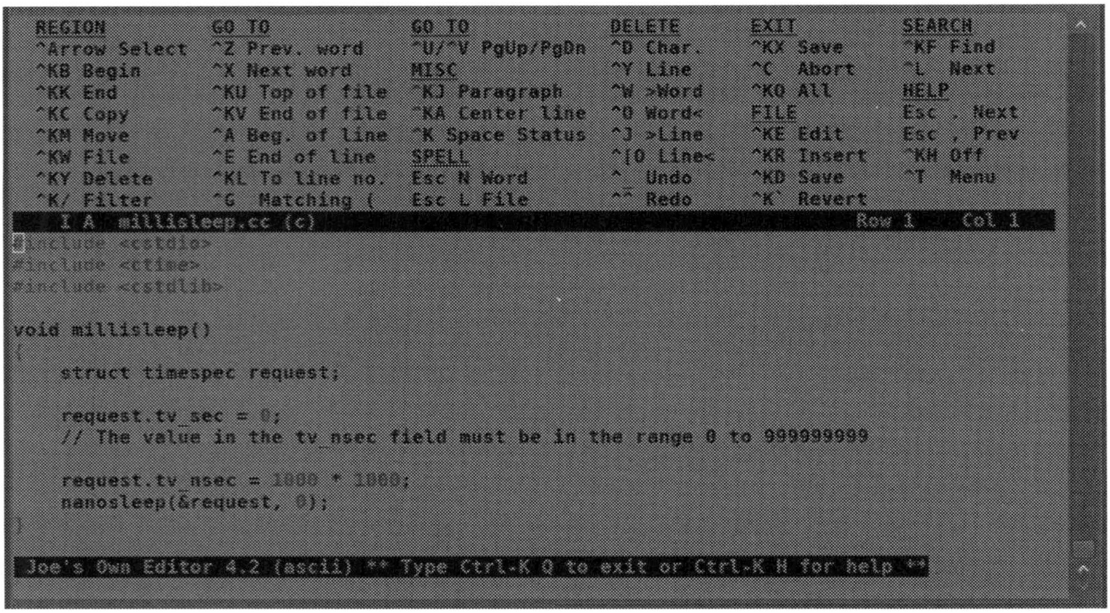

```
REGION             GO TO              GO TO              DELETE        EXIT           SEARCH
^Arrow Select      ^Z Prev. word      ^U/^V PgUp/PgDn    ^D Char.      ^KX Save       ^KF Find
^KB Begin          ^X Next word       MISC               ^Y Line       ^C  Abort      ^L  Next
^KK End            ^KU Top of file    ^KJ Paragraph      ^W >Word      ^KQ All        HELP
^KC Copy           ^KV End of file    ^KA Center line    ^O Word<      FILE           Esc . Next
^KM Move           ^A Beg. of line    ^K Space Status    ^J >Line      ^KE Edit       Esc , Prev
^KW File           ^E End of line     SPELL              ^[O Line<     ^KR Insert     ^KH Off
^KY Delete         ^KL To line no.    Esc N Word         ^_  Undo      ^KD Save       ^T  Menu
^K/ Filter         ^G Matching {      Esc L File         ^^  Redo      ^K` Revert
    I A  millisleep.cc (c)                                                    Row 1     Col 1
#include <cstdio>
#include <ctime>
#include <cstdlib>

void millisleep()
{
    struct timespec request;

    request.tv_sec = 0;
    // The value in the tv_nsec field must be in the range 0 to 999999999

    request.tv_nsec = 1000 * 1000;
    nanosleep(&request, 0);
}

Joe's Own Editor 4.2 (ascii) ** Type Ctrl-K Q to exit or Ctrl-K H for help **
```

Figure 1-2. *Joe's online help system*

Looking at Figure 1-2, you will likely note that you do not need to know Joe beforehand or remember anything about how to work with your text in Joe—except to use -helpon when invoking Joe or use ^KH to toggle the help menu on. The help menu is largely self-illustrating.

A few distributions use -help, not -helpon as the switch for the online help system.

Since Joe's online help elucidates everything, it leaves very little to explain. Still, we will go through some of the elementary paces.

Probably the first thing to keep in mind is that there are two ways to save your file: ^KX saves and exits, while ^KD (followed by a carriage return) saves and keeps the Joe window open.

Editing with Joe tends to be heavily block-oriented. You define a region of text and then operate on that region with a copy/move/delete command.

There are two ways to define a block. You must first move the cursor to the block's starting character, which is the northwest corner.

The traditional way to mark the block is to press ^KB and then travel to the last character of your intended block, where you then press ^KK. That defines (highlights) your block.

There is a newer and easier way too. When at the starting character, hold down the
 Ctrl key and use the keyboard's arrow keys to navigate to the ending character. Your
block gets defined as you move the cursor.

With a block defined, you can press ^KY to delete it. Or else, move to another position
in your buffer, where you can press ^KC to copy it there, or ^KM to move the block there.

Missing from the online help is the indentation system. ^K, unindents the block
(pushes the text to the left), whereas ^K. indents the block (pushes the text to the right).

A lot of people find it irksome to have the block remain highlighted when it has been
operated on. Luckily, there is a fairly straightforward remedy. Press Ctrl + C , the
standard way to cancel an operation in Joe, to undefine the block. If you want the
"undefine" to happen automatically, pass in the argument -lightoff when invoking Joe.

The one most heavily needed editing operation I seem to encounter is deleting the
current line. The command to delete a current line is ^Y

^KF is the interface to find and replace, for which Joe supports a homebrewed
implementation of regular expressions. That brew uses \. to match any single character,
while * matches zero-plus occurrences of the previous token. Word- boundaries are
matched with \< and \>, just as under GNU. Character classes (of the [[:class:]] form)
are not supported.

Joe is an excellent playground for macros too. ^K[(followed by a number between
0 and 9) starts recording a macro tagged as the digit chosen, and ^K] stops the recording.
When you need to play the macro, just press ^K followed by its tag digit.

Joe has a hook into spell checking too. For this, you need to have a spell application
like aspell installed in the backend. To spell check a Joe buffer, press Esc + L .

One fantastic capability of Joe is to filter a block of text through any external
command using the ^K/ command. This has particular significance because Joe does not
have an internal command to comment/uncomment a block.

If you need to comment or uncomment a block, you can work around it by creating a
couple of shell scripts as explained here.

Put the following in $HOME/bin/comment.sh and make it executable (chmod +x
<file>):

```
#!/bin/sh
commenteer='#'
sed 's/^.*$/'"$commenteer"'&/'
exit $?
```

Put the following in `$HOME/bin/uncomment.sh` and make it executable:

```
#!/bin/sh
commenteer='#'
sed 's/^\('"$commenteer"'\)\(.*\)$/\2/'
exit $?
```

You can now filter blocks of code through `comment.sh` and `uncomment.sh` by invoking the respective script with ^K/. Note that these scripts assume that the commenting character is #. If you need to use something else (for instance, //), modify the string assigned to `commenteer` in the scripts accordingly.

Joe throws in a few more kicks for enhanced user-friendliness—command history, find-and-replace history, and tab-based completion (for filenames). Those are better experienced than explained.

One Joe peculiarity worth noting is ⌈Ctrl⌉ key release in Control-based commands. Consider ^KX to illustrate the point. That command works with ⌈k⌉ and then ⌈x⌉ pressed while the Control key is still not released. It also works if ⌈x⌉ is pressed with the Control key released after pressing ⌈k⌉. There are a few commands though, ^K/ for instance, that work only with the Control key released before pressing the Command key (which is ⌈/⌉ in our example). It's simply a matter of getting used to this.

I will close this section with a word about Joe's rich heritage. While a single editor in itself, Joe derives its base from multiple families—Emacs, Pico, and WordStar. A Joe installation usually installs additional links that let Joe emulate Emacs keybindings (if invoked as jmacs), Pico (jpico), or WordStar (jstar). WordStar is deemed the chief inspiration behind Joe, and WordStar lovers almost immediately light up when a discussion about Joe breaks out within hearing distance.

1.4.1 Installing Joe

Follow these steps to install Joe:

1. In Windows:

    Both Cygwin and Babun provide Joe as a package. For Cygwin, you can select Joe under the `Editors` category in Cygwin's setup executable. For Babun, you can use: `pact install joe`

To install Joe as a standalone application under a recent version of Windows (7 or later), you can download `joewin.msi` at the following URL: `https://sourceforge.net/projects/joe-editor/files/JOE%20for%20Windows/`

Windows XP users can use the portable version of Joe available at: `https://www.mirbsd.org/MirOS/dist/jupp/JWIN31V.ZIP`

2. In Linux:

   For Ubuntu, use: `% sudo apt-get install joe`

   For Arch, use: `ROOT#  pacman -S joe`

3. In FreeBSD, use:

   `ROOT#  pkg install joe`

1.5 Summary

Now that you are familiar with the two major console-mode text editors, your Unix love affair is bound to succeed.

People soon start developing preferences when using text editors. You will likely develop a fancy for one over the other, or for other over the one. This is not a cardinal sin by any means. Just be aware that inclinations in the early stages tend to leave a distinct mark on one's evolution in the Unix world.

CHAPTER 2

Essential Unix Commands and Terminology

I am told by reliable sources that, despite ongoing research from the best minds on this planet, scientists are unable to define basic terms like "life" and "time". Fortunately for computer users, computer programming is an easier concept—we can define essential terms. Before we embark on our Unix journey, we'll therefore first define some of the most fundamental terms.

2.1 Kernel, Shell, and Filesystem

The kernel is the operating system's core, without which everything else becomes meaningless. Every single operation you carry out under an operating system has to be executed indirectly by the kernel, which also does many other jobs (memory management, process management, device management, and input-output management) in the background.

Unix kernels in the past tended to be monolithic (with every capability packed into one single file). But modern kernels are modular. Only critical, inseparable capabilities get packed into the kernel, while other capabilities get compiled as modules that can be loaded and unloaded at runtime. Communicating with the kernel is not easy—the kernel does not yet understand the English language and needs special communication procedures known as system calls. This is why Unix creators bundled into the operating system a very helpful application known as the *shell*.

© Manish Jain 2018
M. Jain, *Beginning Modern Unix*, https://doi.org/10.1007/978-1-4842-3528-7_2

The shell (originally the Bourne shell) is the command interpreter—on one side, it accepts from the user commands typed in a derivative subset of plain English; and on the other side, it uses system calls to communicate with the kernel, get your commands executed, and report results back to you. The two most widely used shells today are bash (Bourne Again Shell) and zsh (Z Shell).

That leaves us with one last term—the *filesystem*. You must have come across that term sometime or the other. So what does it mean? A filesystem is the logical, hierarchical representation of electronic data in a disk partition. That sounds a touch abstruse, so let's take the case of a hard disk with one single Windows NTFS partition spanning the disk. When the disk is booted, you get to see C: drive as the top level in *My Computer*.

C: in turn hosts a few subdirectories and files, and then those subdirectories contain still more goods.

So far so good. But the disk partition itself physically is nothing but a huge cluster of 0s and 1s: computers are, after all, binary machines. Translation of the 0s and 1s to present the user with a navigable hierarchy of files and directories is what the term filesystem means. With its NTFS driver, Windows interprets the 0s and 1s in a way such that the operating system gets to see files and directories in a hierarchy rooted under the C: drive. The moral of the story is this: A disk partition is a physical entity; a filesystem is the logical representation of the physical entity.

Every operating system uses a filesystem-specific driver to read from and/or write to a partition. The most widely used native filesystem types in Unix are ext2 (Linux) and UFS (FreeBSD), although I should mention that both Linux and FreeBSD offer alternatives: btrfs (Linux) and ZFS (FreeBSD). Further, modern Unix systems can easily access data under non-native filesystems too (such as FAT and NTFS).

2.2 Files and Special Files

The two most common entities in any filesystem are files and directories. So, before moving ahead to discuss special files, we'll spare a little energy to come up with reasonable, working definitions for both terms.

A *file* is one complete, named unit of digital information, that may be physically contiguous in its storage or spread across a chain of fragments. By complete, what is meant is that you cannot tell the system to delete half of a file.

Directories, on the other hand, are special files that do not contain any data themselves—they are just containers that list names of contained ("immediate child") files and subdirectories. If you want to explore what lies in the directory file, you can open a directory in a text editor (!), just to be sure that it indeed is this way.

Besides directories, there are a few other filesystem entities that do not qualify as regular files, notably symbolic links and device nodes.

Now that we have a reasonable definition of the term file, we can talk about four special ones and then a couple of related terms.

2.2.1 The Null Device

/dev/null is like one big black hole into which you can pump as much data as you want. Everything goes in immediately and nothing ever comes out. In other words, a perfect dustbin.

```
USER>   echo "Hello World" > /dev/null
```

The shell does not say "Hello World".

2.2.2 Standard Input

This is where input comes from. This normally means the keyboard, but it can be redirected to come from a regular disk file using the < operator. Modern Unix systems have the device node /dev/stdin that serves to represent standard input, which the shell denotes as a nameless file with the numeric identifier 0.

We thus can determine how many lines there are in the file /etc/fstab using either of the following:

```
USER>   wc -l < /etc/fstab
```

or

```
USER>   wc -l 0< /etc/fstab
```

Note: There is no space between 0 and <.

Note   Most Unix commands (e.g., wc, grep, and sed) that accept a file as command-line argument also accept input passed in via shell redirection or over a pipe, and vice versa. The wc command shown here could also have been crafted as wc -l /etc/fstab (i.e., no redirection).

Note the difference in wc output when the command is fed a file path, rather than having it process standard input. In the latter case, wc has no idea how the data in its standard input came into being.

2.2.3 Standard Output

This is where output goes. This normally means your monitor, but it can be redirected to a regular disk file using the > operator. Modern Unix systems have the device node /dev/stdout, which serves to represent standard output, which the shell denotes as a nameless file with the numeric identifier 1.

We thus can fetch the listing of the home directory with:

```
USER>    ls -l $HOME
```

This displays the list on the PC's monitor.

```
USER>    ls -l $HOME > /tmp/home.list
```

This command creates the /tmp/home.list file and then saves output in that file.

```
USER>    ls -l $HOME 1>> /tmp/home.list
```

It appends the list to /tmp/home.list using a numeric ID of stdout.

Note   Output redirection to a disk file with > writes the output to a new file. If the file already exists, it will first be truncated to zero-length.

Redirection with >> appends to an existing file. If the file does not already exist, it will be created.

2.2.4 Standard Error

This is where diagnostic and error messages go. This normally means your monitor, but it can be redirected to a regular disk file using the 2> operator. Modern Unix systems have the device node /dev/stderr, which serves to represent standard error, which the shell denotes as a nameless file with the numeric identifier 2.

We can now discard error messages we are not interested in.

```
USER>    ls -l HOME
# Error: 'HOME' should (presumably) have been '$HOME'

USER>    ls -l HOME 2> /dev/null
# No error message: ls quietly returns code to shell indicating failure
```

If needed, standard output and standard error can be merged into a single stream. The following commands do just that.

```
USER>    ls -l $HOME 2>&1
```

The previous command delivers error messages, if any, to standard output.

```
USER>    ls -l $HOME 1> /tmp/home.list 2>&1
```

This command merges output and error streams in the disk /tmp/home.list file.

Figure 2-1 depicts the way the standard input/output/error devices connect the user to a Unix shell.

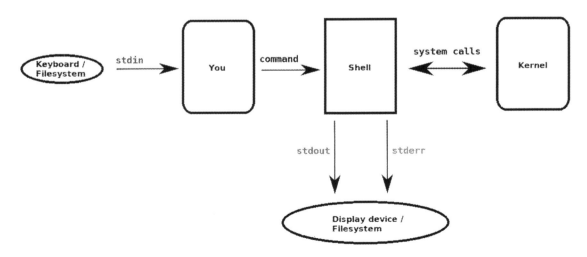

Figure 2-1. *User interaction with Unix*

2.2.5 The Pipe

At this stage, there is one Unix facility that we need to understand: the pipe. The pipe is a way for joining two commands such that the standard output of the first command becomes the standard input of the second.

As an example, let's say we have a string that we need to print in reverse (`'xyz123'` becomes `'321zyx'`).

The following command does the job nicely with a pipe:

```
USER> echo "xyz123" | rev
```

The return value of this command is that the rightmost command in the pipeline returns to the shell. Remember that commands return 0 upon successful completion and some other number when a failure happens.

2.2.6 Console

The last Unix term we discuss is *console*, which can mean one of two things depending on the context. One definition of console is the combination of the keyboard and monitor (i.e., input and output). When used in the qualifier *console-mode,* it refers to your system running in plain-text mode (i.e., with X not running).

2.3 Essential Unix Commands

We are now ready to delve into the world of Unix commands.

Note   Commands return 0 upon success, and some other integer upon failure.

2.3.1 echo \<string>

Prints \<string> on standard output.

Unless -n is used, shell will append a newline.

Unless -e is used, (ba)sh will not honor escape sequences like \t or \n.

2.3.2 cd <path>

Changes the current (working) directory to `<path>`.

If `<path>` is not given, `cd` will change to your home directory.

If `<path>` is – (a single dash), `cd` will change to your previous directory.

If `<path>` is `..` (two periods), `cd` will change to the parent of the current directory.

2.3.3 pwd

Prints the path of the working directory. Not needed often in interactive mode, because most users like to set the shell prompt to the current directory.

2.3.4 ls <path>

Gets the directory listing for `<path>`.

If `<path>` is not given, `ls` will get you a listing of the current directory. If `<path>` is a file, `ls  <path>` will print the complete path of the file. If `<path>` is a directory, `ls  <path>` will get a listing of that directory.

Important switches for `ls` are:

-a   Lists names of hidden items (which start with a period)

-l   Gets a long (multi-column) listing

-d   Prints information about `<path>` itself, rather than listing its contents (applies to directories)

To get colorized output from `ls`, use `--color=auto` under Linux/Cygwin, and –G under FreeBSD.

Under Linux/Cygwin, `ls` likes to put quotation marks around entities with embedded whitespace. To avoid the quotes, use:

```
ls -1 --quoting-style=literal <path>
```

2.3.5 mkdir <path>

Creates the `<path>` directory. If the new directory is being created under a location (parent directory) that does not exist, `mkdir` will fail unless the `-p` switch is used.

```
USER>   mkdir /abc/xyz
```

This fails if /abc is not an existing directory.

USER>   mkdir -p /abc/xyz

This works; mkdir first creates /abc, if it does not already exist, and then creates the subdirectory xyz.

2.3.6 cp <source> <destination>

Copies <source> to <destination>.

If <source> is a directory, cp will fail unless -R is applied.

If <source> ends with a slash, cp behaves differently. Under Linux/Cygwin, the trailing slash is removed. FreeBSD interprets the command as cp <source>/* <destination>.

2.3.7 mv <source> <destination>

Moves/renames <source> to <destination>.

Unlike cp, mv is built as automatically recursive if <source> is a directory. The trailing slash in <source> is removed under Linux/Cygwin as well as FreeBSD.

2.3.8 rm <path>

Deletes <path>.

If <path> is a directory, rm will fail unless -R is applied. A related command is rmdir, which can delete an empty directory.

2.3.9 ln [-s] <path> <additional>

Creates an additional link in the filesystem.

Data in physical storage shows up (gets linked) exactly once in the filesystem. The ln command lets you create additional links. By default, the additional link is hard (meaning the new link is simply another name for the original). If you use -s with ln, you get a symbolic link (meaning the new link is a pointer to the original entity).

USER>   ln /etc/fstab link.hard

This creates an additional hard link for /etc/fstab.

USER>   ln -s /etc/fstab link.sym

This creates a symbolic link to /etc/fstab.

Note   A hard link must reside in the same filesystem as the target. Creating a hard link for a directory is such a bad idea that nobody, not even root, is permitted to do it.

2.3.10 cat <file>

Prints the contents of <file> on standard output. If you need the contents to be line-numbered, use -b or -n.

2.3.11 test <condition>

Tests a <condition> as true or false.

A strange command—possibly the most heavily used shell script command—but is almost never seen anywhere, because users prefer its synonymous cousin:
[<condition>].

Note   Negating a test is done with the ! operator. For example, if !
[-f /boot/grub/grub.cfg] tests whether /boot/grub/grub.cfg is not an existing regular file.

A few conditions that you can check for:

[-f <file>]   True if <file> is an existing regular file

[-d <file>]   True if <file> is an existing directory

[-n <string>]   True if <string> has at least one character

[-z <string>]   True if <string> is empty

[s1 = s2]   True if the strings s1 and s2 are identical

[s1 != s2]	True if the strings s1 and s2 are different
[n1 -eq n2]	True if the integers n1 and n2 are equal
[n1 -ne n2]	True if the integers n1 and n2 are not equal
[n1 -gt n2]	True if integer n1 is greater than n2
[n1 -ge n2]	True if integer n1 is greater than or equal to n2
[n1 -lt n2]	True if integer n1 is less than n2
[n1 -le n2]	True if integer n1 is less than or equal to n2

If you want to concatenate the conditions to be tested, that is done with -a (and) and -o (or).

[<condition1>   -a   <condition2>]

Both must be true.

[<condition1>   -o   <condition2>]

Either must be true.

Note   Note that whitespace is necessary:

1. After [

2. Before]

3. On both sides of = as well as ! =

2.3.12 expr

Evaluates an expression.

If we assign an integer to a shell variable (for example n), we can perform some elementary mathematics with it:

```
USER>    n=7
USER>    expr $n + 1
```

This prints 8 on the console; n remains 7.

```
USER>    expr $n \* $n
```

This prints 49 on the console; n remains 7.

GNU expr has some functionality for strings too, which FreeBSD expr does not:

```
USER>    sz="hello"
USER>    expr length $sz
```

This prints 5 if expr is GNU; it prints an error message if expr is FreeBSD.

Note   To get the length of string sz under FreeBSD, you can use ${#sz} (this portably works under FreeBSD as well as Linux/Cygwin).

You can use GNU expr under FreeBSD too—just install the port sysutils/coreutils, after which GNU expr will be available as /usr/local/bin/gexpr.

2.3.13 dd

Copies raw data in images and block (storage) devices.

This can be used for special copy and USB-burning operations. This is the only command in this chapter that needs a real Unix system to be fully functional. Since Windows does not have device nodes, Cygwin cannot facilitate the examples 2, 3, and 4.

1. This command copies the first 100 bytes of /etc/hosts:

    ```
    USER>    dd if=/etc/hosts of=~/partial.copy bs=100 count=1
    ```

2. This creates an ISO image of a bootable CD attached as /dev/cdrom:

    ```
    USER>    dd if=/dev/cdrom of=cd9660.iso bs=2048
    ```

3. This saves your disk's master boot record in a file on FreeBSD:

    ```
    USER>    dd if=/dev/ada0 of=~/mbr.copy bs=512 count=1
    ```

On Linux, use the corresponding device name /dev/sda:

```
USER>    dd if=/dev/sda of=~/mbr.copy bs=512 count=1
```

4. This "burns" an image file to a USB pen drive attached to the box, assuming that your pen drive is /dev/da0:

```
USER>    dd if=image.img of=/dev/da0 bs=1M
```

2.3.14 grep <regex> [<file>]

Searches for the string pattern <regex> in <file>.

One of the most heavily used Unix commands. Searches for the string (more correctly, the regular expression) <regex> in the file <file>.

If <file> is missing, grep searches in its standard input. Here are a few examples. This determines whether /etc/fstab has any uppercase characters:

```
USER>    grep '[A-Z]' /etc/fstab
```

This would usually produce nothing beyond commented stuff. This searches standard input for a numeric character:

```
USER>    echo Se7en | grep '[0-9]'
```

This produces Se7en because it has the digit 7, which is in the range from 0 to 9. Here's the same search using the more portable way of character class:

```
USER>    echo Se7en | grep '[[:digit:]]'
```

This produces Se7en because it has the digit 7, which is in the character class [:digit:]. Inverse of the previous: Does the input have non-digit characters?

```
USER>    echo Se7en | grep '[^[:digit:]]'
```

This produces Se7en because the input has the non-digit characters S, e, another e, and n.

Another one: Is the first character a digit?

```
USER>    echo Se7en | grep '^[[:digit:]]'
```

This produces no output because Se7en does not start with a digit.

Yet another search: Is the last character a digit?

USER>   echo Se7en | grep '[[:digit:]]$'

This produces no output because Se7en does not end with a digit. There are many important character classes:

      [:alnum:]   Alphabetic or digit only

      [:alpha:]   Alphabetic only

      [:digit:]   Digit only

      [:punct:]   Punctuation character only

      [:space:]   Whitespace only

      [:lower:]   Lowercase alphabet only

      [:upper:]   Uppercase alphabet only

grep has a large number of switches. You'll have to look at the man page (with man grep) to see what the switches do.

This discourse will leave you with a couple of regex builders:

    .   Matches any single character

    *   Means zero or more instances of the previous construct

Leveraging these builders, we can run a fairly sophisticated grep that checks for three conditions—whether input a) begins uppercase, b) ends lowercase, and c) has at least one character between the ends:

USER>   echo Se7en | grep '^[[:upper:]].*[[:lower:]]$'

This produces Se7en: all three conditions matched. A couple of commands related to grep are:

Egrep Which uses extended regular expressions by default

Pgrep Which can search for processes with a given name

2.3.15 awk [<file>]

Prints the field at a particular index in a record.

If <file> is missing, awk operates on its standard input. The default field separator for awk is whitespace, but you can provide your own with the -F switch.

Since /etc/passwd stores the user ID of every user in the third field, the following gets us the user ID of the root user:

```
USER>   grep '^root:'   /etc/passwd | awk  -F  ":" '{ print $3 }'
```

awk (named after its creators—A. V. Aho, P. J. Weinberger, and B. W. Kernighan) is an entire programming language. It does not need the services of grep for this example. awk can handle this on its own:

```
USER>   awk -F ":" '/^root:/ { print $3 }' /etc/passwd
```

2.3.16 sed [<file>]

Streams an editor that edits each line of input to make on-the-fly modifications.

If <file> is missing, sed operates on its standard input.

Let's say we want to retain the digital portion of Se7en and discard everything else, effectively ending up with just 7. A first try could be:

```
USER>   echo "Se7en" | sed 's/[^[:digit:]]//'
```

This produces e7en. We managed to remove the leading S, but there are still two es and one n.

The problem is that sed will only substitute once, unless specifically told otherwise with a trailing g (for "global"):

```
USER>   echo "Se7en" | sed 's/[^[:digit:]]//g'
```

This produces 7.

The sed separator need not be a slash (the / character)—during substitution, sed takes the character immediately after the leading s to be the separator.

So we could just as well have phrased the preceding example as:

```
USER>   echo "Se7en" | sed 's|[^[:digit:]]||g'
```

This also produces 7.

sed has many other uses too, and it's often dubbed a Swiss Army knife. For example, we can fetch the second line of a file with this:

```
USER>   sed -n '2p' /etc/rc.conf
```

This will print the second line of the file /etc/rc.conf.

2.3.17 file <path>

Determines the file type of <path>.

Text files produce ASCII text in the output. So, if you are unsure whether a file can safely be opened in a text editor, run the `file` command on it to find out. This tool is also very handy when files have lost their extension.

```
USER>   file /tmp/somefile
```

This could print something like `/tmp/somefile:  PNG image, 600 x 627, 8-bit/ color RGB, non-interlaced` if the file is a PNG image file.

2.3.18 find

Use this command to find files matching specific criteria and optionally to execute a command on those files.

To non-recursively list sub-directories of the current directory, use:

```
USER>   find . -type d -maxdepth 1
```

To recursively delete all `.jpg` files under /usr, use:

```
ROOT#  find /usr -type f -name '*.jpg' -exec rm {} \;;
```

To recursively list all C files under the current directory modified more recently than makefile, use:

```
USER>   find .  -type f -name '*.c' -newer Makefile
```

2.3.19 updatedb

Creates/updates a database of names of all files present locally.

FreeBSD provides `updatedb` in its base system as `/usr/libexec/locate.updatedb`, while Linux needs you to install the `mlocate` package.

2.3.20 locate <name>

Searches the `updatedb` database for the string called <name>.

FreeBSD provides `locate` in its base system as `/usr/bin/locate`, while Linux requires you to install the `mlocate` package.

2.3.21 basename <string>

Extracts a filename and/or removes the extension from `<string>`.

```
USER>    basename   /etc/hosts
```

This produces `hosts`.

```
USER>    basename   /usr/bin
```

This produces `bin`.

```
USER>    basename ab/cd.txt .txt
```

This produces `cd`.

2.3.22 dirname <string>

Extracts a directory path from `<string>`.

```
USER>    dirname    /usr/local/bin
```

This produces `/usr/local`.

```
USER>    dirname    ab/cd/xyz
```

This produces `ab/cd`.

2.3.23 realpath <path>

Resolves a complete path of an existing file.

```
USER>    realpath    /home
```

This gets `/usr/home`: `/home` is usually a symbolic link to `/usr/home`.

```
USER>    realpath   ab/cd
```

This gets an error message, unless `ab/cd` actually is an existing path.

2.3.24 head [<file>]

Extracts the first few (default 10) lines of input.

To get the first line of /etc/group, use:

```
USER>    head -n 1 /etc/group
```

Or via standard input:

```
USER>    cat /etc/group | head -n 1
```

2.3.25 tail [<file>]

Extracts the last few (default 10) lines of input.

To get the last line of /var/log/messages, use:

```
USER>    tail -n 1 /var/log/messages
```

Or via standard input:

```
USER>    cat /var/log/messages | tail -n 1
```

An important switch for tail is -f. This causes tail to stay alive, waiting for additional data to be appended in real time to the input; it constantly monitors the file for additions:

```
tail -f /var/log/messages
# A good way to list the last few system messages
```

Another handy switch is +<n>. This gets all the lines from input except for the first <n-1>. So if you want to remove the top line from the output of ls -l, you can use:

```
USER>    ls -l | tail +2
```

2.3.26 rev [<file>]

Reverses the input.

If you want to reverse the string xyz123 (to get 321zyx), use:

```
USER>    echo "xyz123" | rev
```

This produces 321zyx.

51

2.3.27 cut [<file>]

Extracts one single character or word from input.

```
USER>   echo "abcd" | cut -c 2
```

This produces b, the second character.

```
USER>   echo "abc lmn xyz" | cut -w -f 2
```

This produces lmn, the second word.
An extended usage is the trailing hyphen, which means "and everything else from here":

```
USER>   echo "abcd" | cut -c 2-
```

This produces bcd , the second character and everything afterward.

2.3.28 tr

Translates characters. This command operates on its standard input only.

```
USER>   echo "abca" | tr 'a' 'A'
```

This substitutes A for a and produces AbcA.

```
USER>   echo "abca" | tr '[:lower:]'   '[:upper:]'
```

This produces ABCA.
Use the -d switch to delete a character:

```
USER>   echo "abc def fed bca" | tr -d 'e'
```

This produces abc df fd bca, having removed all instances of e.

2.3.29 read <arg>

Reads one record from input into the shell variable <arg>.
To illustrate this, we'll use a variable named var. If you type the following in your terminal, the shell will hang, waiting for you to type something and then press Enter :

```
USER>   read var
```

Whatever you typed in before pressing Enter is now held in the variable var.

The other way to use read is to process a file one line at a time:

```
USER>   cat /etc/passwd | read var
```

This command fetches the first line of /etc/passwd into the variable var.
You can process the entire file /etc/passwd one line at a time with this:

```
{

    while read var; do
        echo "line read: $var"
    done
} < /etc/passwd
```

This is a different form for the same purpose:

```
cat /etc/passwd | while read var; do
    echo "line read: $var"
done
```

2.3.30 date

Prints (or sets) the system date and time.

```
USER>   date
```

This produces the system date and time, for example Sat Sep 30 11:11:50 GMT 2017.

```
USER>   date   "+%Y-%m-%d"
```

This prints date in the year-month-date format, for example 2017-09-30.

```
USER>   date "+%H:%M"
```

This prints time in HH:MM format, for example 11:11. The superuser can set the system date and time too:

```
ROOT#   date   2030
```

This sets system time to 20:30 (8:30 PM).

```
ROOT#   date   2501282030
```

This sets system date to 2025 January 28th and time to 20:30.

2.3.31 type <executable>

Prints the full path of <executable>.

If you need to find out whether wget is installed, use:

USER>   type wget

type will report an error if wget is not installed, or else its full path.
A related command is which.

2.3.32 wc [<file>]

Prints the word count (and the character and line count).

USER>   echo "x86 amd64" | wc -c

This counts the number of characters and produces 10. (Nine characters in the string, plus one for the newline that echo appends.)

USER>   echo -n "x86 amd64" | wc -c

This counts the number of characters and produces 9.

USER>   echo "x86 amd64" | wc -w

This counts the number of words and produces 2.

USER>   echo "x86 amd64" | wc -l

This counts the number of lines and produces 1.

2.3.33 less [<file>]

Scrolls the output one screen at a time. less can also be used as a file viewer.

If a command produces a lot of output that you need to study page-by-page, pass the command's output to less and then use `Page Up` and `Page Down` to navigate the output.

To search, press the `/` button, type the text fragment you want to search for, and press `Enter`.

To repeat the search, just press `n` (forward search) or `N` (previous).
To exit from less, press the `q` button.

A couple of examples:

```
USER>    ls -l | less
USER>    less /var/log/messages
```

2.3.34 man <topic>

Prints the accompanying manual for <topic>.

While a man page is on display, you can navigate and search it just as with the less command.

If multiple man pages exist for a topic (most commonly because a shell command is also the name of a C function), you can use the -a switch to summon them one at a time, for example:

```
USER>    man -a stat
```

This command will first display the man page for the stat shell command (from man section 1), and then when you press $\boxed{q}$ to exit, it will display the man page for the C function stat (from man section 2).

If you want to read only the man page for the C function stat (which is in man section 2), use the section number in your command:

```
USER>    man 2 stat
```

2.3.35 set

Sets (or displays) shell behavior characteristics.

Without any parameters, set will display its complete environment. The two most commonly used parameters are -e and -x.

```
USER>    set -e
```

This makes the shell exit upon first command failure from here onward and stays in effect until you use set +e.

```
USER>    set  -x
```

This will trace execution of commands (for debugging) and stays in effect until you use this:

```
set +x
```

55

2.3.36 uname

Prints the name of the operating system. For example, FreeBSD, Linux, or Cygwin.
Important switches are:

-r   Print the release version

-a   Print all system information (hostname, architecture, release
version, and build date)

A related command is hostname, which can display and set the host machine's name.

2.3.37 who

Prints the list of current logins. If a user is logged in from multiple terminals, each login
instance is treated separately. A couple of related commands are as follows.

w   Lists the login names and activities of currently logged-
           in users

users   Lists the login names of currently logged-in users

whoami   Displays the username of the current user

whoami   Also has the variant form who am i

If you just want your user ID instead, use the command: id -u

2.3.38 cmp <file1> <file2>

Compares two files to check whether they are identical.
    The files may be text files or binaries. If the files are identical, cmp exits silently,
returning the exit code 0 to the shell.

2.3.39 diff <file1> <file2>

Compares two text files to check whether they are identical.
    If the files are identical, diff exits silently, returning the exit code 0 to the shell.
    If the files are not identical, diff will display changes to be made to <file1> to make
it identical to <file2>.

2.3.40 ps

List processes currently running in the system.

ps is one of the few applications that accept switches with or without a leading hyphen.

By default, ps will list only those processes that have a controlling terminal. In other words, if you have launched any X applications, they will not show up in the listing.

If you want the list to include processes that do not have a controlling terminal, use the switch -x.

If you want the list to include processes that belong to other users, use the switch -a.

A common ps invocation is ps waux, which is shorthand for ps -w -a -u -x.

A related command is top, which displays system load (CPU usage, memory usage, and process information for running commands) with real-time updates.

2.3.41 kill [<sig>] <pid>

Sends the signal <sig> to process with process ID <pid>.

Only the superuser (root) can send signals to other users' processes.

Important signals are:

    1   HUP (Hang up)

    2   INT (Interrupt)

    9   KILL (Force termination)

   15   TERM (Termination request)

If <sig> is missing, TERM is assumed.

If a user presses Ctrl + C , the process receives INT.

HUP can often be used to make a daemon process re-read its configuration file.

A few other signals are occasionally worth remembering too. SIGSTOP will pause the receiving process, until a SIGCONT is issued to revive it. SIGINFO—generated with Ctrl + T —prints activity/load statistics and is usually available under FreeBSD, but not always under Linux.

Signals can be specified using the number or its name. So kill -1 <pid> is the same as kill -HUP <pid>.

HUP, INT, and TERM can be caught and handled by the process. KILL will kill the process immediately, no questions asked.

A related command is `killall`, which accepts program names associated with running processes instead of PIDs.

2.3.42 sleep <n>

Pauses all activity on the current CPU thread for `<n>` seconds.

```
USER>   echo "Hello"; sleep 10; echo "World"
```

This will print `Hello`, sleep for 10 seconds, and then print `World`.

2.3.43 sort [<file>]

Sorts the input.

`<file>` is usually is a text file: sorting binary files is unheard of. The `-u` switch of `sort` renders approximately the same behavior as the `sort + uniq` implementation.

2.3.44 uniq [<file>]

Lists any unique (non-repetitive) records in input.

`uniq` compares adjacent lines only. So it is pointless to run `uniq` on a file that's not already sorted.

For example, if you have this in a file called `somefile.txt`:

```
abc
xyz
abc
```

`uniq` will process the file and report three unique records: `abc`, `xyz`, and again `abc`, which is just not what you wanted.

So you must first sort the file and then run `uniq` to process its standard input:

```
USER>   sort somefile.txt | uniq
```

The default behavior of `uniq` is to print each record once for every record that is present in the input once or more than one time.

Often, the user needs to find records present in the file exactly one time (i.e., not multiple times). The switch -u does that:

```
USER>   sort somefile.txt | uniq -u
```

This produces just xyz, because abc is present in the input more than once.

2.3.45 chmod <mode> <file>

Changes the permissions of <file> to match <mode>.

There are two equivalent ways to specify the operand <mode>:

- <who>+<perm>:

    <who> can be one of u, g, and o, or a combination of them, where u is the user, g is the group, and o is others (or a is all, shorthand for ugo).

    If <who> is missing, u is assumed.

    The + after <who> enables <perm> for <who>.

    If – is used (in place of +), it disables <perm> for <who>.

    <perm> can be one of the following:

    r = readable; w = writeable; x = executable

    ```
    USER>   chmod +w addresses.txt
    ```

    This makes the file addresses.txt writeable for the user.

    ```
    USER>   chmod o-x myprog
    ```

    This makes the program myprog not executable for others.

    ```
    USER>   chmod a+r calendar.txt
    ```

    This makes the file calendar.txt readable for everyone.

- octal value:

The octal scheme uses a field of three bits:

Left Bit Readable	Middle Bit Writeable	Rightmost Bit Executable
4 when set	2 when set	1 when set

A disabled bit is equivalent to 0.

The previous field above is created three times:

User			Group			Others		
Read	Write	Exec	Read	Write	Exec	Read	Write	Exec
4	2	1	4	2	1	4	2	1

Let's take a file created by the user. If the user wants the file to be:

- Readable + writeable + executable for himself/himself → First field is $4 + 2 + 1 = 7$

- Readable + not writeable + executable for same group → Second field is $4 + 0 + 1 = 5$

- Readable + not writeable + not executable for others → Third field is $4 + 0 + 0 = 4$

The user can invoke the command:

```
USER>   chmod 754 myfile
```

chmod has a recursion switch –R, which lets you operate on a directory's entire hierarchy.

2.3.46 chown <user> <file>

Changes the owner of `<file>` to `<user>`.

If `<user>` is of the form `<name>:<group>`, the specified username and group name will be applied.

chown has a recursion switch –R, which lets you operate on a directory's entire hierarchy.

2.3.47 chsh [<user>]

Changes the login shell.

If <user> is missing, the current user is assumed.

If you want to use the Z shell as your Unix login shell, install zsh and then use:

```
USER>   chsh -s 'which zsh'
```

2.3.48 passwd [<user>]

Changes the account's login password for the user <user>.

If <user> is missing, the current user is assumed.

Only the superuser (root) can change another user's password.

2.3.49 touch <file>

Creates <file> if it does not exist, or updates its modification timestamp.

2.3.50 tar

Creates, tests, and extracts an uncompressed archive, which is like an uncompressed ZIP file. The analogy is for the benefit of folks migrating from Windows—Unix folks would perhaps like it noted that tar is a different application, with its roots in archiving data to the tape (a legacy storage device that's rarely used nowadays).

This is one of the few commands to accept switches with or without the leading hyphen.

In create mode:

```
USER>   tar cf myarchive.tar letters/ images/ calendar.txt
```

This command creates the uncompressed archive file myarchive.tar containing everything present in the directories letters and images (and their subdirectories, if any), as well as the file calendar.txt.

In extract mode:

```
USER>   tar xf myarchive.tar
```

In test mode:

```
USER> tar tvf myarchive.tar
```

In test mode, unlike in extract mode, the archive's contents will be listed, but no files will be written to the disk.

tar has built-in compression support. If you want tar to create a gzip'ed archive, you can do that easily enough:

```
USER>   tar zcf myarchive.tar.gz letters/ images/ calendar.txt
```

To decompress and extract the contents of the archive, you can use:

```
USER>   tar zxf myarchive.tar.gz
```

2.3.51 gzip

Compresses/deflates a file or archive.

If you have an uncompressed archive named myarchive.tar, you can compress it with the standard Unix ZIP application gzip.

```
USER>   gzip myarchive.tar
```

This creates myarchive.tar.gz, which is much smaller than the original uncompressed archive.

To get back to the original archive, you need to run gunzip:

```
USER>   gunzip myarchive.tar.gz
```

This regenerates the uncompressed tar myarchive.tar.

To perform decompression and extraction in one step, you can use tar's built-in decompression support:

```
USER>   tar zxf myarchive.tar.gz
```

gzip can directly work on regular files too, rather than just tar archives. For example, if you want to compress an ISO image file, use this:

```
USER>   gzip FreeBSD-11.1-RELEASE-amd64-disc1.iso
```

This creates the FreeBSD-11.1-RELEASE-amd64-disc1.iso.gz file.

The successor to gzip is bzip2, and the de-compressor equivalent is bunzip2. The tar command also supports this format for compression and extraction using the switch j in place of z.

```
USER>   tar jxf myarchive.tar.bz2
```

2.3.52 xz

Compresses/deflates an archive.

xz is the new ZIP application, which offers superior compression ratios compared to other ZIP algorithms, although at a stiff cost in compression speed. Compressing a 1GB file with xz instead of gzip can lead to a 10% smaller size, and of the order of 10 times the amount of time taken to compress.

You can use xz in place of gzip, and unxz in place of gunzip.

Unlike gzip, xz'ed tarballs cannot always be processed by tar directly using command-line switches (although recent Unix systems do usually enable xz tarballs to be processed with tar zxf). You can, in any case, always get away with a single-line command by yourself to unpack the xz'ed tarball:

```
USER>    xzcat bigfile.tar.xz | tar xf -
```

2.3.53 source <file>

Executes <file> as part of the current shell.

The source command is usually not available in the Bourne shell. You need to be working with a Bourne shell derivative like Bash to make it work. In a strictly Bourne environment, you can use:

```
. <file>
```

2.3.54 wget

Fetches remote data using HTTP or FTP. FreeBSD has a native fetch command, which does pretty much the same.

wget is probably the most convenient way to download remote data. This command has a huge number of switches, one of which is -c (continue partial download). So if, in the first try, you manage to get 999MB of a 1000MB file, you can use wget -c to retrieve the remaining 1MB.

To mirror a complete website (and convert its internal links), use:

```
USER>    wget -r -l 0 -k -nc http://www.example.com/
```

A couple of related commands are wput, which can upload data to an FTP/HTTP server, and scp, which can copy files between machines on an intranet.

2.3.55 md5[sum] <file>

Prints the MD5 checksum of `<file>`.

FreeBSD calls it `md5`, while Linux/Cygwin call it `md5sum`.

2.3.56 sha256[sum] <file>

Prints the SHA256 checksum of `<file>`.

FreeBSD calls it `sha256`, while Linux/Cygwin call it `sha256sum`.

2.4 Summary

You can read this chapter once, and then refer to it any number of times later when you program with Unix. It's inevitable that you will evolve to getting what you need from the Unix man pages, which will likely become your first source for reference information.

We have touched on a large number of Unix commands, and the next chapter gives you the arsenal needed to string these commands into reusable scripts. Once you start using the Unix command line, you will love Unix and its central theme, which is a good one—tools, not policies.

CHAPTER 3

Bourne Shell Scripting

If you are the kind of person who never needs to do the same thing ever again, shell scripting is not for you. Others can greatly benefit, though, by grouping commands into plain text files called *shell scripts.*

Although it is entirely legit to type individual commands directly into the command line, putting them inside a file (then termed a *script*) perks up life at the shell in two ways: a) reusability of a large number of commands in one stroke, and b) reduced chances of operational error afforded by the file's readability. This chapter hence introduces one of the fascinations of working with Unix: *scripting* (also called automation).

3.1 Inside Our First Shell Script

POSIX-compliant scripts are interpreted by the Bourne shell. This makes them portable by nature. So while your interactive shell would understandably be Bash or Zsh, your scripts must be coded for interpretation by sh (the Bourne shell executable).

Every shell script begins with an opening line, called the *shebang,* that sets out the path of the interpreter:

```
#!/bin/sh
```

That line forks off a new shell process that executes the statements in the script. A script without the shebang is still a valid script, but cannot be being executed directly. It can be executed as part of another script, or invoked as a shell argument:

```
USER>   sh myscript.sh
```

The last line of a shebang-ing script is always the same: exit 0. Anything other than 0 implies failure. Without an exit value, the script's return status to the shell is not well-defined. The convention then is for the script to return the exit code of its last operation.

© Manish Jain 2018
M. Jain, *Beginning Modern Unix*, https://doi.org/10.1007/978-1-4842-3528-7_3

There exists a multi-national, cross-cultural agreement that all first-off programs must output Hello World. We'll frame our first script such that we don't break the tradition.

```
#!/bin/sh
echo "Hello World"
exit 0
```

Save the text in hello.sh under ~/bin/ (create that first, if needed, with mkdir ~/bin).

Mark the script as executable, and then execute hello.sh from the command line using these steps:

```
USER>   cd ~/bin
USER>   chmod +x hello.sh
USER>   ./hello.sh
```

This outputs Hello World—pretty much what we would have anticipated.

Before delving any further, we should note that—both on the command line and inside a shell script—the hash sign # marks the beginning of a comment. Everything from there to the end-of-line is ignored by the interpreter. The only exception is the opening shebang, which specifies the path of the interpreter itself.

3.2 Variable Assignment

We'll now try to add some sophistication to hello.sh. For a (rather naive) start, we'll pack the string to be output (Hello World) into a shell variable v1, and then output the shell variable.

```
#!/bin/sh

v1=Hello World
echo v1

exit 0
```

(Hereon, we'll assume the shebang and exit statements as implied.)

Executing `hello.sh` creates two quagmires at once:

```
World: not found
v1
```

Two things went wrong:

- The assignment did not quite work, breaking down at the space character.

- The shell printed the name of the variable `v1`, rather than its contents.

We have fixes:

- First, assign multi-word content, or anything that has embedded whitespace (spaces or tabs, or at times even newlines) in quotes (double or single—more on this later).

- Second, irrespective of what your preferred currency is, reference the contents of a shell variable with a $. In other words, "Write without the dollar; read with the dollar":

```
v1="Hello World"   # or single quotes:  v1='Hello World'
echo $v1
```

Our script works again.

Since the $ is of particularly high value to the shell, you can print a literal $ (and any such special characters) by escaping it with a backslash, as follows:

```
echo \$
```

A touch surprisingly at first—and quite unlike any other programming language—shell variables are of one type only: string. Therefore you never have to worry about the type of a shell variable.

Wherever we have strings, we have string lengths and string concatenation. The string length of the contents of the variable `v1` can be determined with ${#v1}.

As a handy reassurance, if a shell variable has not been assigned anything, it is treated as an empty (null) string. You can assign a null string to a shell variable in any of the following ways:

```
empty1=
empty2=""
empty3='
```

(The term *null* means different things in different environments. In shell, a null string means an empty string. In C, null is equivalent to the number zero.)

For illustrating concatenation, we can break up v1 (which holds 'Hello World') still further and then glue the pieces together to generate v1 on-the-fly:

```
v1a=Hello
v1b=" "                 # a single space
v1c=World
v1="$v1a$v1b$v1c"       # or: v1=$v1a"$v1b"$v1c
```

This code works, but only just about.

Because of the way the preceding assignment is coded, it is quite easy to mess up variable names and surrounding text. To make that last statement more sanguine as well as readable, it is highly advisable—at least whenever there is any scope for ambiguity—to reference a shell variable using the curly braces notation:

```
v1="${v1a}${v1b}${v1c}"    # curly braces strongly advisable
echo ${v1}                 # curly braces optional
```

Variable assignment has some useful default-value modifiers:

```
v2=${v1:-foo}
# If v1 is not empty, use v1; else use the text 'foo'

v2=${v1:=bar}
# If v1 is not empty, use v1; else assign 'bar' to v1 and use it

v2=${v1:?}
# If v1 is not empty, use v1; else exit with an error message
```

If v1 or the text being used contains whitespace, it would have to be referred under quotes. Of course, the safest thing to do is put the assignment within double quotes:

```
v2="${v1:-foo}"
```

With the basic idea of variable assignment laid out, we can now open a new can of worms: assignment via command output (also called command substitution).

For explaining this, we return to the original assignment:

```
v1="Hello World"
```

Let's say we want to determine the number of words in v1. That is readily done with the wc command:

```
echo $v1 | wc -w          # outputs '2'
```

Now, if we want to store the output in its own variable, we can simply run the command within back-quotes (often also called "backticks"). The output then is trapped in the new variable:

```
num='echo $v1 | wc -w'
```

3.3 Arithmetic and Boolean Operations

We'll start with a healthy reminder—shell variables are of one type only, which is the type string.

```
v3=5
v4=true
```

Despite appearances, v3 and v4 are both string variables. Since the contents of v3 are purely numeric, we can perform some basic, external arithmetic operations on it using expr:

```
expr $v3 + 1        # outputs 6 on console; v3 remains 5
v3='expr $v3 + 1'   # prints nothing; v3 is now 6
```

Because using expr is a touch laborious—apart from being an external command, there is a nifty way of performing this arithmetic operation in the shell internally:

```
v3=$((v3 + 1))
```

Despite the fact that the shell is capable of performing arithmetic operations on v3, v3 is not treated specially by the shell. Like all other shell variables, v3 is stored as a string, and arithmetic functions like expr have to be careful to first ensure at runtime that the operand is numeric.

Booleans, in case you are not aware, are true/false conditions. Fortunately or unfortunately, in the world of shell, boolean variables do not exist. If you assign true to a shell variable (like we have done for v4), the shell variable simply remains a string with the contents t, followed by r, followed by u, followed by e.

Instead of true/false, you can use any other combo that you like: on or off, YES or NO, and 1 or 0.

You might be tempted to test (pun not intended) if the C/C++ boolean spirit works in shell too, but it does not:

```
v5=false

if [ $v5 ]; then
    echo "Unexpected"
fi
```

The preceding code prints Unexpected, because the if condition (which presumably was intended to mean if [$v5 = true]; then) was interpreted by the shell as a check whether v5 holds a non-empty string. Since v5 holds the five-character string called false, the test actually succeeds.

Therefore, checking for conditions in shell has to be done the harder way:

```
if [ $v5 = true ]; then
    echo "Unexpected"
fi
```

Since v5 could be a null string or have whitespace in it, it is definitely a very good idea to code this branch with v5 inside quotes. Also, the semicolon can—if you prefer—be replaced with a newline.

Either of the following forms is now equally acceptable:

```
if [ "$v5" = "true" ];  then          if [ "$v5" = "true" ]
    echo "Unexpected"                 then
fi                                        echo "Unexpected"
                                      fi
```

3.4 Command Chaining and Grouping

Very often, you'll need to execute another command based on the outcome of the first command. The shell facilitates this kind of chaining with && and ||:

```
command1 && command2     # if command1 succeeds, run command2 also
command1 || command3     # if command1 fails, run command3
```

Examples:

```
[ -f /etc/fstab ] && echo "exists"
[ -f /etc/fstab ] || echo "does not exist"
```

A particularly handy chaining combination is:

```
command1 && command2 || command3
```

The preceding statement asks the shell to first run command1. Then, if command1 succeeds, run command2. If command1 fails, run command3 instead.

Here is an example:

```
[ -f /etc/fstab ] && echo "exists" || echo "does not exist"
```

Command grouping is another useful shell facility. This lets you execute (or ignore) a bunch of commands as a single group.

Let's say you want to display an error message and exit immediately if the user ID is not 0 (which usually means the root user):

```
[ 'id -u' -eq 0 ] || { echo "root only!"; exit 1; }
```

This example groups the echo command and exit command as a single set of actions which is invoked if the id test fails.

Every command in a group must end with a semicolon ; and there must be whitespace to right of { and to the left of }.

There is an alternate grouping syntax that uses newline characters in place of semicolons and space characters:

```
[ 'id -u' -eq 0 ] || \
{
    echo "root only!"
    exit 1
}
```

3.5 Meta-Character Expansion

There are quite a few meta-characters that the shell expands automatically, unless explicitly told otherwise.

* Zero or more wildcard path characters

? Any single wildcard path character

~ The path of the current user's home directory (i.e., $HOME)

\ Treat the next character specially (\t ~ tabulator;
\\ Z~ literal backslash; \n ~ newline)

A backslash (\) followed by a hard carriage return lets you break up long commands over multiple lines. Each of those lines (except the last) terminates with \ followed by a carriage return.

3.6 Quoting: Single, Double, and Back

For a short while, we'll return to one of the previous examples wherein we generated the string 'Hello World' from its components:

```
v1a=Hello
v1b=" "                     # a single space
v1c=World
```

Since v1b has embedded whitespace, the concatenation has to be quoted. Here is the assignment again: v1="${v1a}${v1b}${v1c}".

What would have happened if we used single quotes rather than the double quotes?

```
v1='${v1a}${v1b}${v1c}'
```

Let's find out with:

```
echo $v1
```

This outputs what had literally been assigned:

```
${v1a}${v1b}${v1c}
```

So single quotes mean literal assignment without the shell making any substitutions whatever. Usually—but not always—this is not what is needed. Even when under quotes, we usually like the shell to help with its goodies: variable name expansion, backslashed escapes, and command substitution for back-quoted text. If you are sure you want none of those, go ahead and use single quotes.

Since you can use the backslash to produce escape sequences, double-quoted strings can have a literal double-quote character embedded in them:

```
sz="abc\"123"
```

While the backslash \ and back-quotes (i.e., '<command>') remain meaningful inside double quotes, many other shell meta-characters (like * and ~) lose their special characteristics.

Since backslash sequences do not work under single quotes, you cannot embed a literal single quote character inside a single-quoted string.

One cool thing to remember is that:

- Double quotes automatically disable any single quote(s) within them

- Single quotes automatically disable any double quote(s) within them

So these are perfectly okay, and are often needed in scripting:

```
sz1="abc'123"
sz2='xyz"789'
```

The third kind of quotes is the back-quotes, which fetch the output of some text interpreted as a command. For example, to populate a shell variable with the listing of the current directory, we can use:

```
dirlist='ls'
```

Back-quotes are programmed to automatically place their output in implicit double quotes. So the previous command is perfectly equivalent to:

```
dirlist="'ls'"
```

3.7 Setting the Shell Prompt

There is one place where you definitely need single quotes: when setting the shell prompt.

Bash users like their shell prompt (PS1) to be the path of current directory. That is accomplished with:

```
export PS1=''pwd' % '        # works for bash; not for Bourne
```

If you use double quotes while setting PS1 in this statement, you will land yourself the rather uncanny outcome that your shell prompt will be set and glued to the path of the directory from which the command was issued. Using single quotes lets PS1 be evaluated at runtime—every time you move to a different directory, your shell prompt will change.

The Z shell similarly can be made to bind the current directory into the shell prompt with the following in ~/.zshrc or issued at the command line:

```
export PROMPT='%d # '
```

Bash and Zsh have built-in string expanders that you can readily use. For example, to get the username into the Bash shell prompt, you can use \u, while Zsh bundles the time into the prompt with %t.

For the sake of completeness, Bash provides a shortcut for the current working directory: \w (which interestingly can be typed using single quotes or double quotes, and equally interestingly works for Bourne shell too).

3.8 Dealing with Whitespace in Filenames

Hopefully, you did not forget my assertion a couple of sections back: back-quotes are programmed to automatically place their output in implicit double quotes. I even gave you an example to prove my point.

Well, I lied. But this is an interesting lie that is intended to forewarn you that dealing with whitespace in filenames can be tricky, at times even a show-stopper unless you write precisely the right code to deal with whitespace.

To get the hang of things that can go wrong, we'll create a shell script with a space character in its name: ~/bin/ab cd.sh (That's a file with the name: ab followed by a space, followed by cd.sh.)

Here is the code to programmatically generate the file:

```
[ -d ~/bin ] || mkdir ~/bin
echo '#!/bin/sh' > ~/bin/"ab cd.sh"         # create
echo 'exit 0' >> ~/bin/"ab cd.sh"           # append
chmod +x ~/bin/"ab cd.sh"
```

(Under Zsh, next run the command `rehash` to recompute the internal shell variables.)

Now let's say we forget where this wonderful script is located. So we run the following commands to find out:

```
USER>    p='which "ab cd.sh"'
USER>    echo "$p"
```

This works perfectly—the path of the script is printed correctly. So what is the problem, if any?

The problem arises when we use the output of `which` for anything other than assignment.

Let's say we want to determine how many lines are in the script. The usual command for that would be:

```
USER>   wc -l 'which "ab cd.sh"'
```

This produces a nasty error:

```
wc: cd.sh: open: No such file or directory
```

Because there is no assignment, the shell will "forget" the double quotes implied by the backticks. You have to put them back in again explicitly:

```
USER>   wc -l "'which \"ab cd.sh\"'"
```

Since the outer double quotes have inner double quotes, the inner ones need to be escaped.

The ability to escape the double-quote character and the backtick is extremely handy in constructing complex commands. If you want to assign the `wc` output to a new variable, you can escape all embedded quotes:

```
USER>   n='wc -l "\'which \"ab cd.sh\"\'"'
```

This command looks fairly arcane to a rookie. But if you are the rookie concerned, you can be fairly certain that in a couple of days, you'll be writing such commands, and possibly ones that are even more complex.

3.9 Shell Functions

Shell scripts can have functions too, and most actually do.

Here is a script that uses a shell function named say:

```
#!/bin/sh

say()
{
    v1="Veni   Vidi   Vici"
    echo $v1
}

say
exit  0
```

If we want the string to be "said" to be passed in to the say() function, we can do that by using $1, a function's first positional parameter:

```
say()
{
    echo $1
}

v1="Veni Vidi Vici"

say "$v1"
# Quiz: What would happen if we don't double-quote $v1 above?
```

Shell scripts and functions can use at least nine positional parameters $1 through $9. Inside a shell function, each positional parameter is what the script's main body passed in as an argument (or else a null string). In the main shell script itself (i.e., outside of any shell function), each positional parameter represents an argument passed in from the command line (or else a null string).

More than nine positional parameters are not often needed, but most modern shells allow you to access more than nine using the curly braces notation. Each positional parameter is read-only.

There is a back-door "hack" to write your own positional parameters. This is usually not needed, but possible. If, inside a function, you want to write the function's positional parameters, you can use the set command, like this example, which sets $1:

```
say()
{
    set "Adios Amigos!"
    echo $1
}
```

No matter what you ask say() to say, it will always print Adios Amigos!

Every shell function implicitly returns 0, which represents success. You can, however, break out from the function at any point by using return <n>. If <n> is not 0, function failure is implied.

3.10 Special Variables

Besides the positional parameters discussed in the previous section, there are a few more important special variables, all of them read-only. You cannot assign anything to these variables (or even the positional parameters) yourself: that can only be done by the shell in the background.

$$ Process ID of the current shell process

$?   Return value of the last command

$0   Name used to invoke the script

$#   Number of arguments

$*   Consolidated list of all arguments

$@   Iterable list of all arguments

$? is frequently used to test/save the return status of the previous command.

$0 is significant because, under Unix, a file could be linked under a different name. The name used to invoke the application may result in altered behavior. Further, when you are inside a shell function, $0 does not change to the name of the function: it remains the script name.

Inside a shell function, $# represents the number of arguments passed in to the function. Outside any function, it represents the number of arguments passed in to the script (i.e., at the command line).

It is important to understand the difference between the last two variables in our list: $* and $@. So important that despite the fact that we are yet to formally touch down on looping (which will happen in the next section), we will use a couple of Hollywood-sanctioned for loops right now to explain the difference.

```
say()
{
    echo "Starting for quoted $*    ..."
    for arg in "$*"; do
        echo "$arg"
    done

    echo    # produce an artificial empty line

    echo "Starting for quoted $@  ..."
    for arg in "$@"; do
        echo "$arg"
    done
}

v1="Bourne  Identity"
v2="Bourne  Supremacy"
say "$v1" $v2
```

Executing this script gets us:

```
Starting for quoted $* ...
Bourne Identity Bourne Supremacy

Starting for quoted $@ ...
Bourne Identity
Bourne
Supremacy
```

Note that, since $v2 is unquoted, the script is passing three arguments to say():

```
"$v1"              # this expands as "Bourne Identity"
Bourne
Supremacy
```

When unquoted, both $@ and $* expand to exactly the same list, which has four items: 'Bourne', 'Identity', 'Bourne', and 'Supremacy'.

When under quotes, $* gets a list with just one item: 'Bourne Identity Bourne Supremacy'.

This normally is not what we would like: we should be able to fetch the three arguments exactly as passed in. The only way to do that is to use $@, which expands as the original list of three items.

It is interesting to note that, even though $@ produces a list of three items, $@ occupies just one line in memory. If you want to be certain that I am not trying to hoodwink you, insert this command

```
echo "$@" | wc -l
```

somewhere inside say(), just to check for yourself what the wc output is.

3.11 Branching and Looping

One of the good things about shell scripting (and programming with C) is that well written, elementary code sounds, reads, and works more or less like plain English. Just so with a touch of scientific precision and with a restricted vocabulary.

We have been using if statements for branching right from the start, without having first discussed the if statement formally. We'll set things right now on that account.

The formal, full-fledged structure of an if statement is:

```
if condition1; then
    <commands_if>
elif  condition2;   then
    <commands_elif>
else
    <commands_else>
fi
```

Not surprisingly, elif stands for "else if". Both branches elif and else are optional. The elif branch can be repeated as many times as the user wants.

The conditions, as denoted by condition1 and condition2 in the formal structure of the if statement, can be generated by either of two methods:

- A test; for example:

```
if [ -f /etc/passwd ]; then
    echo "/etc/passwd exists"
fi
```

- A return value; for example:

```
if cat /etc/passwd | grep --silent '^root:'; then
    echo "/etc/passwd has an entry for root"
fi
```

A second way of branching is with case.

Let's say we have a shell variable var, based on the value of which we have to execute one of three commands: < command1 >, < command2 >, or < command3 >.

The value of var could be one of the following four:

Anything beginning with 'abc' (case-insensitive)	→	< command1 >
'123'	→	< command2 >
'xyz' (case-sensitive)	→	< command2 >
Anything other than 'abc. . . ' / '123' / 'xyz'	→	< command3 >

Noting that '123' and 'xyz' both need the same follow-up command, we can branch with the case switch underneath:

```
case "$var" in
[aA][bB][cC]*)
    <command_1>
    ;;

123|xyz)
    <command_2>
    ;;
```

```
*)
    <command_3>
    ;;
esac
```

Four things to note:

- The variable being switched on should preferably be referred under double quotes because it may have embedded whitespace, or may be null.

- case is smart enough to understand that [aA][bB][cC]* means anything beginning with abc and with no uppercase/lowercase distinction.

- As happens for '123' and 'xyz' in our case switch, multiple patterns can be specified for a single set of commands by separating the patterns with a pipe symbol (|).

- The match for * is the default match. If none of the previous matches succeeded, this one will. Matching for * is optional.

Moving ahead to loops, the Unix shell has two looping constructs that you should know about: while and for.

while is used to repeat an action as long as some condition evaluates as true. The formal syntax of a while statement is:

```
while <condition>; do
    <commands>
done
```

This while loop prints the first 10 integers, beginning with 0:

```
n=0

while [ $n -lt 10 ]; do
    echo $n
    n='expr $n + 1'
done
```

The condition of a while statement is evaluated at the start of each iteration of the loop.

The for loop is used to repeat an action for each entity in a given set of values. The formal syntax of a for statement is:

```
for variable in tokens; do
    <commands>
done
```

This for loop checks if the files /etc/fstab and /etc/passwd exist:

```
for f in /etc/fstab /etc/passwd; do
    [ -f $f ] && "$f exists" || "$f does not exist"
done
```

You might at times need to end a loop prematurely. To exit a while or for loop midway, you can use the break command.

3.12 The shift Command

An easy-to-use and powerful mechanism to parse arguments in the Bourne shell is the shift command, which can operate on the positional parameters ($1 through $9) in general, and on $1 in particular with crafty finesse.

What shift does is discard $1 and move all the remaining parameters one spot farther to the left. So $2 becomes the new $1, $3 becomes the new $2, and so on. Each time this left-shift occurs, the count of the number of arguments (i.e., $#) gets decremented by 1.

With this mechanism in place, you can parse all arguments by just evaluating $1. After each evaluation, you use shift.

Note   If a script does not behave well at runtime, the easiest way to debug it is to put the statement set -x near its top, and then (optionally) the statement set +x near the bottom. When executing the script, the interpreter will display tracing diagnostics that you can use to locate and fix the error.

Here is a script example that sets two options—optX (passed in via -x) and optY (passed in via -y)—at runtime:

```
optX=false
optY=false

while [ $# -gt 0 ]; do
    case "$1" in
    -x)
        optX=true
        shift
    ;;

    -y)
        optY=true
        shift
    ;;

    *)
        echo "Invalid arg: $1" 1>&2
        exit 1
    ;;
    esac
done
```

3.13 Sourcing, Aliasing, and Exporting

For reasons that will become clear later in this section, I will start the section by visiting this chapter's antithesis: non-Bourne scripting. This is permitted, but neither encouraged nor POSIX-compliant scripting. The reason it is permitted is that Bourne shell derivatives like Bash and Zsh have support for arrays, which vanilla Bourne does not—at least as of yet.

If you decide to use bash or zsh as the interpreter, the right way to shebang is:

```
#!/usr/bin/env  <interpreter>
# Example: #!/usr/bin/env zsh
```

Bourne shell also does not have the source command, which both Bash and Zsh have. The source command lets bash and zsh input statements from another script.

A Bourne shell script—for example, named myscript—has to use the . command:

```
. otherscript
# Execute statements in otherscript within the current shell
```

An alias in shell scripting is a nickname tagged to a command, which might be long or complex. With the following statement inside myscript, the script can use dir as equivalent to the command ls -l:

```
alias dir="ls -l"
```

If this statement is located not in myscript but in otherscript, myscript can still use dir as a valid alias for ls -l if myscript inputs otherscript with the . command.

Things change a bit if myscript uses bash as the interpreter, and then inputs otherscript with the source command. An alias defined in otherscript will not by default become available to myscript as well. If the sourcing bash script wants to use aliases defined in the sourced script, it must—before sourcing—issue this command:

```
shopt -s expand_aliases
```

The final point of this section is export of shell variables, best elucidated by throwing into the foregoing mix yet another script, which is executed (not sourced nor inputted via the . command) by myscript with:

```
n=32
yetanotherscript
```

Each time a shell script executes an external command—which could be ls or some other script—the Unix kernel will create a subshell environment for the external command. Variables like n in the parent will not be made available to the subshell. If the parent shell wants to make a variable available to any subshell, it must not just define the variable, but export it as well:

```
export n=32
yetanotherscript
```

yetanotherscript can now access n with the value (32) as originally defined in myscript. If yetanotherscript changes the value of n, the change affects its local copy and not the n inside myscript.

3.14 Putting It All Together

Here are two tasks for you to perform:

1. Create a shell script command named tcase that can convert a parameter string to title case ('abc xYz' → 'Abc Xyz').

   ```
   Tip 1:    echo "abc" | tr [:lower:]   [:upper:]
   Tip 2:    echo "abc" | cut -c 2-
   ```

2. Assuming that you have a text file with multiple occurrences of the word unix, write a shell script called extract.sh to extract all the text between the first and last occurrences. The lines containing the first and last occurrences are themselves ignored for the purpose of output. So if the line number of the first occurrence is 8 and the line number of the last occurrence is 12, you have to print the text of lines 9, 10, and 11 (each of which could itself contain zero or more occurrences of the word unix).

If you flounder, sample solutions are available in the appendix.

3.15 Summary

Although this chapter has largely been restricted to what can be done under Unix emulation environments like Cygwin/Babun, you should now have a pretty good hold of the Unix command line. As you evolve in your shell skills, you will fall in love with shell scripting as a first-choice way of quickly stringing together already available applications to solve problems and automate your system.

You are now ready for real Unix, which will begin in the next chapter and in a new section of its own. If you have been itching to purchase a new PC or hardware upgrade of your existing box, hang on until the next chapter to get tips on what hardware is best suited for running Unix.

Note   Optional detour. If you are starting to feel at home with the Unix command line, you can take a detour and read the first half of Chapter 10, "Advanced Techniques in Shell Scripting," before proceeding to the next chapter. That chapter provides the rest of the common shell techniques, and the material works under Unix as well as Unix emulators (Cygwin/Babun).

PART 2

Preparing for Part II

Very soon, we will be hitting the world of real Unix. This perhaps is just the right place and the right time to ponder: Which Unix?

Wrong answers are permitted—you can always try something else if you don't like what you have. The question itself can be rephrased as a two-pronged poser:

- FreeBSD or Linux?

- For Linux, which distribution?

FreeBSD offers:

Pros:	Cons:
1. Standardization	1. Supports less hardware
2. Higher level of maturity in the code base	2. A pure-text setup process
3. A ports system to build stuff from sources	3. Fewer applications vis-a-vis Linux

Linux offers:

Pros:	Cons:
1. Supports almost all current hardware	1. Fragmentation
2. A graphical setup (except vanilla Arch)	2. Flux in the core of the code base
3. A few more applications vis-a-vis FreeBSD	3. Not as well-documented as FreeBSD

Since the situation is likely to persist in future, the best answer is to install both FreeBSD and Linux. (That's just what we'll do in Chapter 5.)

Linux usually is instantly likeable. As for FreeBSD, the user experience ranges from love-at-first-sight to the graduation:

:-(→   :-| →   :-)   →   ♡

You might dismiss the course of evolution depicted in the last line as just an attempt (on the part of the author) to deliver some humor. But it is more than that. It is equally a note to users accustomed to graphical installation procedures, such as what are used under Windows and (to a large degree) Linux. For users accustomed to graphical installations, there are a couple of important notes:

- There is nothing more educational about a computer than a command-line installation of an operating system (and any associated desktop environment). Once you have installed FreeBSD a couple of times, you will, more likely than not, fall in love with the process. You might even start wishing, just as I do, that all operating systems use a curses/ncurses (text-mode widgets) based installation procedure.

- While eating into the dividend outlined here, a graphical installation also (and even more) disturbs the FreeBSD operational motto: *We make things as simple as possible, but not any simpler.*

That leaves us with the second question—which Linux distribution? You should remember that Linux distributions mostly come in one of three flavors (based on the package manager):

- `rpm`-based (mostly not documented in this book): Red Hat, Fedora, and CentOS

- `apt`-based: Ubuntu, Linux Mint, and elementary OS

- `pacman`-based: Arch, Manjaro, and Antergos

If this is the first time you are installing Linux, my suggestion is not to think about this part of the question too much, and simply try Linux Mint (Cinnamon) before anything else. Linux Mint is an outstanding distribution, and the Cinnamon desktop is fast and gorgeous.

Those wanting to try something other than Linux Mint should keep in mind a couple of distributions I tried recently and liked: Manjaro and Parrot.

You can always go Linux-hunting at the URL: `https://distrowatch.com/`.

If you do opt for Linux Mint, besides FreeBSD, you will have precisely the same setup as I do in this book.

## CHAPTER 4

PC Hardware for Unix

Is it a good idea to suggest hardware?

Hardware purchases are supposed to be entirely a function of the user's likes and dislikes. It is only when the user gets stuck with hardware that refuses to budge under the operating system of the user's choice that the user begins to wonder—why can Unix/Linux forums not create a portal where hardware advice and ratings are easily available? There are many OEMs (Original Equipment Manufacturers) out there who still take pride in asserting the adage, "Works with Windows," which at times is just another way of saying, "We have no idea whether this thing works with Unix".

This chapter tries to fill in the gap that OEMs forcibly create. Of course, the hardware suggestions in this chapter are based on my own views. If there is anything you seriously disagree with, you can always email me. If it's feasible, I will update the suggestions accordingly.

4.1 A Shopping List

If you are going to build a PC, it's helpful to have a shopping list that you can readily tick items off. The following list is arranged in order of component importance. You can build a PC without a printer (the last item in the list). But if you manage to build a PC without a CPU (the first item), it will be in the newspapers.

89

© Manish Jain 2018
M. Jain, *Beginning Modern Unix*, https://doi.org/10.1007/978-1-4842-3528-7_4

- CPU
- System board (motherboard)
- RAM
- Hard disk
- SMPS (power supply)
- Cabinet
- Graphics card
- Optical drive (CD/DVD reader & writer)
- CPU cooler
- Printer/scanner

I have left out console devices (monitor, keyboard, and mouse) from the list, as well as from the PC's budget. Those things are pretty much standard, but some notes might help.

- You can use standard wired USB devices for keyboard/mouse. Or for a few dollars more, opt for wireless USB, with the USB protocol implemented by an OS-independent receiver. Wired and wireless USB work equally well, using the same driver in the Unix kernel.
- You should stick to the basic 101/104/105 keyboard (i.e., no multimedia keys). But you can opt for one with those hip-looking LED backlights (which cost at least US $20 extra).

4.2 Preparatory Notes

Compared to a couple of decades back, building a PC has become less costly (as long you do not "Add To Cart" with abandon) and an increasingly messy business. Even within the same architecture (AMD64), you have different product lines (AMD and Intel). And then, in each line, there are different hardware configurations possible (e.g., CPU socket types and even different RAM types, such as DDR3 and DDR4).

We'll keep things simple and geared for economy, while still aiming for a power-packed PC. The chapter's guiding principles are:

- For desktops, AMD delivers significantly better value for the money than Intel.

- Using a dedicated graphics card leads to notably better system performance.

- DDR4 does not lead to a clear performance advantage over DDR3 for desktop usage, but does lead to clear cost disadvantages (both for the motherboard and for the actual RAM modules).

Working around these principles, we'll derive a PC configuration with plenty of oomph and muscle, and within a budget of US $500 (excluding console devices and printer/scanner). Most importantly, everything in our build will work out-of-the-box under FreeBSD and Linux—which is the whole point of this chapter.

If you want to economize, here is a formula you can try (on your own) to shave about $200 off the bill for the standard course:

- AMD A6-6400K Richland processor (3.9GHz; socket FM2; dual-core)

- MSI A68HM-E33 V2 motherboard (socket FM2; SATA3; USB3; mATX)

This formula derives its savings in part from the onboard graphics (Radeon HD 8470D; works with FreeBSD/Linux), which means you do not need to buy a dedicated graphics card. Instead, your CPU and part of system RAM will be used for delivering the graphics payload to the output device (the monitor). Further savings can be yielded by using the stock CPU fan or scaling the RAM size down to 4GB. If you use 4GB RAM with onboard graphics, set the video memory size in BIOS to 256MB or less.

Either way, you have to remember one point. The two most trouble-prone components in a Unix PC build are the graphics chip and the printer. For the graphics (video) chip, FreeBSD is the highest common factor. If it works under FreeBSD, it works under any Unix. For the printer, just make sure you select something that has an open-source driver. The printer driver support under FreeBSD and Linux is pretty much the same, at least with an HP device.

Note   Prices mentioned in this chapter represent the list prices in US dollars that were current at the time of writing. These will change per market dynamics.

4.3 CPU (Central Processing Unit)

Even though a dual-core processor is enough for desktop purposes (my system is a dual-core Athlon), I suggest you spend about a dozen more dollars to equip the PC with four cores. It's an investment of a lifetime.

AMD's four-Core, 3.8GHz FX-4300 (socket AM3+) is a top-notch CPU, with performance in the league of Intel's Core i5 series offerings. It's priced well under half as much. Figure 4-1 shows an early bird view of the package you will get (price: $69).

```
https://www.amazon.com/dp/B00907YU3S
```

Once you select a CPU, you need to narrow down the motherboard search to fit the CPU's socket.

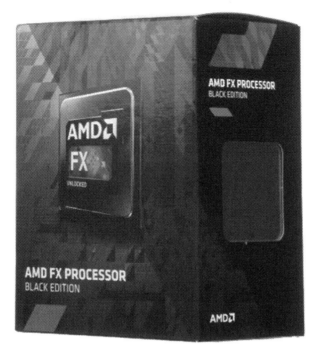

Figure 4-1. *The AMD FX-4300 processor (socket AM3+)*

Note also that AMD's processors typically consume more power than Intel's. So we'll do the wise thing here by building a top-dog CPU cooler (with its own fan and heatsink) into our PC. The cooler does not cost much, compared to the benefits it begets.

4.4 System Board/Motherboard

With an AM3+ socket, the Gigabyte GA-970A-DS3P is a very nice fit for our CPU. It has USB3 ports (for frontside and backside connections) as well as SATA3 (6Gbps) ports. One particular nicety is that the board has both PCI Express (new style) as well as PCI (old style) expansion slots, the latter not often found on motherboards these days.

This link will take you to Amazon, with the GA-970A-DS3P ready for you to cart off with: `https://www.amazon.com/dp/B00CX4MUCC` (price: $90).

The board is shown in Figure 4-2, and its specs are listed next.

Figure 4-2. *Gigabyte GA-970A-DS3P motherboard (AM3+)*

It might be of interest to you that all major motherboard manufacturers—Asus/ Gigabyte/MSI/any other name you can think of—are based in Taiwan, which seems to enjoy a monopoly in the motherboard manufacturing business.

Here are the complete specs for our motherboard, as available at Amazon:

Model: Gigabyte GA-970A-DS3P

Socket: AM3+

Chipset: North Bridge AMD 970 and South Bridge AMD SB950

Memory: 4 × DDR3; 2000(OC)/1866/1600/1333/1066 DIMM;

     : Dual-channel; max capacity 32GB

CPU: AMD AM3+ FX/AMD AM3 Phenom II/AMD Athlon II

LAN: Realtek GbE LAN chip (10/100/1000Mbit)

Expansion slots: 1 × PCI Express x16 slot, running at x16 (PCIEX16)

: 1 × PCI Express x16 slot, running at x4 (PCIEX4)

: 3 × PCI Express x1 slots

: 2 × PCI slots

Storage interface: 6 × SATA 6Gb/s connectors;

: Support for RAID 0, RAID 1, RAID 5, and JBOD

USB: Up to 12 USB 2.0/1.1 ports; 4 USB 3.0/2.0 ports

Audio: Realtek ALC887 (high definition audio, 8-channel)

This motherboard does not have any onboard (integrated) graphics, and thus no VGA/DVI/HDMI output ports. Such boards (often judged as high-end) must use a dedicated graphics card. Not having integrated graphics in the motherboard leads to two advantages:

- The most expensive CPU operations (graphics) get delegated to a separate system, which has its own dedicated processor and memory.

- The motherboard is decoupled from the problem of graphics support, which usually is the most pressing concern with the operating system's support for the motherboard itself. Just get a good video card once, and you will never have to worry about whether graphics will work for you under FreeBSD/Linux—even if later you switch to a different motherboard.

I should expressly mention at this point that I find overclocking an abhorrent idea. Trying to overclock is like trying to run a 500 kmph TGV train on a track built for an optimum speed of 100 kmph. Your system will overheat frequently and wear out quicker. A motherboard is built to perform best and last long in its default configuration. Gains from overclocking are miniscule anyway, considering a modern CPU's speed.

Also note that choosing a motherboard narrows your RAM search to just the type the motherboard supports, which in our case means DDR3. It also limits your RAM speed to the highest frequency supported by the motherboard, which in our case means 1866MHz. If your RAM module clocks a higher frequency, the motherboard will restrict the DIMM (dual in-line memory module) to what the motherboard itself can support.

4.5 RAM (Random Access Memory)

We would like to pick a RAM module with a frequency rating that matches the maximum supported by our un-overclocked motherboard (1866MHz).

The Kingston HyperX FURY 8GB 1866MHz DDR3 CL10 DIMM, for $76, is one such module. It's found at `https://www.amazon.com/dp/B00J8E92I0`. Figure 4-3 shows this model.

Figure 4-3. *Kingston HyperX FURY DDR3 RAM*

Besides excellent performance and a generous size, this module is a single-piece module, which usually is preferable to a 2 × 4GB configuration. While the dual-channel mode (2 × 4GB) comes off marginally better than single channel (1 × 8GB) in performance benchmarks (owing to two memory bands instead of one), what should concern you more is the prospect of going up from 1 × 8GB to 2 × 8GB.

If you opt to economize with just one DIMM of 4GB (anything less is unacceptable), you can expect about 75% as much zip as the standard 8GB system. But you must create a mid-sized swap partition (5GB should be okay) in your hard disk. Even with more RAM, a small swap partition would never hurt, while having no swap partition at all will hurt sooner or later. Swapping always adds to the amount of memory available. When the operating system runs out of RAM, it uses swap space to extend memory.

4.6 Hard Disk

This is where you can go beyond the budget of $500, without necessarily being extravagant.

There are two storage media widely used as today: rotating SATA disk (magnetic, 3Gbps, called SATA2) and Solid State Drive (SSD) disk (electronic, 6Gbps, called SATA3). An SSD provides roughly a three-fold performance advantage over traditional SATA and a four-fold cost disadvantage too, which calls for user judgment when economy is needed.

For the standard storage solution, I propose having two disks: one small SSD (64GB, which hosts the operating system installation) coupled with a much larger normal SATA disk (500GB, which you can use to store large multimedia files).

Although you can use any 64GB SSD and any 500GB internal 3.5 inch (desktop) disk, the following couple is shown in Figure 4-4:

- Silicon Power 60GB S60 MLC SSD (SATA3) for $30 (`https://www.amazon.com/dp/B01M2UUACN`)

- Western Digital AV-GP 500GB (32MB cache, SATA2, Green Power) for $28 (`https://www.amazon.com/dp/B00X95ROOS`)

Figure 4-4. *Silicon Power 60GB S60 MLC SSD and Western Digital AV-GP 500GB (green)*

If you find it repugnant to have your data spread across multiple disks, you can opt for a 500GB SSD, although this will cost you about $90 extra. What follows—and is shown in Figure 4-5—would certainly not be a bad choice if you decide to go the all-SSD way.

Samsung 850 EVO 500GB SSD
(SATA3, firmware MZ-75E500B/AM)

https://www.amazon.com/dp/B000BRE5UE
(USD 150)

Figure 4-5. *Samsung EVO 850 500GB SSD*

Disk manufacturers do not bundle a SATA cable into the disk parcel. Those cables (usually a 2-pack) instead are made available by the motherboard manufacturer. I always find it handy to have one or two SATA cables lying around in my spare stock. If you like the idea, you can use the UGREEN offering shown in Figure 4-6 below.

UGREEN SATA 90-Degree Cable, 3 Pack

www.amazon.com/dp/B01LYC6A8M
(USD 8)

Reliable and firm

Figure 4-6. *UGreen SATA Cables*

4.7 SMPS (Switched Mode Power Supply)

The most undervalued component in a PC build tends to be the power supply (transformer and AC-to-DC converter). This is due almost entirely to user ignorance—I myself was unaware of this factor until I had to trash a whole system because of a faulty SMPS.

A bad power supply will slowly (or perhaps even quickly) spread cancer in your PC's guts, providing faulty electrical signals, evidenced as weird noise problems and high power intake. So do not under-invest in this particular component.

Besides keeping the PC itself in good shape, a good power supply (at least 80% power efficiency) will let you recover costs in the long run via lower electricity bills. The Thermaltake 500W Bronze-rated ATX Power Supply Smart DPS G (seven-year warranty) is a fine, Bronze-rated (about 85% efficiency) SMPS, which at $53, is priced quite agreeably.

See https://www.amazon.com/dp/B01FA092N0. Figure 4-7 shows it in all its glory.

Do not try to open the SMPS to find out what its innards look like—the left side of Figure 4-7 should be enough to satisfy any curiosity. Opening an SMPS is a serious health hazard—at least for the power supply.

Figure 4-7. *Thermaltake 500 W Bronze-rated ATX Power Supply Smart DPS G*

If you are not comfortable with the idea of hooking the power supply into the PC yourself, you are not alone. I usually call in the hardware guy for this sacred task.

4.8 Cabinet

What good is a PC if it just performs well and does not look dapper? A cabinet is what lets your computer be nicely "object-oriented".

You can choose any cabinet you like, although I will mention the one shown in Figure 4-8, as it:

- Is superbly built, yielding handsome and elegant looks

- Is priced agreeably

- Has plenty of racks to tuck SATA disks and SSDs on

- Has generous room that can accommodate the fat-bellied CPU cooler that you'll learn about shortly

- Has a frontside USB3 port, which is pretty useful

This is the Thermaltake Versa H21 ATX Mid Tower Computer Chassis, found at `https://www.amazon.com/dp/B072T268WZ` (price: $38).

Figure 4-8. *Thermaltake Versa H21 ATX midtower computer chassis*

Chassis fans have a delectable knack for being noisy, no matter how expensive the cabinet. Luckily, the chassis fan is never needed and can safely be unhooked.

4.9 Graphics Card

This is where folks like to overspend. But we won't. We'll use a basic 1GB graphics card that will play any video file with perfect ease. Since I am not into gaming, I will simply ignore the gaming suitability of the card(s)—you should too.

I'll mention a card each from both the major players: AMD/ATI Radeon and NVIDIA.

For the Radeon, I would have liked to refer the card that I use myself—Sapphire Radeon R5 230 (HD6450, 1GB). But, for some reason, that card was not available for order with Amazon Prime in the United States at the time this was being written.

Figure 4-9 shows the Radeon offering at left, which works equally well. The right side caters to NVIDIA buffs.

- XFX ATI Radeon HD5450 DDR3 1 GB ($35) at `https://www.amazon.com/dp/B004TCM634`

- MSI Computer NVIDIA GT710 DDR3 1GB ($35)at `https://www.amazon.com/dp/B01AZHOWL0`

Figure 4-9. *1GB graphics cards: XFX (ATI Radeon) HD5450; MSI (NVIDIA) GT710*

Both cards mentioned here are known to work with FreeBSD (which, because it supports fewer graphics chipsets, usually becomes the HCF, or highest common factor, when choosing a video chip) as well as Linux, under which the chip will always work if it works under FreeBSD. To get information about which graphics chips do work under FreeBSD, visit `https://wiki.freebsd.org/Graphics`.

About the worst thing you can do with your graphics card is use the VGA (Video Graphics Array) cable to hook it to with the monitor. That VGA cable delivers to the monitor an analog signal, whereas modern monitors (LCD/LED/OLED) are purely digital devices, so they are much happier to work with digital input—DVI (Digital Visual Interface) or HDMI (High-Definition Multimedia Interface).

When you connect the graphics card to the monitor using the VGA cable, what happens is that upstream, the card has to convert the digital signal to analog. And then downstream, the monitor has to convert the analog signal all the way back to what it originally was—a digital signal. Not funny at all, and not uncommon at all as well. I reckon at least half of PC users still use the VGA cable for graphics delivery to output.

Trash the VGA cable and get a proper digital cable: DVI-DVI/DVI-HDMI/HDMI-HDMI. Amazon retails superb offerings for digital cabling under its in-house brand AmazonBasics, each cable priced very economically. Probably the most flexible solution for digital cabling is to use an HDMI-HDMI cable and—if needed at either end—adapt for DVI using an HDMI (female), DVI-D (male) converter. See Figure 4-10.

- AmazonBasics HDMI Cable, 6 Feet ($7) at `https://www.amazon.com/dp/B014I8SSD0`

- CableCreation HDMI female, DVI-D male adapter ($7) at `https://www.amazon.com/dp/B01FM52438`

Figure 4-10. *HDMI cable and DVI-D adapter*

A new fad that might break out in the coming days is the HDMI/DVI-only graphics card. Such cards are already available. Figure 4-11 shows one such card—Gigabyte's GeForce GV-N710D5-2GL:

Gigabyte NVIDIA GV-N710D5-2GL (2GB, DDR5) at `https://www.amazon.com/dp/B073SWN4ZM` ($50).

Figure 4-11. *Digital-only graphics card*

The card's DVI-I port will accept DVI-I cable as well as DVI-D. A DVI-I port has four extra pin slots that are not used when you plug in a DVI-D cable. Also, DDR5 is the configuration of the card's own internal memory (video RAM). The card will work with any DDR3/DDR4 board.

4.10 Optical Drive (CD/DVD Reader and Writer)

I doubt whether there is any real advantage in using a Blu-Ray optical drive, at least under Unix. So we will just stick with a normal DVD drive. Again, you can choose any one to suit yourself, although I mention this one:

ASUS Internal 24X SATA Optical Drive DRW-24B3ST, available at `https://www.amazon.com/dp/B0056UV96I` ($22).

Figure 4-12 shows this optical drive in full bloom.

Figure 4-12. *Asus DRW-24B3ST DVD writer*

You might be wondering what holy algorithm I used to cherry-pick this model from a whole range of DVD R+W drives—all of them equally good. I will be honest enough to share the selection criteria with you:

- For just a couple of dollars more than the other DVD drives, Asus DRW-24B3ST gave me a screenshot I could not easily have imagined to be as aesthetic as what I finally managed to get.

- It somehow seemed unjust to me that I should go through an entire chapter on PC hardware without somewhere mentioning a product from Asus. I have a lot of regard for those folks.

4.11 CPU Cooler

Whether your CPU is AMD or Intel, it gains a lot of peace of mind if you can supply a good cooling solution. In the case of AMD in particular, the stock fan and heatsink often do not do a job worth writing home about (at least in a good spirit).

The Cooler Master Hyper 212 LED CPU Cooler with PWM Fan at `https://www.amazon.com/dp/B005065JXI` ($30) claims to be the best in the business—it can pare down your CPU temperature by as much as 30°C (vis-a-vis cooling achieved with the stock fan and heatsink), all very silently. I can vouchsafe as much from personal experience. Figure 4-13 can only tell you what the cooler looks like, not its cooling finesse.

Figure 4-13. *Cooler Master Hyper 212 CPU Cooler*

The CM cooler comes with its own very special fixing/cooling liquid. Putting together a Cooler Master cooler requires some engineering expertise. Consider calling in someone who won't feel intimidated by the prospect of working with the motley pieces on the left to deliver the juggernaut on the right in Figure 4-14.

Figure 4-14. *Cooler assembly*

4.12 Printer/Scanner

The generic solution to printing under Unix is CUPS (Common Unix Printing System), which replaces the old line printer daemon. CUPS supports all current printing standards (PostScript, PCL, and PDF). While most HP inkjet printers use PCL, other printers can be made to work under Unix if they provide a PostScript Printer Definition (PPD) format file that CUPS can readily use, or else a native driver. Two OEMs that provide open-source drivers/PPDs for at least some of their printers are HP and Epson.

4.12.1 Buying an HP Printer

HP (Hewlett Packard) is the leading open-source camp follower. It even has its own Unix printing software HPLIP (HP Linux Imaging and Printing) that enables most of HP's current-generation printers to work under Unix. If you want to buy a printer for your FreeBSD/Linux box, choosing an HP is a smart choice.

I will start by mentioning the very cheap printer that I myself use very happily under FreeBSD as well as Linux—the HP DeskJet 1112 Compact Printer, available at `https://www.amazon.com/dp/B013SKI4QA` for $26.

If you have a slightly deeper pocket, you can get the Multi Function Device shown in Figure 4-15, which can print and scan, and is an all-time best seller at Amazon.

The HP Envy 4520 All-in-One Photo Printer at `https://www.amazon.com/dp/B013SKI4LU` ($67) looks gorgeous too, as Figure 4-15 might convince you.

Figure 4-15. *HP Envy 4520 Multi Function Device*

Note   A wireless printer can also be hooked with its USB cable

For laser buffs, HP has a very agreeably priced monochrome laser printer (which, at least in theory, should yield per-page cost savings vis-a-vis inkjet printers). The HP LaserJet Pro M102w Laser Printer is available at `https://www.amazon.com/dp/B01LBWELIW` for $88.

This piece is equally peachy and is depicted in Figure 4-16.

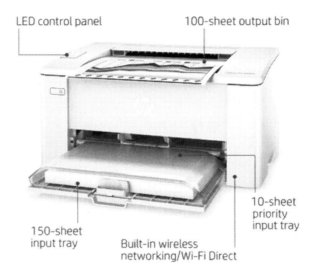

Figure 4-16.   HP LaserJet Pro M102w laser printer

4.12.2 Buying an Epson Printer

Epson has created a Linux line of printers called L*nnn* where *nnn* usually is a three-digit or four-digit number. Epson provides open-source drivers for that series, printers of which therefore work with Linux—and many under FreeBSD too.

The list of printers under the L-series can be viewed at the following URL, which delves into Epson India's support website:

`https://www.epson.co.in/Support/Printers/Single-Function-Inkjet-Printers/L-Series/sh/s112`

At the time of this writing, the list cobbled up at the URL was:

L800 L100 L110 L120 L200 L210 L220 L300 L310 L350 L355 L360 L365 L385 L455
L485 L550 L555 L565 L605 L655 L805 L810 L1300 L1455 L1800

Surprisingly, Amazon USA does not retail L-series printers (but Amazon India does).

Epson printers from outside of the L-series can be made to work with Linux (but not FreeBSD) by downloading a closed-source Linux driver package from http://download.ebz.epson.net/dsc/search/01/search/?OSC=LX.

FreeBSD supports the following Epson printers for which a native driver is available.

- epson-inkjet-printer-201401w: L456 L455 L366 L365 L362 L360 L312 L310 L222 L220 L132 L130

- epson-inkjet-printer-201601w: L380 L382

- epsonepl: (for laser printers) EPL-5700L EPL-5800L EPL-5900L

Readers in Europe can order Epson's L382 inkjet color printer/scanner at Alza Shop: https://www.alzashop.com/epson-l382-d4514535.htm. It was listed, when this was being written, at the price of €156.45. Figure 4-17 shows Alza's L382 offering.

Figure 4-17. *Epson L382 Multi Function Device*

4.13 Summary

You now have everything needed to assemble your PC—except perhaps a screwdriver, which I will let you research on your own.

If you can assemble the PC yourself, nothing like it. If you can't, you are like me and should call in the hardware guy. If you pay him anything up to $28, you still remain within our budget of $500 (excluding the printer).

The next chapter is where you'll start playing Unix using your own box.

CHAPTER 5

Installing and Configuring FreeBSD/Linux

A few decades back, installing Unix yourself was not possible—most of the time, Unix makers would only sell machines that were fully preinstalled.

Times have changed. Unix now runs on the PC—something AT&T was highly averse to, mostly for commercial reasons. Since the PC is a personal computer, Unix installation is now very much a personal task. You can—and must be able to—install FreeBSD and Linux yourself. This is not difficult at all, as this chapter will hopefully elucidate.

5.1 Disk Partitioning

We'll start this chapter by revisiting a fundamental term: *partition*. What is meant by that?

Essentially, a partition is a contiguous portion of a hard disk, the start and end of which are recorded in the first sector of the disk (which hosts a partition table). Every disk can be broken into chunks, each of which can be presented to the operating system as a single storage source (filesystem).

There are two widely-used partitioning schemes for managing disk partitions: MBR and GPT.

© Manish Jain 2018
M. Jain, *Beginning Modern Unix*, https://doi.org/10.1007/978-1-4842-3528-7_5

5.1.1 MBR (Master Boot Record)

Under the MBR partitioning scheme, which is the traditional scheme in use since the days of DOS, there are a maximum of four such chunks (minimum, of course, is one). Those chunks are referred to as *primary partitions* (Windows/Linux) or *slices* (FreeBSD). One of the four slices can optionally be subdivided. If there is such a slice (which is configured for subdivision), it is called an *extended partition* (more correctly, a DOS extended partition), and its subdivisions are *logical drives*. FreeBSD refers to the DOS extended partition as an *EBR slice*.

Let's say we have a hard disk with three slices, the second being an extended partition. Linux will call the slices sda1 (primary), sda2 (extended), and sda3 (primary). The first subdivision in the extended partition is indexed (4 + subindex = 4 + 1) 5, which makes its device node sda5. The second subdivision is sda6, and so on.

FreeBSD uses ada0s* in place of sda*. If you hook in a second hard disk, its partitions show up as sdb* under Linux and as ada1s* under FreeBSD.

Note   The 4+ EBR nomenclature owes its heritage to the fact that the partition table in the MBR accommodates information for the four slices only. EBR break-up information is recorded in the first sector at the start of the EBR slice.

Besides a fundamental limitation that MBR can handle disks only up to a maximum of 2TB, there are a couple of points to remember for MBR partitioning.

- Every operating system needs its own primary partition. Since our example disk has only two primary partitions (sda1 and sda3), it is limited to a maximum of two operating systems.

- FreeBSD can internally carve up its slice to make it work more or less as an extended partition. If ada0s3 is a BSD slice with two subdivisions, the subdivisions get denoted as ada0s3a and ada0s3b. FreeBSD refers to ada0s3 as a slice, and to ada0s3a and ada0s3b as partitions. In the BSD world, you do not mount slices. Rather you mount partitions, unless the slice is undivided and hence itself a partition—as is the case with ada0s1 (Linux sda1) in our example disk. MBR slices of type BSD (freebsd) and extended partition (ebr) are nests (enclosing subdivisions) and thus not mountable themselves. Instead, each partition inside the nest is mountable.

Here is a table of oft-used slice/partition type IDs under the MBR partitioning scheme:

```
ebr slice / Extended Partition:    0x5 (5)
                         ntfs:     0x7 (7)
                        fat32:     0xc (12)
                   linux-swap:     0x82 (130)
  linux-data (Ext2/Ext3/Ext4):     0x83 (131)
               freebsd slice:      0xa5 (165)
```

The filesystem type (NTFS/FAT32/Ext2) created in a partition almost always corresponds to the partition type. But it is possible to use a different filesystem type. This book uses a linux-swap partition that flips between FreeBSD Swap (when FreeBSD is booted) and Linux Swap (when Linux is booted).

The biggest virtue of MBR partitioning is never noted anywhere: the scheme forces the user to plan and adapt. That happens because everything possible under GPT is possible under MBR too, and MBR provides only the least number of choices possible for achieving all the objectives possible. As you will hopefully one day agree, it is a boon to be furnished a small set of choices at the most basic levels in computer usage. I should perhaps repeat, though, that MBR cannot address disks sized over 2TB.

5.1.2 GPT (GUID Partition Table)

The other partitioning scheme is the newfangled GPT, where the G stands for GUID. GUID in turn stands for Globally Unique IDentifier. Unlike MBR, GPT works for very large disks too. GPT further lets you create as many partitions in the disk as you want, unlike MBR, which restricts you to a maximum of four slices. GPT partitions are always actual partitions, not nests.

If you are working with a very large disk (> 2TB), you should use GPT. FreeBSD denotes a GPT disk's partitions as ada0p1, ada0p2, and so on, while Linux device node names remain the same as in MBR: sda1, sda2, and so on.

The downside to GPT is that it makes multi-booting trickier (and one can never use FreeBSD's boot0cfg, the nifty MBR boot code configurator that I personally am very fond of). For this book, which uses a dual-boot setup, we keep things simple by using MBR as the default partitioning scheme. Section 5.10 has notes for GPT partitioning tailored for dual-booting Linux and FreeBSD.

5.2 Do We Have Enough Disk Space?

At this point, we'll put in a word about how much disk space you need to install Unix. We don't want a bare-minimum system—on the contrary, we want a full-fledged box with at least 10GB still lying around free after installation of a desktop environment.

For Linux, 20GB should be enough for the root partition. Because FreeBSD packs more punch in its base system, it needs more disk space. 35GB should be enough for FreeBSD's root partition. But, on this particular account, you should choose to err on the side of being generous. You can't go wrong—if your disk's size permits—giving 30GB to Linux and 50GB to FreeBSD.

Perhaps more important than disk space is number of slices available. If you are working with a brand new disk, you don't have anything to worry about. You can have up to four of them as mandated by the MBR standard.

The trickier case is you are working with a disk with something already on it. Let's say you have Windows on it.

Note   The following hold for Windows hard disk partitions:

The C: drive is a primary partition at the start of the disk. This is true without exception.

The D:, E:, F: (and so on) drives are usually logical drives in the extended partition.

If, as likely, all drives except C: are logical drives in an extended partition, you can delete all existing logical drives and then the EBR slice (extended partition) itself to create free space that you can use to create two new primary partitions—one for Linux and the second for FreeBSD. Any remaining space can be used to create an extended partition.

If you can't free up sufficient space, it is a good time—and a very good reason—to buy another hard disk (preferably a solid state drive). For Windows XP users, there is an additional reason, even if you have sufficient disk space: Windows XP understands neither SSD functions (e.g., discard) nor AHCI, the newer and more efficient configuration mode for SATA devices. If you install FreeBSD/Linux alongside Windows XP, you have to put your hard disk in legacy IDE mode—with a performance penalty.

Existing Windows users should always prefer to buy a new SSD and install FreeBSD/Linux.

5.3 The Default Partitioning Scheme

The rest of this discussion assumes brand new disks, to be partitioned MBR.

This section illustrates the MBR partitioning schemes for the following couple of hard-disk pools (which correspond to the hardware we purchased in Chapter 4):

- A small 64GB SSD paired with a large 500GB SATA disk, under which operating system installations and swap space are hosted inside the SSD. The large SATA disk hosts an EBR slice that nests a storage partition and a spare primary partition that can be used, for instance, to create backups.

- A single, large 500GB SSD that hosts everything within itself.

You can use any partitioning scheme that you consider best suited for your needs. The following couple—which use embedded rectangles to depict nested partitions—is a good starting point.

Figure 5-1 is the suggested scheme for the 64GB SSD and 500GB SATA pair.

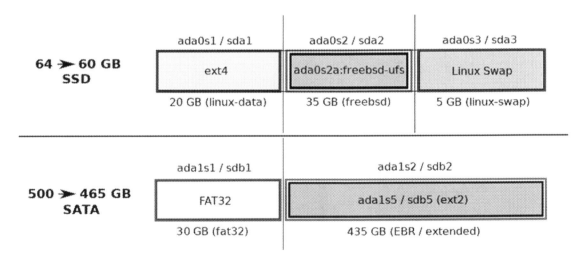

Figure 5-1. *MBR partitioning scheme for a small SSD and a large SATA disk*

This scheme puts the swap partition (created as `linux-swap`) in a slice of its own. You can, if you want, create it as a logical drive nested in an EBR slice—the next scheme does precisely that.

The singleton 500GB SSD can be partitioned as shown in Figure 5-2.

Figure 5-2. *MBR partitioning scheme for a large SSD*

Both schemes use a spare primary partition (created as `fat32`) that can be used for a variety of tasks later: creating backups, a spare installation, and storage. The filesystem type FAT32 is purely nominal. From the scheme's perspective, it is just a way of saying "Disk space reserved for future use".

Both schemes also use a single swap partition, created as `linux-swap`. FreeBSD and Linux can share the swap partition. Refer to Section A.4 in the appendix for how to enable swap sharing. This is very simple, and it saves you precious space inside the SSD for a second swap partition. (Reminder: Swap works three times faster inside SSD.)

5.4 Preparing the Computer's CMOS for Unix

One of the recent additions to computer terminology is UEFI (Unified Extensible Firmware Interface), which was supposed to be the next-gen BIOS (Basic Input/Output System) that solves the problems and limitations of legacy BIOS. In the context of UEFI, I should note that I am not a big fan of new computer technologies adding to the technology swamp, particularly when the legacy technology is still sufficient for the purpose.

Note   BIOS, as well as its apparent-heir-to-be UEFI, is a meta-system for hardware configuration that decides the rules and limitations the actual operating system has to comply with. For instance:

- Is the first-boot device the hard disk or the CD drive?

- Should the keyboard/mouse be able to wake up (power on) the system?

- Should the hard disks use IDE mode or AHCI mode?

BIOS/UEFI configuration is saved in a chip called CMOS (Complementary Metal Oxide Semiconductor).

While both FreeBSD and Linux can work with UEFI, it makes life easier if you disable UEFI entirely in the CMOS settings. Your system's CMOS quite likely has a compatibility support module, which can be used to enforce legacy BIOS functionality. So boot into the CMOS and disable UEFI.

While we are in the CMOS, check on a few other settings as well. If your CMOS has EHCI handoff (USB2) support and XHCI handoff (USB3) support, enable them.

Note   Here's some USB jargon to remember:

OHCI stands for Open Host Controller Interface ↔ USB 1.0/1.1 (1.5Mbps)

EHCI stands for Enhanced Host Controller Interface ↔ USB 2.0 (35MBps)

XHCI stands for eXtensible Host Controller Interface ↔ USB 3.0 (400MBps)

(b = bits; B = bytes)

One particular setting is crucial for Linux: if your system's CMOS flaunts a feature named IOMMU (Input Output Memory Management Unit), enable it. Otherwise Linux quite likely will not be able to ping the network and USB ports might not work well.

There is one final tweak: AHCI (Advanced Host Controller Interface). SATA disks traditionally were presented to the operating system in native IDE mode. An alternative mode called AHCI has emerged over the last decade. AHCI offers significant performance benefits over IDE mode. If your BIOS offers AHCI functionality, you can use that in preference to IDE. The one point to remember for AHCI is that if a SATA disk is in AHCI mode, you cannot install old, AHCI-unaware operating systems (e.g., Windows XP) on the disk.

Note   One point that might be pertinent to mention is the architecture name quagmire created by the use of the artificial name x86_64. Until the AMD64 architecture was created, the term x86 was reserved to denote the 32-bit architecture i386 (created by Intel) and any of the derivatives of i386: i486, i586, and i686.

Since the 64-bit PC architecture was created by AMD, it is quite properly named AMD64. Intel, quite naturally, is not pleased about the prospect of having to sell its 64-bit processors with the name of its rival proudly advertised on the packing. Intel has therefore pushed hard to get the name x86_64 substituted for AMD64.

A lot of Linux distributions (the Arch family in particular) have been eager to please Intel, and thus publish their 64-bit ISO images tagged as x86_64. This, quite clearly, is a problem on multiple counts. The name x86 was originally coined to mean i386/i486/i586/i686, all of them 32-bit. The concoction x86_64 implies (from everyone's point of view, not just Intel's viewpoint) that x86 now means the very strange mix (i386/i486/i586/i686/AMD64).

If you find the situation pleasant, you don't have anything to worry about. Otherwise, you should question your Linux distribution (if it tags its ISO as x86_64, not AMD64) why this absurdity is being allowed to perpetuate.

5.5 Downloading and Burning Installation Media

For FreeBSD and Linux, it is recommended to install from optical media (CD or DVD), not USB memory sticks.

For FreeBSD, point your browser to this URL:

```
https://download.freebsd.org/ftp/releases/ISO-IMAGES/
```

Choose the release version you like. At the time of this writing, 11.1 was the freshest release. To fetch the CD installer for 11.1 for AMD64 architecture, you can download the 11.1/FreeBSD-11.1-RELEASE-amd64-disc1.iso file in your browser or via wget on the command line.

Tip   If your environment has the unxz command, you can save some time by downloading the compressed .iso.xz file, which you can unpack with the unxz <iso> command.

Along with the ISO image, you should also get the CHECKSUM.SHA256 file for your architecture, so that you can be sure the ISO downloaded is a good one. Once you have the ISO file, run sha256 <iso> (if your environment has the sha256 command) on the ISO file and match the result with the CHECKSUM.SHA256 file.

If the checksum matches, you are good to go ahead and burn the ISO to a CD. You can burn the CD with a graphical application like Nero or K3b, or from the command line if your environment has a CLI-burner such as cdrecord or cdrdao.

If, for some reason, you are unable to use optical media for the installation, you can wget the memstick.img (memory stick image):

```
11.1/FreeBSD-11.1-RELEASE-amd64-memstick.img
```

After matching its checksum with sha256, you can "burn" it to a USB pen drive:

**ROOT#   dd if=FreeBSD-11.1-RELEASE-amd64-memstick.img **
of=/dev/da0 bs=1M conv=sync

If you are trying to burn the USB image to a pen drive under Windows, this is not possible natively but can be accomplished (with fingers crossed) using dedicated tools like Rufus, which is available at https://rufus.akeo.ie/.

Linux installation media HowTo is pretty much the same in principle. The one major difference is that Linux distributions usually come wired with a graphical desktop environment, which gets installed automatically along with Linux installation.

We'll take Mint as our Linux distro of choice. The URLs for Linux Mint are:

https://linuxmint.com/download.php (ISO download page)
https://linuxmint.com/verify.php (checksums page)

Linux uses the same (hybrid) ISO image for DVD media as well as a USB memory stick. To burn the ISO to a USB memory stick attached as /dev/sdb, use:

ROOT#   dd if=linuxmint-18.3-cinnamon-64bit.iso of=/dev/sdb bs=1M

5.6 Our Example Hard Disk

It's good to note that booting an operating system broadly involves two separate boot blocks: one in charge of the entire hard disk (located in the hard disk's first sector), and the other that can boot the operating system in a particular slice (located in the slice's first sector). The former, executed by BIOS, invokes the latter.

We will take the 64GB SSD in Figure 5-1 as our disk for installations. Our bootstrap strategy for the disk (which will be the device /dev/ada0 under FreeBSD and /dev/ sda under Linux) is illustrated in Figure 5-3.

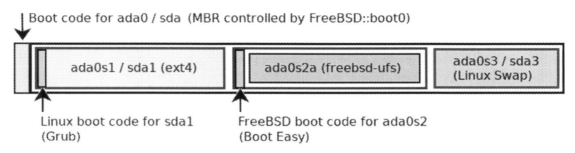

Figure 5-3. *The bootstrapping strategy*

We will place FreeBSD's boot0cfg in charge of the MBR: the boot0 code (which fits inside the disk's first block of 512 bytes) can readily bootstrap FreeBSD/Linux/Windows. OS-specific bootmanagers (Grub under Linux, Boot Easy under FreeBSD) will occupy the first sectors in their respective slices. Note that what is called a *bootloader* in Linux is called a *bootmanager* in FreeBSD. Under FreeBSD, the bootmanager's home run yields control to /boot/loader, which takes over for the last stage of the bootstrap process— loading the kernel into memory.

5.7 Installing FreeBSD

Boot with your CD. You will meet Beastie, the lovable FreeBSD mascot—see the left side of Figure 5-4. Just press ⎡ Enter ⎤ to move up to the second screen (right side), where you can again press ⎡ Enter ⎤ (with Install selected) to kick off the installation.

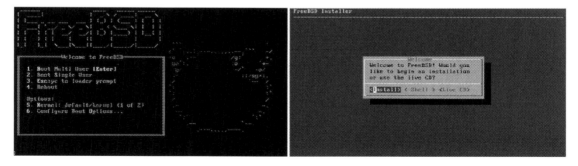

Figure 5-4. *FreeBSD initial boot screens*

Select your keymap (the default is US English). Then set your hostname, which can be any string, with no spaces or special characters.

The next screen, Distribution Select, is for choosing additional components (besides the base system) for your FreeBSD installation. Press the spacebar to un-select the ports distribution and select src. Your screen should now look as shown Figure 5-5.

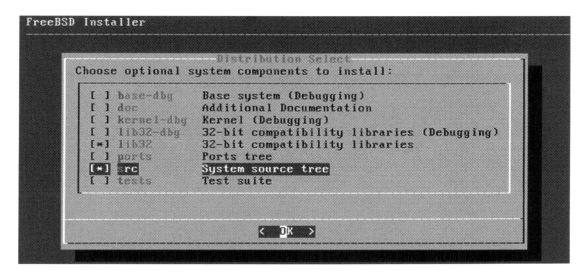

Figure 5-5. *Select distributions*

Press ⎣Enter⎦ to continue.

The reason we un-select ports is that FreeBSD ports are a dynamic collection. What you would have on the installer CD would be outdated by at least a few months. You can get the latest ports collection after installation is over. We'll do that in the next chapter.

The reason we select src is that a few ports and other system facilities need the system sources. For example, if you want to build the NVIDIA driver from ports, you will be prompted for the system sources if those are missing. It anyway is a good idea to always have the source code for the system you are running, and it can be tricky (or at least inconvenient) getting the system sources later. So we do that right now and rest happily afterward.

Choosing the Manual partitioning mode, move ahead to the partitioning screen.

Note   The next few steps assume a new disk with no data in it. If the disk has any data that's still important, you should alter the next couple of steps to remove and recreate only those partitions that have no existing data of significance.

This next step deletes all existing partitions and the partition scheme itself. So do this only if you are sure you do not need anything on the disk.

Once you're at the partitioning screen, select the disk's device ada0 and tab onto the Delete button. Press [Enter] to delete any existing partitioning scheme. (You can, as an easier alternative, press [d]—the equivalent to Delete and [Enter]). Your screen should now look like Figure 5-6.

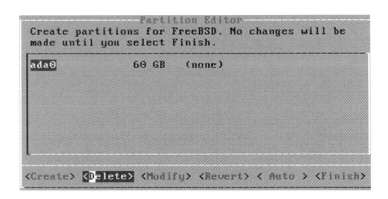

Figure 5-6. *Delete any existing partitioning scheme*

You now have a new/like-new disk with no partitions, or even a partition scheme. So the first thing you must do is create a new partition scheme (MBR or GPT) in the disk— this is also called *initializing* the disk.

With your disk ada0 selected, tab onto the Create button and then press [Enter]—you can also just press [c]. Setup will prompt you for the kind of partitioning scheme you want. Choose MBR. Refer to Figure 5-7.

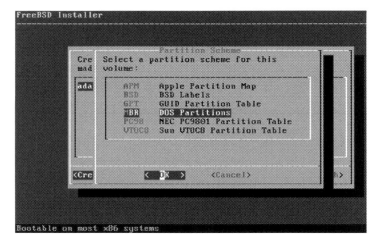

Figure 5-7. *Create a new partition scheme*

When you're done, your screen will appear as in Figure 5-8. Don't click Finish yet.

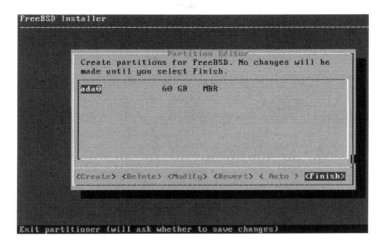

Figure 5-8. *The initial partition table*

Your hard disk now has a partitioning scheme. The next step creates a table of slices. Do not try to set any mountpoints yet, and do not click Finish.

Press ⓒ (or Create) to create a slice of type `linux-data`, sized 20GB. Refer, if needed, to Figure 5-9. `/dev/ada0s1` thus created is where our Linux installation—to be made after the FreeBSD installation currently underway is done—will reside.

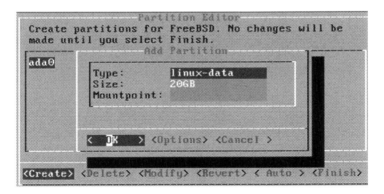

Figure 5-9. *The first slice: ada0s1*

Press ⓒ (or Create) a couple of times to create a slice of type `freebsd`, sized 35GB, and then a slice of type `linux-swap` spanning the remaining disk space—nominally assumed 5GB. Refer to Figure 5-10 for the final layout—and remember not to click the Finish button.

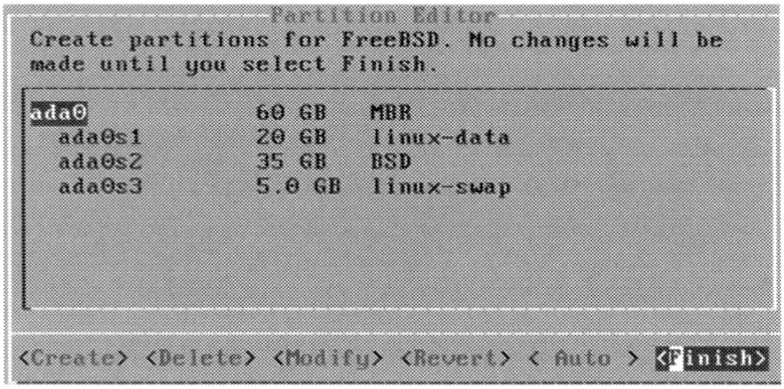

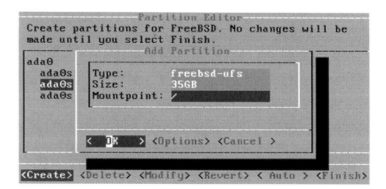

Figure 5-10. *The final partition table*

Inside the BSD slice ada0s2, we'll create just one nested partition: ada0s2a (UFS), the
/ mountpoint for our FreeBSD installation.

With your BSD slice ada0s2 selected, press C (or click the Create button) to create
ada0s2a. Let the partition's default size (35GB) and filesystem type (freebsd-ufs)
remain unchanged. Set its mountpoint as /. Refer to Figure 5-11.

Figure 5-11. *UFS partition configured*

If your hard disk is a solid state drive (SSD), you can tab onto Options and set
ada0s2a to use TRIM support. Refer to Figure 5-12.

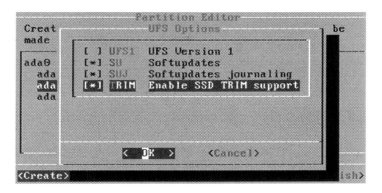

Figure 5-12. *TRIM enabled for UFS*

TRIM (discard) enables prompt and efficient recovery of disk space following deletion of files from solid state storage.

Refer to Figure 5-13. The disk layout is now final.

```
                       Partition Editor
   Please review the disk setup. When complete, press
   the Finish button.

 ada0               60 GB    MBR
   ada0s1           20 GB    linux-data
   ada0s2           35 GB    BSD
      ada0s2a       35 GB    freebsd-ufs   /
   ada0s3           5.0 GB   linux-swap



 <Create> <Delete> <Modify> <Revert> < Auto > <Finish>
```

Figure 5-13. *The final disk layout*

Click Finish and then Commit. Setup will format partitions, and then extract the necessary distributions (base, kernel, lib32, and src) into the root filesystem (/). Next, it will prompt you to set the root password. Set the password you like.

Setup will then probe for an Ethernet device. If it finds a wired network card, setup will prompt you to configure network—whether you want to use IPv4 and DHCP. DHCP (Dynamic Host Configuration Protocol) auto-configures IPv4 settings and is possible only if your intranet has a DHCP server. Choose Yes for IPv4. If your intranet has a DHCP server, choose Yes for DHCP too. Otherwise, you must manually configure IPv4.

To manually configure IPv4, you need the IP address of your router/gateway—pretty often this is 192.168.1.1. With that router IP, you can choose an unused IP address in the 192.168.1.* series, and subnet mask 255.255.255.0.

Setup will next let you turn on IPv6 and SLAAC, if you need them. SLAAC (StateLess Address AutoConfiguration) is quite like DHCP of IPv4.

When prompted for resolver (DNS) configuration, you can use your preferred DNS servers, or simply use OpenDNS servers: 208.67.222.222 and 208.67.220.220.

See Figure 5-14. When setup is at the finish line, it will ask if you want to run any command in the system freshly installed (from within the CD installer—this facility is known as chroot). Choose Yes.

Figure 5-14. *Entering installer's chroot*

See Figure 5-15. Inside the chroot'ed shell, run the following command, which inserts the FreeBSD boot0 code into the MBR:

```
boot0cfg -B /dev/ada0
```

```
This shell is operating in a chroot in the new system. When finished making conf
iguration changes, type "exit".
# boot0cfg -B /dev/ada0
#
```

Figure 5-15. *Installing boot0 code to MBR*

When you exit from chroot (with the command exit), the system will reboot. Upon reboot, quickly remove the installer CD; otherwise you will encounter FreeBSD setup again. To visit your freshly installed FreeBSD system, press F2 at the boot prompt.

Next, we'll install Linux, which will be readily bootable with F1, courtesy of boot0.

5.8 Installing and Configuring Linux

As long as you read the opening discussion of this chapter (relating to partitions and BIOS settings), you need very little by way of explanation about how to install Linux. Even so, there is a fair panoply to worry about.

But the first thing to do is boot your box with the Linux installer media and then fix things if/as needed. Screenshots in this section have been generated with the installer for Linux Mint (Cinnamon) 18.3, 64-bit.

One glitch might nip your enterprise in the bud—Linux setup sometimes fails to recognize a USB keyboard and mouse if those are connected via a USB hub. If you find setup not responding to keyboard/mouse input, you should first check in the BIOS as to whether EHCI handoff—as well as IOMMU, if present—is enabled. If that does not resolve the issue, hook those devices directly to motherboard ports, not via a hub.

The next hiccup is a big one. Unlike FreeBSD, Linux setup hardwires default Internet settings for DHCP, and does not give the user a chance to enforce manual IP configuration, even if needed. This is a problem, even more confusing because the Linux installer does have the capability for configuring manual IPv4/IPv6 settings.

If you are fine with DHCP configuration for your box, you can skip past the next screenshot on to the next step.

For manual IPv4/IPv6, don't launch the main installer right away. Instead, first check in the installer's taskbars for a Network Connections icon. Or else you might end up—if your box needs manual IP settings—with a full-fledged Linux installation that does not connect to the Internet.

Figure 5-16 shows the Network Connections icon highlighted.

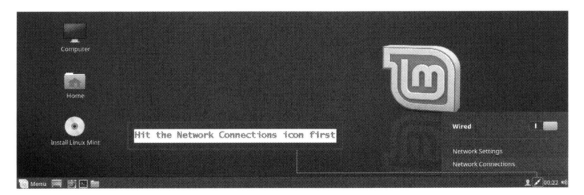

Figure 5-16. *The big hiccup: enforcing a manual IP configuration (if needed)*

When you find the Network Connections icon, click/right-click to get the network configuration tool, which in Linux Mint appears as shown in Figure 5-17.

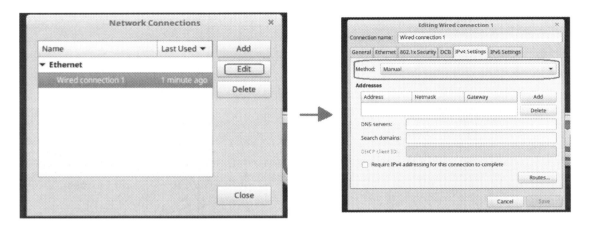

Figure 5-17. *Network connection editor*

Use Edit and then the tab to your network type to set your network parameters. You can use manual IPv4 as well as OpenDNS for this, just as with FreeBSD.

When network configuration is done, open a terminal and test Internet access with this command:

```
$   ping www.google.com
```

If this command fails, try pinging an IP address:

```
$   ping 8.8.8.8
```

If pinging IP addresses succeeds, it just means your DNS resolver is not configured correctly; if it fails, your network configuration is not a good one. For any DNS woes, you might like to remember that OpenDNS servers are 208.67.222.222 and 208.67.220.220.

Once your Internet access is working seamlessly, you can continue further onto the filesystems screen in Linux installer, where you should use the Something Else option so as to reuse the layout we created earlier (during FreeBSD installation).

Among the myriad filesystem options for Linux, the two of most interest are Ext2 and Ext4. Ext2 has been the standard Linux workhorse for quite a while. Its offshoot Ext4 has built-in support for SSD TRIM with the discard filesystem attribute. The Linux Mint installer does not seem to offer the facility to use custom options for mkfs.ext4, but this is not a serious problem. You can still enable discard as a mount option in /etc/fstab once Linux installation finishes.

When you reach the filesystems section, your screen will look like Figure 5-18.

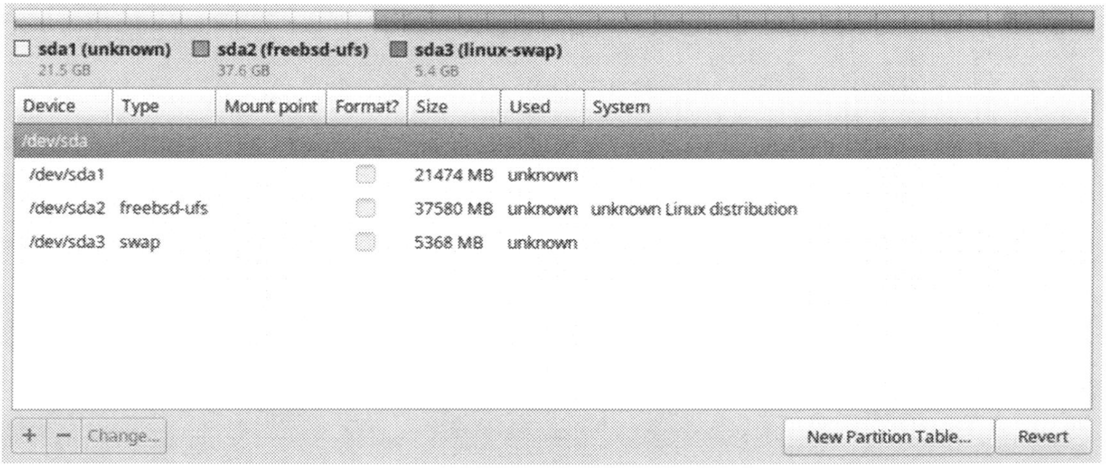

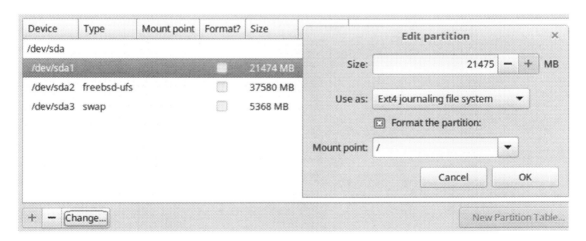

Figure 5-18. *Partition layout (as created by FreeBSD)*

This layout is created by FreeBSD. You can click on /dev/sda1, and then click the Change button to have Linux setup format the partition as Ext4 and mount it as the / filesystem for Linux. Refer, if needed, to Figure 5-19.

Figure 5-19. */dev/sda1 configured as an Ext4 partition (to host/filesystem)*

Linux setup will usually pick up /dev/sda3 on its own as a Linux Swap partition to be formatted and used as such. If not, you can enforce the necessary change.

Refer to Figure 5-20. The black rectangle is the final filesystem layout.

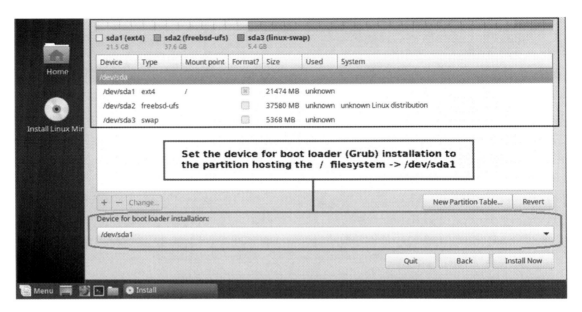

Figure 5-20. *Where to install Grub*

Next, change the device for bootloader (Grub) installation to /dev/sda1. The lower half of Figure 5-20 illustrates that too. When being written to the MBR, Grub has the strange habit of not writing out a proper boot sequence (which can be chain-loaded by other bootloaders) to the first sector of Linux's root partition. Installing Grub to the first sector of Linux's root partition fixes that problem.

Note   On an MBR disk, FreeBSD boot0 can readily boot FreeBSD, Linux, and Windows.

Because Linux Grub (GRand Unified Bootloader) is not able to boot FreeBSD without extra work, the ideal bootstrap mechanism is FreeBSD boot0 manager on the MBR, and Linux Grub on its own partition.

If someone or something overwrites the MBR, you can reinstall FreeBSD's boot0 by booting into a Fixit/Live shell with your FreeBSD installer CD, and then issuing the boot0cfg -B /dev/ada0 command.

On a disk partitioned GPT, the reverse becomes true: it is easier to boot FreeBSD with Linux Grub than to boot Linux with FreeBSD. In Section 5.10 (which discusses dual-booting FreeBSD and Linux on a GPT disk), we use that convenience to our advantage.

You can now click the Install Now button and complete the installation of Linux. When you reboot, you can switch to the freshly installed Linux system with F1 .

One peculiar problem you could run into booting a fresh Linux box installed from a USB memory stick is device name bungling. It occasionally happens that the USB stick gets enumerated as /dev/sda at the time of installation, and your hard disk gets enumerated as /dev/sdb. After installation is over, when you boot into Linux from the hard disk (with the USB stick removed), the bootloader will fail to find the root filesystem (which was enumerated during installation as sdb1, but now is sda1).

If such a malady afflicts you, there is a workaround: boot into Live mode with Linux setup, mount your Linux installation at /tmp, and then alter its /etc/fstab (which now is /tmp/etc/fstab) such that its root filesystem matches the device node it would be with the USB stick removed (in other words, sdb1 → sda1). Unmount /tmp and reboot (with no USB stick attached).

Of course, the best solution is still the original recommendation—install Unix from optical media, not USB.

Unlike FreeBSD, Linux needs very little post-install configuration. The three points that I can mention as relevant to Linux configuration (which are anything in the nature of widely-needed) would be use of the discard option (if your hard disk is SSD); use of UTC (Coordinated Universal Time) for timezone configuration; and addressing possibly non-functional USB3 ports.

If your hard disk is an SSD, check whether the option discard has been applied to your Linux /filesystem's mounting options. If you find the flags in /etc/fstab to be rw, change the flags to rw,discard. Linux kernel honors the discard mount option for all native filesystem types (Ext2/Ext3/Ext4), not just Ext4.

Linux setup by default turns on UTC, which means your CMOS clock's time will hold what the Queen of England would consider the local time. This can be a problem for other operating systems, and perhaps unwelcome from the user's own viewpoint. You can, if you want, disable UTC and revert to the actual local time in CMOS clock with:

```
timedatectl set-local-rtc 1
```

XHCI (USB3) might not work out-of-the-box for you under Linux. If the USB3 ports are not working, you can do the following:

1. Boot Linux. Press `e` at Grub's loader prompt to edit startup parameters.

2. Locate the line starting with `linux`.

3. Append to that line: `iommu=soft`.

4. Boot (pressing the `F10` key usually does this).

5. When the system is up, run this command (as root / via `sudo`): `update-grub`.

5.9 Post-Install Configuration of FreeBSD

All commands in this section use > to denote the root user's shell prompt.

FreeBSD requires extensive post-install configuration. This can be a challenge the first time you are installing FreeBSD. But luckily, most of the work can be automated. You can write a few shell scripts to do the work for you unattended in future. The `mkdesktop` utility—written by the author of this book and discussed at the end of this section (see Subsection 5.9.9)—is perhaps the easiest-to-use automated system for post-install configuration of FreeBSD.

But before using any automation products, you must first become extensively familiar with the basic steps. Shying away from this preliminary stage is the most frequent reason users fail to adapt to (and then possibly be fascinated with) the FreeBSD operating system.

Note   Your FreeBSD box has no swap space yet. If you want FreeBSD to share the `linux-swap` partition with Linux, refer to Article A.4 in the appendix.

To list all disk devices (optical drive as well SATA/SSD disks), FreeBSD provides a handy command: `camcontrol devlist`.

5.9.1 Networking

Boot up and log in as root. If there are no error messages, test your Internet access:

```
> ping 8.8.178.110
> ping www.freebsd.org
```

If pinging the IP address fails, your network configuration is not a good one. If pinging the IP address succeeds and pinging www.freebsd.org fails, it just means your DNS resolver is not configured correctly. For any DNS/network failure, you can reconfigure network with this command:

```
> bsdconfig networking
```

5.9.2 Software Packaging Subsystem

The heart of FreeBSD's package management is pkg, which ships as a stub in the base system (/usr/sbin/pkg). Once FreeBSD has been installed, you can use the stub to pull in the full-fledged software manager (/usr/local/sbin/pkg):

```
> pkg bootstrap -f
```

5.9.3 A Friendlier Shell

The root user's default shell under FreeBSD is C shell. FreeBSD recommends this not be altered—otherwise, you might disrupt certain system facilities, e.g., chroot environments.

You can, though, use the shell of your choice for *toor*, the root user's mirror that has all the privileges of root. This is what we do next.

Two equally good, modern and user-friendly shells are the Bourne Again SHell (Bash) and Z shell (Zsh). Real estate is split as (left, Bash) and (right, Zsh):

```
> pkg install bash                   > pkg install zsh
> chsh  -s /usr/local/bin/bash toor  > chsh  -s /usr/local/bin/zsh  toor
```

5.9.4 X Server

Install the X server and associated utilities:

```
>   pkg install xorg hal dbus
```

While Xorg does not need DBus (Desktop Bus; facilitates inter-process communication) and HAL (Hardware Abstraction Layer; allows desktop applications to discover and use the host system's hardware via an API), most desktop environments under FreeBSD need both of them.

At this stage, many system files will need to be tweaked.

Append the following lines to /etc/fstab:

```
fdescfs      /dev/fd      fdescfs     rw     0     0
procfs       /proc        procfs      rw     0     0
```

Append the following lines to /etc/devfs.conf:

```
own /dev/pci root:operator
perm /dev/pci 0664
own /dev/dri/card0 root:operator
perm /dev/dri/card0  0664

own /dev/cd0 root:operator
perm /dev/cd0 0664
own /dev/xpt0 root:operator
perm /dev/xpt0 0664

own /dev/pass0    root:operator    # This configuration is for:
perm /dev/pass0   0664             # CD/DVD drive & 1 hard disk.
                                   # If you have 2 hard-disks,
own /dev/pass1    root:operator    # repeat pass1 lines to add
perm /dev/pass1   0664             # settings for /dev/pass2
```

Append the following lines to /etc/devfs.rules (you will almost certainly need to create this file):

```
[system=10]
add path 'usb/*'  mode 0664 group operator
add path 'cd*'    mode 0664 group operator
```

```
add path 'da*'    mode 0664 group operator
add path 'video*' mode 0664 group operator
```

Append the following lines to /etc/rc.conf:

```
devfs_system_ruleset="system"
dbus_enable="YES"
hald_enable="YES"
```

Append the following line to /boot/loader.conf (you may need to create this file):

```
kern.vty="vt"
```

Note   Under FreeBSD, the default kern.vty driver often is sc. This is now being phased out in favor of vt. Recent versions of X.org do not work well with sc, and need vt as the kern.vty driver.

5.9.5 NVIDIA Graphics Driver Addition

Unlike ATI Radeon (as well as Intel) graphics support, which is shipped with FreeBSD in its base system, NVIDIA graphics support needs you to install a package.

If your box has an NVIDIA graphics card, install the NVIDIA graphics driver:

```
>  pkg install nvidia-driver
```

5.9.6 NVIDIA and ATI Radeon Graphics Configuration

If your box has an NVIDIA/Radeon graphics chip, put the following in /etc/rc.local:

```
kldload nvidia              kldload radeon
kldload nvidia-modeset      kldloadradeonkms
```

The right place to load kernel modules is /boot/loader.conf, wherein appending XYZ_load="YES" would load the module XYZ.ko into the FreeBSD kernel at boot time. Radeonkms, however, currently fails from /boot/loader.conf, which is why the alternate route via /etc/rc.local is suggested here.

5.9.7 User Accounts

If you did not create any normal user accounts at the time of installation, now is a good time to make reparations for your sins. If you did create a normal user account, you have another kind of sin to atone for—the FreeBSD user's ID (UID) would likely be different from the UID under the Linux system. For a box that dual-boots between Linux and FreeBSD, it is preferable that the UID of the normal user account is the same across Linux and FreeBSD. This avoids permissions woes when accessing files used under both installations.

Linux usually adds the first normal account with the UID 1000 and the group ID (GID) 1000 as well. You can use the interactive command adduser to add a normal user account under FreeBSD—and then force the UID 1000 during the interaction. If you want, you can make the normal user "pretty powerful" by telling adduser to create the user with additional membership of the groups wheel and operator.

Note   Under FreeBSD, only members of the group wheel can switch to the root user account with su. Members of the group operator are granted some additional privileges for dealing with devices (e.g., the printer).

If you need to modify an existing FreeBSD user—let's say named uvanilla (primary group name gvanilla) so that IDs are in sync with Linux (username and group name can differ from Linux; only the IDs matter), use the non-interactive command pw:

```
>   pw  groupmod -n gvanilla -g 1000
>   pw  usermod -n uvanilla -u 1000 -g 1000
>   pw  usermod -n uvanilla -G wheel,operator   # Optional extra groups
```

Note   With all this done, it is time to reboot (with the command reboot). Upon reboot, log in as the normal user and then issue the command startx. If everything is working correctly, startx will launch an X session using the TWM (Tab Window Manager) mini-desktop environment embedded into the X.org distribution.

If an X session comes up, your FreeBSD installation is raring to go up to the next level—installation of a full-fledged desktop environment.

If not, you can find out what went wrong by looking up /var/log/Xorg.0.log in a text editor or file viewer. For example:

```
>   less /var/log/Xorg.0.log
```

About half a dozen desktop environments work well under FreeBSD: KDE, GNOME, Mate, Xfce, LXDE, (work-in-progress) and Lumina.

We consider KDE and GNOME in the discussion that follows.

5.9.8 Graphical Desktop Environment

To install KDE or GNOME, execute one of the following two commands:

```
>  pkg install kde            >  pkg install gnome3
```

KDE and GNOME have their own display managers to perform the login, which can be enabled for boot-time launch via /etc/rc.conf:

```
gnome_enable="YES"     # boots into GNOME display manager gdm
kdm4_enable="YES"      # boots into KDE display manager kdm
```

If you want to start X sessions manually, create the file $HOME/.xinitrc under your normal user account and put one of the following two lines in it:

```
exec /usr/local/bin/gnome-session    # starts GNOME desktop
exec /usr/local/bin/startkde         # starts KDE desktop
```

You can now start your desktop environment from the shell with startx (as the normal user).

5.9.9 Making Things Easier: A Simpler Way to Configure FreeBSD

For newcomers—and occasionally veterans too—it might seem a rigmarole configuring a fresh FreeBSD installation. Luckily, there is a new way to configure FreeBSD lets you configure the entire system in a single shot. You can use the port mkdesktop:

```
>   portsnap fetch extract
>   cd /usr/ports/sysutils/mkdesktop
>   make install clean
```

Now just run `mkdesktop`.

The default desktop environment that `mkdesktop` currently uses is a lightweight version of KDE4 (use `kde-runtime` + `kde-baseapps` + `kde-workspace`).

If you want to use GNOME3, run the following command in a separate terminal `Alt` + `F2` after `mkdesktop` has gone through its initialization routine:

```
echo "gnome3" > ~/mkdesktop/pkg_list/desktop
```

This command must be executed after `mkdesktop` says it has initialized itself.

By default, `mkdesktop` works with five stages:

```
   [ pre_x:    The stage where you can get console-mode applications ]
         x:    Usually just gets xorg
  [ post_x:    X applications not specific a Desktop Environment (DE):
               firefox; xmms ]
   desktop:    What you define as the DE – wired by default for
               lightweight kde4
[ post_desktop:    DE stuff the desktop stage itself does not get:
               ksnapshot; kcalc ]
```

Stages listed in square brackets are ones that start out as empty lists by default. Each stage—as well as the number of stages—can be customized as per user requirement.

Once the stages have been processed, a `postproc` routine lets you install emulation layers (Wine; Linuxulator) and set up the most important configuration files under `/etc` to function out of the box upon reboot.

If you run `mkdesktop` with the argument `--begin 0`, it will additionally configure the graphics subsystem for you.

5.10 Dual-Booting FreeBSD and Linux on a GPT Disk

Let's say you have a disk-sized 4TB. You have to use GPT for such a disk, because MBR can only address 2TB (maximum).

Let's further say you want FreeBSD / to be 50GB, and Linux / to be 30GB.

Points to note:

- FreeBSD under GPT needs one extra partition: type `freebsd-boot`, maximum size 512 KB. This is besides a partition of type `freebsd-ufs`, which serves as the root filesystem (`/`) and which can be of any size. As a side note, the `freebsd-boot` partition is never mounted. It just holds extra boot code that can (and should) be ignored by the user during normal work.

- Dual-booting Linux and FreeBSD under GPT is easier done with Linux Grub. When booting FreeBSD, Linux Grub should directly boot the partition that corresponds to / (and not the `freebsd-boot` partition).

Install FreeBSD first and create six partitions:

ada0p1: type `freebsd-boot`; size 512KB

ada0p2: type `freebsd-ufs`; size 50GB

ada0p3: type `freebsd-swap`; suggested size would be amount of RAM + 1GB

ada0p4: type `linux-data`; size 30GB

ada0p5: type `linux-swap`; suggested size would be amount of RAM + 1GB

ada0p6: type `linux-data`; size is whatever is left ($\approx$ 3.9TB)

Unlike in the MBR strategy, this time around we use separate swap partitions for FreeBSD and Linux—owing entirely to the humongous size of our disk. You can, if you want, continue to share a single swap partition between the two operating systems.

Go through and complete the FreeBSD installation.

Next, install Linux using `sda4` as the / mountpoint. Set the device for bootloader (Grub) installation as `/dev/sda` (which should be the default), and not `/dev/sda4`.

Once your Linux system is functional, open the file `/etc/grub.d/40_custom` in a text editor and add a new entry for the second GPT partition (which is our FreeBSD /):

```
menuentry "FreeBSD" {
    insmod ufs2
    set root=(hd0,gpt2)
    kfreebsd /boot/loader
}
```

Then run `grub-mkconfig -o /boot/grub/grub.cfg`. You can now reboot and happily choose which OS to launch: Linux or FreeBSD.

For the sake of reference, GUIDs for some partition types are mentioned here:

```
        linux-data:   0fc63daf-8483-4772-8e79-3d69d8477de4
        linux-swap:   0657fd6d-a4ab-43c4-84e5-0933c84b4f4f
       freebsd-ufs:   516e7cb6-6ecf-11d6-8ff8-00022d09712b
      freebsd-swap:   516e7cb5-6ecf-11d6-8ff8-00022d09712b
fat / fat32 / ntfs:   ebd0a0a2-b9e5-4433-87c0-68b6b72699c7
```

Note   Beware of one GPT pitfall: the scheme encourages poorly planned, *ad hoc* partitioning. If you create 100 partitions in your disk, it won't be easy to locate which file dwells under which partition.

5.11 Summary

Installing and configuring Unix is as much fun as it is rewarding. Unix is incredibly scientific in its philosophy and implementation. Each time you install and configure FreeBSD and/or Linux, you come away with a sense of having been educated. Everyone struggles a bit the first time around, but this chapter lumps together all that can be delivered generally for you to successfully set up Unix on your PC.

Now that we have it, we are going to have to look at administering it, which happens in the chapter that follows.

CHAPTER 6

Basic System Administration

There used to be a time when administering Unix was considered a hallowed task, open only to super-experts whose salaries were a source of much envy. With the onset of the GNU revolution, that happily has changed to a situation in which administering a Unix desktop requires less overhead than Windows, which still uses the obsolescent search-download-install-configure cycle for every small change in the system.

Administering a Unix server (to host services like mail, firewall, and DNS) still requires a fair bit of knowledge, expertise, and willingness to tinker. But luckily our discussion is not about Unix services—just a good, modern desktop box. That is something that everyone can—and should—do by himself or herself.

6.1 Being Root

Under FreeBSD, you can be root whenever you need. Under Linux, one cannot be sure. (Commands in this chapter assume root credentials, unless noted otherwise.)

The first thing you need to be sure of under Linux is that you can switch to the superuser (root) account:

```
USER>   su -
```

Ubuntu-flavored distributions encourage the user not to switch to root user account and use sudo instead. The system installer is automatically granted sudo privileges. So to run any command as root, just feed the command as an argument to sudo. To actually switch to the root user account, you must first set the root user's password:

```
% sudo passwd root
```

© Manish Jain 2018
M. Jain, *Beginning Modern Unix*, https://doi.org/10.1007/978-1-4842-3528-7_6

If you are on a freshly installed Linux box, update the system to retrieve all the important fixes issued since the installer was rolled out:

```
ROOT#  pacman -Syyu  # Arch
%  sudo  apt  update  &&  apt  upgrade    # Ubuntu
# The rest of the chapter assumes the lead 'sudo' as and when needed
```

6.2 Local Filesystems

Most of the time, the only mounted filesystem after a fresh installation is the / filesystem. You must make a note of—and then remember—the device node that gets mounted as /.

Linux defaults to using UUID to denote filesystems in /etc/fstab. This has minor advantages and major disadvantages. The traditional device node nomenclature is more transparent and easy to remember—you anyway do not want / to be loaded via dynamic references. Imagine if you needed to carry out a filesystem consistency check with fsck and without any fond memories of the device node for /.

If there are any partitions (beyond /) in your hard disk you need to access, create a mountpoint directory, typically under /mnt, and add an entry in /etc/fstab. For example, let's say you have a logical drive (formatted as Ext2) in your extended partition. You can mount it with the following entry in /etc/fstab:

```
/dev/ada0s5   /mnt/ext2   ext2fs   rw   0   0          # FreeBSD fstab
/dev/sda5    /mnt/ext2   ext2   rw   0   0             # Linux fstab
```

With this line, you can now mount the filesystem of ada0s5 (FreeBSD)/sda5 (Linux) with the mount /mnt/ext2 command.

Note   Under FreeBSD, you need to first load the ext2fs driver into the kernel with kldload ext2fs. This can be automated by appending the following line to /etc/rc.conf:

```
linux_enable=YES
```

If you do not want to create an entry in /etc/fstab, you can simply use the full-fledged mount command:

```
mount -t ext2fs /dev/ada0s5 /mnt/ext2     # FreeBSD
mount -t ext2 /dev/sda5 /mnt/ext2         # Linux
```

When the system reboots, /mnt/ext2 will get automatically mounted if an entry is made in /etc/fstab. If you want automatic mounting disabled, change the mount flags in /etc/fstab from rw to rw,noauto. rw, as you might have guessed, stands for read+write, which has a read-only counterpart, called ro.

Optical media can be mounted similarly (with a mountpoint directory first created):

```
/dev/dvd   /mnt/dvd   cd9660   ro,noauto  0  0        # FreeBSD fstab
/dev/sr0   /mnt/cdrom  iso9660  ro,noauto  0  0        # Linux fstab
```

Removable USB disks can be mounted easily too. If you have a USB stick formatted as FAT/FAT32, create a mountpoint (/mnt/stick) and then alter /etc/fstab:

```
/dev/da0s1  /mnt/stick  msdosfs  rw,noauto  0  0   # FreeBSD fstab
/dev/sdb1   /mnt/stick  msdos    rw,noauto  0  0   # Linux fstab
```

This assumes the USB stick is attached as da0 (FreeBSD) or sdb (Linux). If you are unsure of the correct device node, check the output of the command dmesg.

Note   Unix user-level access to non-optical disks does not differentiate between the connection interface: SATA/SSD/USB disks are all treated uniformly with the same commands.

FreeBSD does though score a minor yet significant point over Linux in the device nomenclature for disks. While SATA/SSD devices show up as /dev/ada* entries (ada = ATA Direct Access), USB media use a different series: /dev/da* (da = Direct Access).

This clarity is missing under Linux, wherein all disks—whether SATA/SSD or USB—use the same series: /dev/sd*. This could at times result in confusion and the need to troubleshoot the system.

If the USB stick is formatted as NTFS, it needs a bit more effort.

Under Linux, use `modprobe ntfs` to load the NTFS module and then alter
`/etc/fstab`:

```
/dev/sdb1    /mnt/stick    ntfs    rw,noauto   0   0          # Linux fstab
```

FreeBSD does not support the NTFS driver in the kernel itself—you need to use the
fuse library:

```
pkg install fusefs-ntfs
kldload fuse                                   # if not loaded already
ntfs-3g -o rw /dev/da0s1 /mnt/stick
```

If you need to format a USB stick or disk partition afresh, avoid using FAT/NTFS:
those filesystems have no understanding of Unix permissions, as a result of which every
entity placed therein is marked as universally writeable and executable.

Perhaps the best candidate for formatting removable media now is Ext2, support for
which is available under all major operating systems:

- Windows users can use ext2fsd, the Ext2 filesystem driver for
  Windows available at `https://sourceforge.net/projects/`
  `ext2fsd/`.

- FreeBSD can access Ext2 filesystems with the ext2fs driver, and
  further can format a partition as Ext2 with the `mke2fs` utility, which is
  part of the e2fsprogs package: `pkg install e2fsprogs`.

Linux can mount UFS partitions read-only once you have loaded the UFS module:

```
modprobe ufs
```

FreeBSD can mount Ext2/Ext3 partitions read+write once either or both Ext2fs and
Linux modules have been loaded: `kldload ext2fs` -or- `kldload linux`

Ext4 partitions can be mounted under FreeBSD as read-only via `fuse` support:

```
kldload fuse                                   # if not loaded already
kldload linux                                  # if not loaded already
pkg install fusefs-ext4fuse
ext4fuse <ext4_partition_node> <mountpoint>
```

The final—and the most important—point in this section is manual filesystem consistency check you must carry out on every filesystem mounted in read+write mode whenever there is an improper shutdown. Since we are not dealing with alternative filesystems such as btrfs (Linux) and ZFS (FreeBSD), this section deals with the traditional fsck for Ext2 (Linux) filesystems and UFS (FreeBSD).

When you experience an improper shutdown, boot into single-user mode using the bootloader menus. For FreeBSD, this is usually done with 2 at the bootloader menu. For Linux, you need to press e to edit the boot command sequence, locate the line beginning with linux, append either single or S to that line, and then press F10.

When you have entered the single-user shell, execute the following commands, which assume that Linux / is /dev/sda1 (Ext4) and FreeBSD / is /dev/ada0s2a (UFS):

For Linux ext4: fsck.ext4 -fy /dev/sda1

`# Or, for an ext2 partition: fsck.ext2 -fy /dev/sda1`

For FreeBSD UFS: fsck -fy /dev/ada0s2a

- The foregoing commands perform checks for / only: You need to carry them out for each filesystem mounted rw (read+write) at the time of the improper shutdown.

- fsck may report that a second run is needed. If so, re-run fsck.

- If e2fsprogs is installed, FreeBSD can carry out fsck.ext2 / fsck.ext3 / fsck.ext4 on Linux filesystems too. But this is not necessarily recommendable: FreeBSD fsck.ext[234] has not yet matured to the point where it can reliably do the job. But there are no penalties either: if FreeBSD fsck.ext[234] fails, all that happens is that you get an error message clearly stating the failure, in which case you can boot into Linux and use Linux fsck.ext[234] to finish the job.

6.3 Partition Management

Partition formatting is done with newfs (FreeBSD) and mke2fs (Linux).

A newfs invocation usually turns on soft updates, the FreeBSD counterpart of journaling in Linux (Ext3) filesystems:

```
newfs -U <node>
# where <node> is the device node of the partition to be formatted
```

If <node> lies in a solid state disk, you can turn on discard (TRIM) support with the additional argument -t to newfs. Later, you can use the tunefs command:

```
tunefs  -t enable  <node>
# enable TRIM in existing (but unmounted) UFS filesystem
```

To format a partition under Linux (or FreeBSD) as Ext2, use mke2fs <node>.

For SSD TRIM, you can add discard support, which works best in Ext4 format:

```
mke2fs -t ext4 -E discard <node>
```

You can add discard support to an existing (unmounted) Ext2/Ext3/Ext4 partition too:

```
tune2fs -o discard <node>
```

FreeBSD does not yet recognize/honor the discard attribute when mounting partitions of type Ext2/Ext3/Ext4. So when mounting Linux filesystems under FreeBSD, omit the discard option in FreeBSD's /etc/fstab; otherwise, the mount will not succeed.

To add or delete partitions in a disk, the standard commands are gpart (FreeBSD) and fdisk (Linux). Linux fdisk is interactive, and hence readily usable with no prior experience. A cute variant is cfdisk, which uses ncurses widgets.

FreeBSD gpart needs some getting used to. The USB-stick tutorial is a start. The example underneath creates the MBR schema and then two slices (primary partitions) in a USB stick attached as /dev/da0. One slice, sized 1GB, contains a UFS partition and the other slice is Ext2 (spanning the rest of the stick):

```
type mke2fs &>/dev/null || pkg install e2fsprogs
gpart destroy -F da0 2>/dev/null
gpart create -s MBR  da0
```

```
gpart add -s 1G -t freebsd da0    # adds da0s1 as a slice
gpart create -s BSD da0s1         # creates BSD nesting schema on da0s1
gpart add -t freebsd-ufs da0s1    #  creates partition da0s1a in the slice
gpart add -t linux-data da0       # adds da0s2 spanning remaining disk
newfs -U /dev/da0s1a
mke2fs /dev/da0s2
```

The bootcode subcommand of gpart can also insert booting code into a disk/slice. You can read man gpart for usage, while a few points are noted here.

- For MBR partitioned disks, there are two versions of the bootcode that can be put into the first sector (512 byte block) of the disk:

  1. /boot/mbr is the non-interactive version, and it will simply boot the slice marked as active in the disk's MBR table. If that slice is of type freebsd, it needs to have the bootcode /boot/boot written to it (with gpart again).

  2. /boot/boot0 is the interactive version, and it will present a list of bootable slices in the disk, each of which can be booted with a corresponding Function key: F1 , F2 , F3 , F4 . Again, if any of the (max four) bootable slices is of type freebsd, it needs to have the bootcode /boot/boot written to it.

- GPT partitioned disks too must use a version of the MBR known as *Protective MBR* for the disk's first sector. The code for that version is /boot/pmbr.

Each MBR disk reserves the disk's first block of 512 bytes, as follows:

- 446 bytes for the boot code

- 64 bytes for a table that records the start/end/fstype of four slices

- Two bytes for a checksum

6.4 Console Configuration

Console-mode usage of the computer has been falling out of favor for a while now, and that trend will probably continue.

Linux essentially has very little by way of console-mode usage. The only console-mode usage under Linux happens when you need to run fsck in a single-user shell.

FreeBSD still has a significant (but rapidly dwindling) console life. If you just feel like having fun without X, FreeBSD can deliver some nice juice: text editing (Vim or Joe), email (alpine), music (mp3blaster), chat (irssi), and even a few games (vitetris, the Tetris game). And then, on a dull day, you might flirt with the cookies: /usr/games/fortune.

To drop into console-mode FreeBSD, this is what you can do:

1. Run the command bsdconfig console. This sets your console preferences: saver; key-rate.

2. Append this line to /boot/loader.conf: kern.vty=sc.

Note   The line above will prevent start-up of X server, which needs vt as kern. vty driver.

---

3. Disable any X login manager (gdm/kdm) in /etc/rc.conf.

4. Reboot.

While you are at the console, remember that you can open additional terminal windows with Alt + F2 , Alt + F3 and so on.

When you have had enough console-mode fun, you can return to the X environment. For that, you will likely need to readjust the kern.vty driver in /boot/loader.conf from sc to vt (and then reboot). Otherwise, the X server might refuse to start.

6.5 Internet Connectivity

Since wired Ethernet cards are supported under Unix as well as—perhaps even better than—Windows, wired NIC (Network Interface Card) drivers are usually not an issue. This is in stark contrast to wireless cards, for which OEM (Original Equipment Manufacturer) support to the open-source community ranges from scandalously poor to zilch. The only OEM that provides good open-source support for its wireless NIC is Atheros, and these cards are not easy to find in the market.

For this discussion, we assume that you are using wired Ethernet for your Unix box. Just in case you are not aware, we'll first discuss a couple of abbreviations.

- DNS (Domain Name Service)

  When you call John Doe on his mobile, it is good to have his name. But the more important part is his mobile number. Precisely in that spirit, when you want to open the URL `www.yahoo.co.uk` in your web browser, you need the numeric (IP) address of `www.yahoo.co.uk` (which would be of the form 1.2.3.4). Since it is unlikely that you or the browser has that address, somebody must fill in this crucial part of the jigsaw puzzle: what is the IP address of `www.yahoo.co.uk` ?

  That's where DNS comes in. Your web navigation request first goes to a predesignated DNS resolver, which tells your browser the IP address for `www.yahoo.co.uk`.

- DHCP (Dynamic Host Configuration Protocol)

  Just as `www.yahoo.co.uk` maps to an IP address, your computer too must have a valid IP configuration when connecting to the Internet. Manually supplying your host an IP configuration needs a few tidbits strung together: host IP address; netmask; address of the machine (gateway/router/modem) that will send/receive packets on behalf of your computer; and address of the DNS resolver.

  Often, the gateway (or perhaps the modem your box connects to) can automatically supply your host with a valid IP configuration when the host machine boots up. That happens when the gateway is running a service known as DHCP. In such a case, your host can simply accept DHCP configuration for connecting to the Internet—everything happens auto-magically thereafter.

Both FreeBSD and Linux use a couple of files for DNS resolution: `/etc/resolv.conf` lists the DNS resolver addresses.
`/etc/hosts` lists hostnames that get resolved locally without querying DNS resolvers.

147

You should not insert anything in /etc/resolv.conf manually (except for one-time usage)—your changes will likely be wiped out by a reboot.

If you need to navigate to www.yahoo.co.uk without assistance from any DNS resolver, you can ping www.yahoo.co.uk on the command line, make a note of the responding IP address, and put that address in /etc/hosts:

```
106.10.160.45 www.yahoo.co.uk
```

That hack works only as long as www.yahoo.co.uk continues to service under the IP address 106.10.160.45. When that changes, you can delete the line in /etc/hosts and return to good, old DNS-based navigation.

FreeBSD configuration for network interfaces is done with:

```
bsdconfig networking
```

This command lets you set a variety of networking parameters—hostname; local host's IP address (if not using DHCP); DNS resolvers; default router/gateway; and (optional) use of IPv6. In case you do not have any preferred DNS resolvers of your own, you can always use OpenDNS: 208.67.222.222 and 208.67.220.220.

If you need to restart FreeBSD network services, use the following command:

```
service netif restart &&  service routing restart
```

Linux has equivalent commands:

```
service network-manager restart       # Ubuntu
systemctl restart NetworkManager      # Arch
```

If your Linux Ethernet configuration gets messed up, use the nmtui command to generate a new Ethernet connection profile.

An easy way to generate a new Ethernet connection profile under Linux is to first run the ip link command and get your NIC's MAC (hardware) address, which is a colon-separated hexadecimal string in the output.

Then run nmtui, delete all Ethernet profiles (if any), and create a new one. Put eth0 in the Profile Name field, and use the MAC address in the Device field. If needed, adjust the connection properties—for instance, Automatic (DHCP) or Manual. Refer to Figure 6-1.

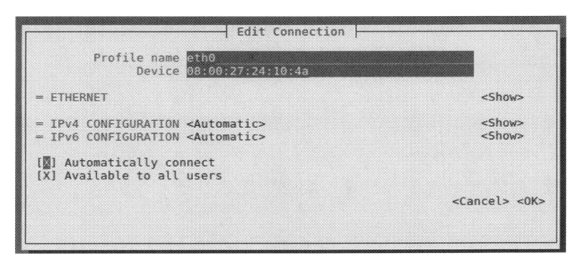

Figure 6-1. *Generating a new Ethernet profile with nmtui*

When you save the profile, it should automatically be activated.

If you need any further help, it promises to get messy. True to its bleeding-edge flux, Linux networking varies between red and green and blue—things that should be handled in the base system are handled instead by the flavors and distributions, each of which is deterministically avowed to do things its own way and break any degree of compatibility with other distributions:

- nmtui might not be available. The distributor chose to omit it from the base distribution.

- nmtui installation occurs as part of another package, the name of which could be networkmanager, NetworkManager, or network-manager.

For the case nmtui is not installed, we'll take up the following example for nmtui installation under Arch (with Ubuntu notes in comments), assuming that the system currently has a wired Ethernet card with no Internet connectivity as yet.

To get one-time Internet connectivity, first run ip link to extract a couple of important tidbits, which we save as the placeholders:

```
ip link
# Note your ethernet card's name (e.g. enp0s3)         => <eth>
# Note your card's MAC address (e.g. 08:00:27:24:10:4a)  => <mac>
```

Make sure you save <eth> and <mac> in a plain-text file somewhere.

If /etc/resolv.conf is empty, put in the following:

```
nameserver 208.67.222.222
nameserver 208.67.220.220
```

Then continue as follows (assuming you want your box to be 192.168.1.100):

```
ip link set <eth> up
ip addr add 192.168.1.100/24 broadcast 192.168.1.255 dev <eth>
ip route add default via 192.168.1.1
pacman -Ssy                     #skip for Ubuntu
pacman -S networkmanager        #Ubuntu: apt-get install network-manager
systemctl enable NetworkManager #Ubuntu: systemctl enable network-manager
systemctl start NetworkManager  #Ubuntu: systemctl start network-manager
```

Adjust the preceding snippet if and as needed for:

- <eth>: This should be the device name as reported by ip link; e.g., enp0s3

- Your host's IP address (assumed to be 192.168.1.100)

- Gateway/default router IP (assumed to be 192.168.1.1)

- Netmask (assumed to be 24)

At this stage, you must reboot. When you come up afresh, you will not have any Internet connectivity, but you do have the all-important nmtui command.

Run nmtui to generate a new, persistent Ethernet profile that will survive the next reboot. All that you need for that is the MAC address, which we so wisely saved as <mac> at the outset. That MAC address corresponds to the Device field, while for the Profile Name you can use eth0. If DHCP is not to be used, change automatic to a manual configuration.

6.6 Sound Configuration

Just as with Ethernet, sound chipsets used nowadays are shipped onboard as part of the motherboard. Since motherboard manufacturers are strongly inclined to provide drivers to all major operating systems, your sound card is virtually certain to work out-of-the-box, even better than under Windows, where a driver installation would usually be needed. Unix kernels ship with support for every major sound chipset in the market.

The most you might need to do is to manually load the driver into the kernel (with `kldload` under FreeBSD or `modprobe` under Linux). That happens if the sound card is not plug-and-play, which luckily is nowadays an almost nonexistent scenario.

FreeBSD provides an easy way to check whether your sound card is recognized for what it is. The first couple of lines you get from `cat /dev/sndstat` should match your sound card, with an example of the output from my system:

```
Installed devices:
pcm0:  <CMedia CMI8738> (play/rec) default   # My CMedia 8738 chip
```

The more pressing concern might be to configure your sound card's play characteristics, such as volume. For that, you can use a mixer application to tune the card. For example, `aumix` is a command-line utility that can set and save your mixer settings. Some desktop environments have an integrated mixer that does the job. For instance, KDE provides `kmix`.

6.7 X Configuration

Here's the good news: X nowadays needs no configuration. Over the years, X has matured so handsomely that the system takes care of the entire configuration innately: graphics, keyboard, and mouse—the whole caboodle.

Since Linux distributions usually ship with X and a wired desktop environment, the system will automatically launch into an X session when booted.

If you need to disable Linux's automatic X startup at boot time, use `systemctl`:

```
systemctl set-default multi-user.target   # Boots into console-mode
```

Besides `multi-user.target`, the other chief target is `graphical.target`, which usually is the default-as-shipped and starts X at boot time. To get the current target, you can use `systemctl get-default`.

For FreeBSD, remember that if you are using a Radeon or NVIDIA graphics chip, you need to `kldload` a couple of modules:

(`radeon, radeonkms`) for ATI Radeon cards

(`nvidia, nvidia-modeset`) for NVIDIA cards

The right place to automate loading any kernel module into the FreeBSD kernel usually is /boot/loader.conf. But radeonkms currently fails to load from that file, which is why it is suggested you automate the loading of a graphics chip's modules via /etc/ rc.local. Any other kernel module, let's say ums.ko, can be loaded at boot time by appending to /boot/loader.conf: ums_load=YES.

Since your keyboard and mouse will likely be standard USB devices, they should work flawlessly with the generic drivers in the kernel. The only "add-on" feature that has gained popularity of late in this segment is the use of keyboard backlights, which make it very easy to work with the keyboard even in the dark. You may be able to use a dedicated key on the keyboard to switch backlights on or off. If not, there is command-line fallback, called xset led on.

You can even automate backlights to be switched on when you log in with X, by putting this line into your shell's configuration, perhaps $HOME/.bashrc:

```
pgrep -x Xorg >/dev/null && xset led on
```

A couple of X informational/troubleshooting utilities are xlogo and xkill, available via package names with the same respective names. xlogo displays the X logo, while xkill gives you a Jolly Roger cursor that you can place on the window of an X application that has run amok: Roger's skull will kill the misbehaving application.

We'll now look at a worst-case scenario: you happen to be using a graphics chipset for which a Unix driver is not yet available.

That's bad news, agreed. But still not as bad as it initially sounds. If a driver is not available for your graphics chip, that does not hinder your usage of the computer for "normal" work. What is affected is your ability to play multimedia files (video playback in your .avi/.mp4/other such files, and some games, which there anyway are not so many of under Unix, at least compared to DOS/Windows).

Video content uses a hardware acceleration facility known as Direct Rendering Infrastructure (DRI), which is only available with a full-fledged driver. If you try to play a video file with no DRI support available, its frames will move in jerks rather than fluidly. If video playback is not high on your list of priorities, your graphics chip can usually be made to work very satisfactorily—while open-source developers work assiduously in the background to remove the driver hiccup for you.

In such cases, this is what you can do (as root):

1. Run this command while in text mode: Xorg -configure

2. Open the file generated in Step 1 in a text editor.

3. Locate the line with the setting for `Driver` in the section titled `Device` (recheck the section title: `Device`; not `InputDevice`).

4. Replace the value of the `Driver` setting (whatever it is) with `vesa`.

5. Move the altered configuration file to `/etc/X11/`.

Now use `startx` (as a normal user; not as root) to start the X server with the generic `vesa` driver. Your system will work absolutely fine—just with the rider that video playback for movie files will be fidgety.

6.8 Running X Applications as Root

You must never run the X server directly as root—that is supposed to be a major security loophole. The only time root is permitted to use the `startx` command is to check that X was installed correctly.

Run the X server as a normal user with the command `startx`. It goes without saying the X applications (clients) should also be run as the normal user—that happens automatically anyway.

There are a few (not zero, but, yes, very few) X applications that currently need to be run as root directly. One such application is `xconsole` under FreeBSD, which lists console messages that appear on `/dev/ttyv0` for example, whenever you plug in/out a removable disk or when there has been a kernel-level error.

This is how you can run the useful-and-unwieldy `xconsole` under FreeBSD.

Remember that you have started the X server as the normal user. Once the X server has started, it will only accept commands from you. But since `xconsole` will be run not as you and as root instead, it creates a problem—how do you enable root to launch `xconsole` under an already running X server? That can be done with `xauth`, which can authorize an additional user to issue commands to the X server that you started.

You can install `xauth` and `xconsole` in one shot: `pkg install xauth xconsole`

Then run once as root, with `<user>` as a placeholder for your normal user account:

```
ROOT#    touch /var/xauth.extract
ROOT#    chown <user> /var/xauth.extract
```

Now run as the normal user (with an X session already started):

```
USER>    xauth extract /var/xauth.extract $DISPLAY
```

The root user can pick up the authorization and launch X applications:

```
ROOT#    export DISPLAY=:0
ROOT#    xauth merge /var/xauth.extract
ROOT#    xconsole &
```

To confirm that xconsole is working as intended, just plug in a USB stick and watch the messages appear in the xconsole window.

As root, do not overuse the authorization. Use it strictly for the useful-and-unwieldy genre of X clients.

6.9 Finding Local Files Quickly

Every now and then you'll need to find filenames in the local system that match a certain path string. Since the matching files could be under your $HOME or under /var or /etc or /usr, the search would have to be rooted at /. But recursing down / with the find command is less than ideal. If you are not convinced, try it right now:

```
find / -type f -name *.svg  # When fed up, press Ctrl+C to stop the search
```

The solution is a database-backed search with locate:

```
type locate        # FreeBSD default: always available; Linux default: never
                     shipped
```

If locate is not installed in your Linux box, you need to install the mlocate package.

```
Ubuntu: ROOT#  apt-get install mlocate
Arch:   ROOT# pacman -S mlocate
```

Once that package has been installed, run updatedb as root:

```
ROOT#    /usr/libexec/locate.updatedb      # Path under FreeBSD
ROOT#    /usr/bin/updatedb     # Path under Linux
```

Now, for system-wide queries for file paths, you can query the updatedb database:

```
locate svg         # Find all files in the system with the string "svg" in
                     the path
```

Each time you run `locate`, it will query the existing `updatedb` database. If your database is old, you should first run `updatedb` (as root) and then query the refreshed database. `updatedb` is fast. It returns within a few seconds, perhaps a high value of a minute per TB (terra byte) in the host system's storage. `locate` returns instantly.

6.10 Configuring the Printer

Printing under Unix is mostly done with PostScript, a page description language originally created at Adobe Systems. For a printer to work under Unix, the OEM releases—at the very least—use what is known as a PostScript Printer Description (PPD) file, which allows the printer to interface with the Common Unix Printing System, CUPS.

This is a good stage to check whether the `cups` package is installed. You should also install `cups-pdf` so that you can use the Print-To-File facility to export any document as a PDF. Use your system's package manager to install both. FreeBSD users should also append the following line to `/etc/rc.conf: cupsd_enable=YES`.

When CUPS is installed, the installation process will create a group named `cups`. Add your normal user account (`<normal>` in the following commands) to that group:

```
ROOT#   pw groupmod cups -m <normal>    # FreeBSD
ROOT#   usermod -a -G cups <normal>   # Linux
```

After you added yourself to the group `cups`, it is strongly suggested that you reboot. Your new group membership will not come into effect immediately.

For a USB printer, next make a note of your printer's USB port. This is easy—just run `lsusb` (Linux) or `usbconfig` (FreeBSD) twice. Once with the printer turned off, and then the second time with the printer turned on. The additional port that shows up in the second run is your USB printer.

OEM support for open-source printing has steadily improved over the last few years. You must still query about a printer's open-source driver status before any purchase.

Two major OEMs that provide Unix driver-level support for at least some printers are Hewlett Packard (HP) and Epson.

HP has created a framework called HPLIP (HP Linux Imaging and Printing), which readily recognizes all HP printers (at least the USB ones) under Linux as well as FreeBSD. HP inkjet printers often use HP's own print format (PCL) for communicating with the printer.

For an HP printer, all that the user usually needs to do is install the package `hplip` (as root). Then run the command `hp-setup` (as the normal user) to create a queue for the printer, which you can start feeding print jobs into.

155

If hp-setup fails to locate your USB printer, check the permissions for the USB port it is being hooked into. If the port is configured for root-user access only, set more generous permissions for the port.

TROUBLESHOOTING USB DEVICE PERMISSIONS

In the output of usbconfig, my HP 1112 printer shows up at the USB port ugen2.4, which in the filesystem is /dev/usb/2.4.0, so I put the following line (as root) into my FreeBSD configuration file /etc/devfs.conf:

perm usb/2.4.0 0664

Then, still as root, I restarted the devfs service:

```
/etc/rc.d/devfs restart        # HPLIP now sees the printer
```

If HPLIP still fails to find your printer, run hp-doctor to find the diagnosis.

Once the queue for the printer has been created, you can run hp-toolbox to get its status, and perhaps print a test page. At this stage, it can also be expected that HPLIP will automatically insert a handy system tray icon somewhere in your desktop's panels—the system tray icon will persist across a reboot.

Epson created an increasingly healthy line of inkjet printers in a series named as L*nnn*, where the L presumably stands for Linux. This is as opposed to the line named M*nnn*, which presumably is Microsoft-specific.

If you have an Epson inkjet printer under your Unix box, you want it to be from the L-series, PPDs for which should generally be available.

Epson printers from outside of the L-series can be made to work with Linux (but not FreeBSD) by downloading a closed-source Linux driver package at http://download.ebz.epson.net/dsc/search/01/search/?OSC=LX.

As on date, FreeBSD has a couple of ready-to-use ports for Epson inkjet printers.

/usr/local/ports/epson-inkjet-printer-201401w supports the L456, L455, L366, L365, L362, L360, L312, L310, L222, L220, L132, and L130 models.

/usr/local/ports/epson-inkjet-printer-201601w supports the L380 and L382 models.

Installing any of these ports (or their corresponding packages, the names of which simply strip out the leading /usr/local/ports/) would result in PPD files being generated, which you can then feed to CUPS as "drivers".

Once a PPD is available for your printer, switch your printer on and use your web browser to open the CUPS administrative site, which is:

```
http://localhost:631/admin
```

If you are prompted for user credentials at any stage, you can use root as the username and root's password as the password.

Click the Add Printer button to create a new queue (and make very sure that your printer is online). Your printer will likely be listed among the Local Printers: in which case, half the battle is won. Click that entry and move ahead.

The CUPS framework will then attempt to locate a suitable PPD for the printer discovered previously. If the system cannot find a good PPD for the printer by itself, it lets you browse and locate a suitable one.

When a PPD for your printer has been found—which is the remaining half of the battle, a CUPS queue will be created—which all applications in your system can print to.

CUPS also creates network-oriented URLs (of the form ipp:// and socket://) that any application in your intranet can utilize to print via your box. We'll leave those for you to play with on your own, if you like.

6.11 Using the Scanner

Scanners normally do not need any configuration. They usually are independent devices that advertise scanning capabilities over the USB infrastructure. Even when part of an MFD (Multi Function Device: Printer/scanner/anything else), the unit's scanner works largely independently of the remaining device.

If you have a scanner attached to your box, you need the SANE (Scanner Access Now Easy) backend package, the name of which varies between distributions:

```
pacman -S sane       # Arch
pkg install sane-backends      # FreeBSD
apt install sane-utils      # Ubuntu
```

Once you have the backend package, your system will have a couple of important commands: scanimage and sane-find-scanner.

The `scanimage` application is your scanning frontend:

```
scanimage -L   # Lists all the scanners attached to your box
```

If `scanimage -L` finds nothing, you need to investigate:

1. Run `scanimage -L` as root. If the scanner shows up, you simply have a permissions problem.

2. If the scanner is still undetected, run `sane-find-scanner` (again as root).

`sane-find-scanner` performs a vigorous vetting of devices that advertise scanning capabilities. If `sane-find-scanner` fails to spot your scanner, you probably need to write to your distribution's email forums.

For any permissions woes, refer to the troubleshooting guidelines highlighted in the previous section.

Once your scanner has started making its presence felt, you can scan:

```
scanimage --format jpg > scan.jpg
```

If ImageMagick is installed, the system can convert the output to PNG format (or any other compatible format as needed) readily:

```
convert scan.jpg scan.png
```

6.12 Using an APC Powerchute UPS to Shut the System Down

If you have a UPS that supports shutting the system down in case of extended power failure—for example an APC UPS with the Powerchute feature—you can ensure that your Unix box never shuts down unclean.

For this, you need to install the package `apcupsd`, a task which you can surely do with `pkg`, `apt`, or `pacman`.

For FreeBSD, there is an additional step after installation:

```
echo "apcupsd_enable=YES" >> /etc/rc.conf
```

Now locate the file `apcupsd.conf`. Under Linux, the typical path is `/etc/apcupsd/apcupsd.conf`, while FreeBSD uses `/usr/local/etc/apcupsd/apcupsd.conf`.

Edit the following six settings, for which we assume a USB UPS:

UPSNAME AnyNameThatSuitsYou

UPSCABLE usb

UPSTYPE usb

DEVICE BATTERYLEVEL 50

MINUTES 9

The DEVICE setting should be blank for any UPS of type USB. With the preceding configuration, the UPS will take control in case of power failure, and then halt the system when either the batter level dips under 50% or time-to-live dips under nine minutes.

You can launch the service immediately:

```
/usr/local/etc/rc.d/apcupsd start         # FreeBSD
systemctl enable apcupsd && systemctl start apcupsd   # Linux
```

You might like to check the output of ps waux | grep apcupsd. If apcupsd is not running under Linux, check if the file /etc/default/apcupsd exists. If the file exists, edit it to change ISCONFIGURED=no to ISCONFIGURED=yes. Then retry.

6.13 Building Stuff from Sources

This usually is never done under Linux (unless you are a developer yourself). But under FreeBSD, building from sources still happens. So I will dedicate this section to a quick word about the FreeBSD ports system.

While Linux has just one make system (GNU make) that interprets makefiles, FreeBSD has two—GNU make (the one imbibed from the Linux world) which is called gmake, and a native make. So what is make in Linux is gmake in FreeBSD, and what is make in FreeBSD has never been made in Linux. GNU make has no understanding of the FreeBSD ports system, and therefore cannot work well thereunder.

We'll take the example of [/usr/ports/mail/]alpine, a wonderful console-mode email client (which allegedly is Linus Torvalds' favorite email client, not surprisingly too). One reason folks like to build alpine from sources is that the pre-built package does not have support for saving passwords to the hard disk. If it rankles your blessed soul to have to type in your password each time you start alpine, you will have to delete the package and build the port instead.

The first step, in case you don't have the /usr/ports/ hierarchy yet, would be (as the root user) portsnap fetch extract.

Once your port's tree has been populated, navigate to /usr/ports/mail/alpine, set the options as suits you, and then start the build:

```
cd /usr/ports/mail/alpine
make config              #set your preferences: eg, save passwords
# Note you might have preferred for above: make config-recursive
# Read the following para to get a gist of why so

make install clean
```

The ports system is recursive: if alpine needs 100 other ports to be built, they will get automatically built along the way, with alpine the last one to finish. If any of those 100 ports need their own configuration options, you will be prompted as and when the port's build commences. This results in a stop-start-stop-start chain of builds, which might not suit you. This is why—at least for ports that have a lot of dependencies—folks prefer to use config's own recursion capability. If you use make config-recursive when setting options for alpine, the make system will *at the very beginning* invoke make config for alpine as well as any of the 100 ports that have any configurable options. You can spend a couple of minutes upfront reviewing the options for all the ports, for most of which you just want to accept the defaults with a simple OK. Once the configuration issue is fully settled, the download/build/install cycle will kick off in one, final swoosh and you won't be prompted at all.

If someday you want to deinstall alpine, just run make deinstall under the directory /usr/ports/mail/alpine. There is no deinstall-recursive.

That is our two-minute tutorial to the world of FreeBSD ports. Just before we close this section, it is handy to note that ports and packages use a common installation database, which does not differentiate between stuff that got in via pkg and stuff that got built via ports. If you install alpine as a port, pkg info alpine will recognize alpine as a locally installed application.

6.14 Unix Virtual Filesystems

This section is entirely optional. It is not intended to be a meaty discussion—just a gentle "awareness" exercise. It may or may not help—but it certainly does not harm—you to know a little bit about virtual filesystems in Unix.

If you are on Linux, you might have noticed that running the mount command gets a listing of many, many filesystems when you might have just created one / mountpoint. So what exactly are the others?

Every Unix installation, particularly Linux, automatically sets up a variety of additional filesystems that mostly reside in main memory (RAM). The purpose of these filesystems is to let various components of the kernel and the applications running in userspace memory communicate with each other faster but transparently.

One such filesystem is /proc, which automatically gets set up under Linux, but needs to be set up manually under FreeBSD. /proc provides a view of the table of the processes currently running in the system, complete with related information—for example, what were the command-line arguments passed in to the command when launched.

A working /proc is mandatory—and therefore automatically setup by the installer—under Linux, and strongly recommended under FreeBSD. You can mount /proc under FreeBSD with the following line in /etc/fstab:

```
procfs /proc procfs rw 0 0
```

Linux /proc yields other benefits—all major OS information is available as zero-sized files with data (!): cmdline (boot-time arguments to the kernel), filesystems (list of mounted filesystems), modules (list of loaded kernel modules), and other files. You can also, when you have gained expertise, change the parameters of a running kernel by manipulating /proc entries under Linux. But not under FreeBSD, which uses sysctl for controlling tunable parameters. For example, to prevent users from seeing information about other users' processes, a FreeBSD user would need to use sysctl security.bsd.see_other_uids=0.

There are many other such virtual filesystems—tmpfs, fdescfs, and sysfs, for example. But the one virtual filesystem that you should know just a bit about is the one that no one seems to know nowadays—devfs, the device filesystem (udev under Linux).

Until about the year 2002, both Linux and FreeBSD used the device node implementation as largely imbibed from AT&T Unix. Every device for which a driver was available in the kernel would show up as a node under /dev when the system booted. But while AT&T Unix catered to a very small set of hardware, GNU has to deal with an ever-ballooning explosion. In 2002, a Red Hat 7.3 box would typically have over 5,000 nodes under /dev. It was a real jungle, with users finding it difficult to figure out which files were actually relevant to him/her and the installation.

The problem was solved with devfs, a highly intricate paradigm that lets the system create nodes at boot time under /dev—not for all hardware supported, but for hardware actually present in the box. From 5000+ mostly-junk nodes in 2002, the listing for /dev has been slashed to typically something like 100 nowadays in 2018—with each node relevant to the box.

Since devfs is itself mounted at /dev, no one can create device nodes manually thereunder. That can only be done via system calls by a driver in the kernel.

6.15 Additional Commands to Administer Your Desktop

At this stage, you should be familiar with a few commands, some of which you might meet once a year, others a few dozen times a day. That depends on how you use your desktop Unix box. It is likely that you already know some of these commands, but there is no harm to a recap.

6.15.1 df

The diskfree command determines filesystem usage. How much has been used and how much is still free. Note that, since Unix filesystems reserve a percentage of every filesystem (ranging from 0% to 12%; with 8% being a typical value) for the root user's "emergency" operations, the two halves won't yield, upon addition, the filesystem's actual total size.

df -h is the human-readable variant that will use 1G instead of 1,073,741,824. (Reminder: Computer jargon uses 1K to denote not 1000, but 1024; which disk manufacturers very happily ignore when selling disks—as a result of which, when you buy a 256GB disk, you actually get 256 divided by 1.024 three times.)

If you are just interested in a particular filesystem, you can tell df that:

```
df -h /              # Stats for /, whichever device it maps to
df -h /dev/ada1s3a   # Stats for device node ada0s3a
```

6.15.2 du

du is similar to df, but instead of stats for a filesystem, it reports disk usage of a file or a directory. Just as df, it has a human-readable version:

```
du -h <path>    # If <path> is missing, a . (current directory) is assumed
du -sh <path>    # If <path> is a directory, print summary only
```

If images is a directory, this is what you can expect:

ls -ld images

drwxr-xr-x 2 bourne bourne 1536 Nov 10 15:50 images

du -sh images

2.1M images

What this means is that the directory file images itself uses just 1536 bytes, while those colorful files inside images/ occupy another 2.1MB (minus 1536 bytes).

Since du has to compute a directory's size at runtime by recursing over all its constituents, running it over a very large directory (/usr, for example) can take a huge amount of time. Contrast this with df, which always returns immediately—that is possible only because the operating system maintains a stats table for each filesystem, which gets updated in real time whenever the filesystem gets written to. Of course, the operating system cannot maintain such stats for every single file and directory in the system.

A related command is stat.

6.15.3 at

at schedules a job to be performed by the system using /bin/sh.

There is a large number of formats deemed valid for specifying the date and time, which you can read with man at. For an example, it will serve our purpose to know that HH:mm is recognized as a valid time.

at 23:59 will give you an input section, into which you can type in your command, followed by `Enter`, and closed by `Ctrl`+`D`. `Ctrl`+`D` is the standard way in Unix to denote end-of-input when feeding input from the keyboard.

If successful, this at command will schedule your job to run at 23:59 later today. The major reason for failure, if your command does not get queued, is that root blacklisted you in the file at.deny, the location of which is distribution-specific.

You can list your at jobs with atq and delete job number <N> with atrm <N>.

A related command, which lets you schedule repetitive jobs, is cron.

6.15.4 cdrecord

One of the great things in Unix is to be able to do from the command line what others can accomplish only via graphical toolkits—it certainly adds to your bragging rights when in company. If I were to place my finger on one such application, it would be cdrecord, which can record DVDs too, by the way.

In case your box does not have dvd+rw-tools, this is a good starting point. Install the package dvd+rw-tools, which automatically pulls in cdrtools, the package that contains the command cdrecord, and its buddy mkisofs.

To work with cdrecord, you must have an existing file in the standard ISO format. There are a couple of distinct ways to use cdrecord: burn a pre-existing ISO image you downloaded or write your own data—first into an ISO image with the associate command mkisofs, and then to the optical medium.

Since I like to go things in the order of fulfillment, I will first take up mkisofs—the ISO image compiler. To create an ISO image containing all .pdf files and the images/ directory, this is what you could use (as a normal user or as root):

```
mkisofs -iso-level 4 \
-allow-lowercase -allow-multidot -relaxed-filenames \  # Leniency hacks
-J -R \     # Pull in the Rockridge (Unix) and Joliet (Microsoft)
extensions
-o cdimage.iso \       # The image to be compiled
*.pdf images/      # The paths for the input data
```

You now have the ISO. The next step is to find the SCSI address of your CD writer, which is done with the --scanbus argument to cdrecord. If your CD writer was manufactured by Asus, you could run:

```
ROOT#   cdrecord --scanbus | grep -i asus | awk '{print $1}'
```

On my system, I get 0,0,0 as the SCSI address.

If you have no idea about the device manufacturer, just browse the output of cdrecord--scanbus for the most likely candidate. The SCSI address is a substring of the form <digit1>,<digit2>,<digit3>. FreeBSD provides an additional way to get the CD writer's SCSI address: camcontrol devlist.

Now you can insert a blank CD and write the image via your CD writer (as root):

```
cdrecord -dao dev=<scsi> speed=8 driveropts=burnfree cdimage.iso
```

<scsi> is a placeholder for the SCSI address we located with --scanbus.

The writing speed can be decreased (min 1) or increased (max 48 on most systems).

6.15.5 Loop Device Configuration

Sometimes—instead of burning to optical media—you need to loop and mount a CD/DVD ISO image through the kernel's looping ability. Note that Linux calls the CD image format iso9660, while FreeBSD calls it cd9660.

Under Linux, you can set up a loop for a CD image data.iso at /mnt/iso with:

```
mount -t iso9660 data.iso /mnt/iso -r -o loop
```

FreeBSD has a similar toolbox, which is kicked off with mdconfig:

```
mount -r -t cd9660 /dev/'mdconfig -f data.iso' /mnt/iso
# 'mdconfig -f data.iso' will usually output md0
```

When done, you can optionally unmount the image (umount /mnt/iso) and then destroy the loop device allocated by using:

```
mdconfig -d -u 0
```

6.15.6 smtp-cli

Sooner or later, you will want one important capability: shooting an email from the command line. More than the issue of bragging rights, it serves the need to inform—and be informed—at the critical moment.

There are a few tools that do the job, with my favored solution being smtp-cli.

The first step, as always, is to install the package smtp-cli. On first run, smtp-cli would likely complain about a few missing Perl modules. Install them one-by-one (as a normal user) with cpan. For example: cpan IO::Socket::INET6.

We'll use the following sender, which essentially is me:

```
fromaddr="bourne.identity@hotmail.com"
fromname="Manish Jain"
password="12345678" # For very good reasons, I am mistelling the password
SMTP="smtp-mail.outlook.com"
PORT=587
```

We'll use the following receiver, which is where my alter-ego resides:

```
sendto="jude.obscure@yandex.com"

smtp-cli --ipv4 --auth \
--server="$SMTP" \
--port=$PORT \
--user="$fromaddr" \
--pass="$password" \
--from="$fromname <$fromaddr>" \
--to="$sendto" \
--subject="Scripting with Transmission" \
--body-plain=$HOME/notes/transmission-scripting.txt
```

If a blank email with no body text is to be sent, delete the `--body-plain=` line.

If you need to send an attachment, that can be done easily by supplying `--attach=<path>` (`--attach=<>` can be repeated as many times as you like).

Just as `cpan` needs no administrative rights to invoke (it installs modules by default into the user's `$HOME`), emailing with `smtp-cli` can be done as a normal user too.

Cygwin has an add-on package named `email`, which has roughly equivalent capabilities, but `smtp-cli` is a touch more flexible.

6.15.7 rsync

I am going to be infamous with the next section, wherein I will profess the counter-revolutionary line: there's (almost) no need to back up. This section opens a mutually-convenient escape route for the cases where a system-wide backup actually is needed, with all operations performed in this section as root.

When you want to copy an entire filesystem, there are multiple ways to do it (`dump/ restore` for example). My favorite solution is `rsync`. If you don't have `rsync`, just install the package with the same name.

The rest of this section is illustrated with FreeBSD, documenting which is significantly easier—Linux users will need to adapt. (Creating a bootable backup under Linux is not easy—you have to use `grub`, an incredibly volatile component. Any attempt to insert boot code under Linux quickly turns into a PhD thesis.)

In this example, we'll back up the / filesystem, along with its boot code.

Let's say the backup device is /dev/da0, a USB disk not yet mounted and the current data in which can be trashed. You need to ensure the USB disk is larger than the used part of your / filesystem.

Let's also say the mountpoint location for the backup device is /mnt/bk—you need to create that beforehand.

We prepare the device to receive the backup:

```
gpart  destroy -F da0 2>/dev/null
gpart create -s MBR da0
gpart add -t freebsd da0
gpart create -s BSD da0s1
gpart add -t freebsd-ufs da0s1
gpart bootcode -b /boot/boot0 da0
gpart bootcode -b /boot/boot da0s1
newfs -U /dev/da0s1a
mount  /dev/da0s1a  /mnt/bk
```

(If you are on Linux, use fdisk /dev/sdb → mke2fs /dev/sdb1 → mount. We will simply ignore the boot code insertion. You can try on your own, though.)

The next thing to do is prepare a list of exclusions:

```
/dev/*          # devfs populates this directory at boot-time and as-needed
/media/*        # Auto-populated as and when you mount/eject media
/mnt/*          # Mountpoints should be established afresh
/proc/*         # Temporal entries
/sys/*          # Temporal entries
/tmp/*          # Temporal entries
/usr/ports      # freebsd user can just run 'portsnap fetch extract'
/var/tmp/*      # Temporal entries
/lost+found/*   # linux user does not need this in the backup - or so
                I hope
```

You can adjust the exclusions list as needed, although I feel inclined to note that the list presented here is a fairly mature one.

Save your exclusions list in the file /root/excl and initiate the sync:

```
rsync -aAHXv --delete --exclude-from /root/excl / /mnt/bk/
```

```
# Under Linux, adjust the next line for device node and fstype: echo '/dev/
da0s1a / ufs rw 0 0' > /mnt/bk/etc/fstab
```

```
# Save the current fstab too for reference (optional):
cp /etc/fstab /mnt/bk/etc/fstab_original
```

```
umount /mnt/bk
```

If and as needed, you can do three things with your backup:

1. You can open a shell with its root filesystem in the backup. The command for that is `mount /dev/da0s1a /mnt/bk && chroot /mnt/bk`.

2. You can boot off the USB disk (if you are using FreeBSD).

3. You can also carry out a reverse sync to mirror the backup into a new (possibly larger) root filesystem (/) in the hard disk.

6.16 Mitigating the Need for Backups

It does not please me one bit to have to deal with backups in my daily life. It pleases me still less to lose any important data.

Keeping Scylla and Charybdis satisfied is luckily not so difficult. It just requires you to work out a sound strategy that takes care of your data. For most desktop users, the following strategy is good enough. (I use it myself.) But the strategy needs to be executed with a fresh disk.

Let's say your hard disk device is `ada0` (`sda` under Linux; Linux names are stated in parentheses). Since the MBR schema permits one extended partition and three primary partitions, create four slices in your disk:

- `ada0s1` (`sda1`): 30GB; created as fat32; unformatted; reserved for future use.

- `ada0s2` (`sda2`): 30GB; Linux-data (Ext2/3/4); the / for a Linux installation.

- ada0s3 (sda3): 50GB; FreeBSD with one UFS partition ada0s3a; the /
  for FreeBSD.

- ada0s4 (sda4): Spans the remaining disk, is an extended partition,
  known as EBR in FreeBSD documentation. Our strategy's crux
  revolves around the EBR slice.

The ada0s4 slice (sda4) contains a single partition (Logical Drive) ada0s5 (sda5),
formatted as Ext2. (If you want to set up a swap partition, refer to the appendix for
creating ada0s6 as a swap partition shared by FreeBSD and Linux.)

Here are the FreeBSD commands to create ada0s4 and its nested ada0s5 (although
you can just as easily use Linux fdisk to create this schema):

```
type mke2fs &>/dev/null || pkg install e2fsprogs

# Assuming ada0s1, ada0s2 and ada0s3 have already been created:

gpart add -t EBR ada0   # creates ada0s4 spanning remaining disk space

gpart create -s MBR ada0s4
# A gpart bug often prevents use of the EBR schema in the command above
# Else the proper command  would be:   gpart create -s EBR  ada0s4

gpart add -t linux-data ada0s4
# Reports addition of ada0s4s1, which shows up as ada0s5 upon reboot
# So reboot and then create the ext2 filesystem:

mke2fs ada0s5
```

Create a directory /perm and map it to /dev/ada0s5 in /etc/fstab:

```
mkdir /perm

echo '/dev/ada0s5 /perm ext2fs rw 0 0' >> /etc/fstab
# Linux adaptation: echo '/dev/sda5 /perm ext2 rw 0 0' >> /etc/fstab
```

Mount /perm and create a few directories in it as the per the commands (left side) or the corresponding schema (right side):

```
                                          /perm
    mount /perm                           |-- home_freebsd
    mkdir -p /perm/home_freebsd/root      |    |-- root
    mkdir -p /perm/home_linux/root        |-- home_linux
                                          |    |-- root
```

This completes one-time disk initialization activities. The ensuing discussion details per-installation follow-up.

Whenever you make a fresh FreeBSD/Linux installation, do a few things—denoting your installation as <os> and your user name as <user>:

1. Make /home point to /perm/home_<os>:

```
cd /
rm -rf home

ln -s /perm/home_freebsd home    # if the new install is FreeBSD
ln -s /perm/home_linux home      # if the new install is Linux
```

2. Make /usr/home point to /perm/home_<os>:

```
cd /usr
rm -rf home

ln -s /perm/home_freebsd home    # FreeBSD
ln -s /perm/home_linux home      # Linux
```

3. Make /root point to /perm/home_<os>/root:

```
cd /
rm -rf root

ln -s /perm/home_freebsd/root root    # FreeBSD
ln -s /perm/home_linux/root root      # Linux
```

4.   Delete hidden entries in the path that will soon be your $HOME. Otherwise, those could interfere with programs that need to be reinitialized:

```
cd /perm/home_<os>/<user>

find .  -maxdepth 1 -name '.?*' -delete
```

Note the following points:

- First back up any important hidden files as unhidden. For instance:

```
.vimrc → vim.rc
```

- Repeat Step 4 for /perm/home_<os>/root as well.

If you are going to install Linux and FreeBSD—which is always a wise thing to do—delay creation of the normal user account under FreeBSD until after Linux installation.

Pick up the numeric user ID (quite often 1000) of your Linux user account from /etc/passwd (or use id -u), and then create your FreeBSD user with that UID. In other words, force the UID in the second system to match the first system's UID.

You might at this stage like to adjust permissions:

```
chown -R <user> /perm/home_<os>/<user>
chown -R root /perm/home_<os>/root
```

With this complete:

- All your data—whether as the normal user or as root—automatically gets stored in persistent storage, which will survive a complete reinstall.

- You will never run into any permissions woes.

You must make sure that you *never delete the EBR slice ada0s4 or the logical drive ada0s5 inside it*. That partition represents your persistent storage solution.

When reinstalling FreeBSD/Linux afresh, you can delete/recreate/resize the primary partitions ada0s1/ada0s2/ada0s3 as many times as you like. But the EBR slice ada0s4 (or its nested ada0s5) must never be touched by the partitioning software. Also, keep the disk's count of primary partitions constant: three.

Store all your important data—configuration files, source code, audio-visual content—somewhere under /perm/. That ensures it is saved under /dev/ada0s5. Of course, if you can get an external USB disk, you could once a month or once a year mirror /perm into the USB disk.

There is a small price to pay for having your data saved in persistent storage: under single-user mode Linux, carrying out fsck on /dev/sda5 is now a two-step operation:

1. Boot into single-user mode and comment out the entry for sda5 in /etc/fstab.

2. Reboot into single-user mode again and then carry out fsck on /dev/sda5. Then uncomment the entry for sda5 in /etc/fstab. You can now reboot for normal mode (graphical/multi-user) operations.

6.17 Summary

You can now mount/unmount filesystems, configure Internet access, print, scan, create backups, and use administrative command-line tools.

That's quite a lot. If you got this far, you'll do very well under your Unix box. We have now covered all important Unix concepts and system tools. The rest of this book will be progressively easier. Actually, for most readers, the next chapter—"The Best of the Graphical Unix World"—should be as easy as a walk in the park.

## CHAPTER 7

The Best of the Graphical Unix

Not to run afoul of Darwin's theory of survival of the fittest, nerds needed to evolve and adapt—which is just what has happened. In the 1970s and 80s, nerds used the keyboard. Nowadays most of them can also use the mouse.

As a well-architectured operating system with immense flexibility and stability, Unix has always been iconic for its role as a server. But that was not going to be enough for the 21st Century, when it had to reach out to the masses with an interface that was, in its ease of use, a match for the brilliant underlying systems-level programming. If there is one thing that today unites all of Unix and GNU's Not Unix, it would the graphics system: X or X.org. The X window system is what makes Unix user-friendly.

X is almost entirely a user-space system. The only bits that get hosted in kernel-space are the drivers: for the graphics chip and for console devices.

7.1 X Is a Client-Server System

People sometimes get dazzled with the use of terms like client and server, mistaking them as highly technical jargon of the geek world. But that is not true.

A server is just some computer program that can act as a servant (the not-so-insulting term is *daemon*). A client is a computer program that asks the server to do a job for it. The requested job must be of a kind the server is known to be capable of; otherwise, the situation becomes akin to asking the laundry-man to cook your food.

The term *server*, as is usually clear from the context, can mean one of two things: the computer program (service) running as a daemon, or the computer hosting the concerned service. Likewise for *client*. That situation is akin to using "laundry" to refer to the dirty-linen-washing service, or to refer to the honorable establishment that washes your dirty linen (in other words, hosts the dirty-linen-washing service).

173

© Manish Jain 2018
M. Jain, *Beginning Modern Unix*, https://doi.org/10.1007/978-1-4842-3528-7_7

If you ask Thunderbird to pop off all your Hotmail email, you are using Thunderbird as an email client to collect mail from the Hotmail machine (server) that runs multiple services—collecting your email; storing the email as long as needed; and then relaying the email to Thunderbird. The club of all those associated services running together is designated the Hotmail server.

You might at this stage like to note a couple of things:

- The address of the Hotmail machine (or any server) must be known in advance and must remain static. Otherwise, the client has no way of contacting the server.

- There is no such thing as a machine that's a 100% forever-and-pure server. If a machine is set up to be a mail server, there might be other jobs (e.g., printing) it needs some other machine to do for it. So the mail server could itself be the client of a print server, which might in turn be the client of a database server.

When the X window system (in short, X or X.org) was created, there were two options for its architecture. One was the model Microsoft used later in Windows—a kernel-level graphics subsystem that applications could use via an API (Application Programming Interface). Since Unix has been increasingly modular in its implementation—particularly since the time around 1990 when GNU took over the mantle from AT&T—a client-server model was deemed more suitable for a GNU implementation. The client-server model also fits in well with the need for distributed computing, which was a rage in the days when the architecture of X was being sculpted.

In the X system, the X server listens to some reserved sockets. Applications communicate with the X server over those sockets. This framework allows the X server to run on one machine, and X clients to run anywhere on the intranet. That does not often happen, but is possible with the architecture—actually, during the 80s and 90s, it was regular for companies to run the X server on one machine, with X clients hooked in via the intranet.

You might have already noticed that your Unix shell, when in X mode, exports a variable $DISPLAY, the value of which often is :0. That simply is a shorthand for 127.0.0.1:0.0—in TCP/IP networking, 127.0.0.1 is always your local host and 0:0 is the socket. If X applications on your system were to need services of a remote X server, it would be a simple matter of fixing the IP address.

7.2 Desktop Environments

Although there is only one X server (which earlier went under the moniker XFree86), there is a plethora of desktop environments to choose from. Each of them is a collection of sub-services that tell the X server, for example, how to treat your keyboard or mouse input; what fonts to use where; what should window buttons (such as Close and Maximize) look like; and many other such things: menus, panels, wallpaper, widget style, and window background color.

The two desktops that have been around the longest are GNOME and KDE, both of them have about two decades in the business. Some other good desktops have emerged of late: Xfce, Cinnamon, and Mate. The last two are GNOME forks. GNOME itself has been struggling of late with issues that seem perpetual.

For completeness and sheer number of features, KDE would be hard to beat. Among GNU desktops, KDE also happens to resemble most closely the Windows 2000/XP interface, and further happens to be my preferred desktop—which will inevitably taint some of the remaining discussion in this chapter. KDE is resource-intensive—you should have at least a 2GHz processor and 4GB of RAM for a smooth desktop experience. On the plus side, KDE is bug-free—my grandmother says so.

No discussion of current Unix desktops would be complete without a peek at the beautiful as well as functional Cinnamon desktop environment, a Linux Mint specialty.

Figure 7-1 provides a scent of Cinnamon.

Figure 7-1. *The Cinnamon desktop environment*

If you are relatively new to Unix and have not settled on a desktop, my suggestion would be to first try KDE under FreeBSD, and Cinnamon under Linux.

If you need a leaner desktop, you can dabble with Mate or Xfce—neither of which is as resource-hungry. Beyond that, it would largely be personal preference—Unix gurus are often addicted to tiling window managers, which we'll take a look at shortly.

Whichever desktop you use, you can rest assured of a few things:

- You can install and use any of the widely used X applications: Firefox, Chromium, Thunderbird, SMPlayer, XMMS, LibreOffice, and Pidgin.

- Each desktop environment automatically bundles useful utilities: A file manager, a calculator, a ZIP frontend, and a text editor.

- You can install any of the utilities of another desktop environment under yours: So a KDE user can install GNOME's gedit text editor, and a GNOME user can install KDE's PDF viewer Okular.

The last item in the preceding list perhaps needs a bit of elaboration. Each desktop environment packages basic runtime functionality into a few modules of their own. Under KDE4, for example, those modules are the packages named `kdelibs`, kde-baseapps, and kde-runtime. With the base packages installed, you can install utilities from that desktop environment. Since modern package managers are clever systems, installing a desktop's utilities automatically installs its base packages first.

A crucial ingredient in the desktop environment mix is the window manager (wm for short). Each desktop has its own window manager: kwin under KDE, metacity under GNOME, and xfwm under Xfce. The wm is the component of a desktop that manages windows and virtual desktops. It draws a window's borders and title bars, and provides buttons for common window operations: move, maximize, minimize, and close. While you can largely ignore the wm when using a desktop environment, it is good to know that some window managers can run independently.

7.3 Window Managers

If you have an old PC with limited hardware, you would want to consider running a window manager, not a complete desktop. A window manager has the streamlined task of simply managing how you interact with your application windows without all of the extra bloat of a desktop environment. Window managers are usually quite customizable and—in principle—do one job only: manage your windows, which means they move/resize/close any application windows.

Because the window manager implements a minimalist philosophy, using a window manager lets your old/limited hardware remain speedy and functional. There are quite a few window managers that can work standalone: Awesome, Enlightenment, Fluxbox, and FVWM. They differ a lot in functionality and capabilities—Enlightenment, sized roughly a couple of dozen megabytes, is at one end of the spectrum where it can almost qualify as a desktop environment in its own right; Awesome and Fluxbox weigh in under 1MB each.

Note   A nice Unix utility is scrot, which is a screenshot capture from the command line. scrot -d 5 scr.png will grab the desktop after five seconds in the file scr.png. scrot -d 5 -q 100 scr.png additionally forces 100 % quality (default is 75).

A purely functional, tiling window manager is Awesome, which uses tiles of xterm windows (launched via right-click). The scrot'ed Figure 7-2 is really Awesome.

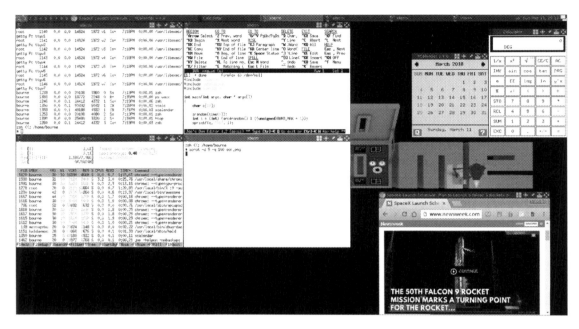

Figure 7-2. *Being functional with Awesome*

Each xterm window (four in the northwest section of Figure 7-2) is launched via right-clicking and choosing Open Terminal. The windows are neatly stacked by the Awesome window manager.

You can, of course, use the xterm windows to bring up more applications, the placement of which is not tiled. As you can see in Figure 7-2, I opened three additional windows (deliberately moved to the right, and also resized with mouse right-click-and-drag in the window's title bar): Chromium, X Calculator, and X Calendar.

Awesome works incredibly well. It's highly customizable and has a tiny memory footprint. To run Awesome, execute awesome from your normal user account's ~/.xinitrc:

```
exec  /path/to/awesome
# If ~/.xinitrc does not exist, first create it with your text editor
```

With the .xinitrc in place, just run the command startx (as the normal user).

Note   Unix package names are usually (but not strictly always) all lowercase. So the package name for Awesome is `awesome`.

FreeBSD is working on a BSD-centric desktop Lumina that promises to be the ultimate go-between: a desktop environment with the resource-footprint of a window manager. Lumina is already at the finishing stages, producing the alternate desktop on my box.

In its current state, Lumina is not a full-fledged desktop. It's more of a window manager with part of the entourage of associated utilities that make up a desktop—some of them available (file manager, for instance); some of them not yet available (keyboard/mouse configuration applet, for instance).

Lumina does furnish a handsome outlook; see Figure 7-3.

Figure 7-3. *Lumina: The FreeBSD desktop*

The startup script for Lumina is `start-lumina-desktop`, which you can execute (exec) from `~/.xinitrc` as a normal user.

7.4 Starting X and the Desktop Environment

Under Linux, this section is of little use—the installation procedure sets up X and the desktop to be kicked off at boot time. Everything happens automatically thereafter.

Under FreeBSD, you have to manually install the xorg meta-package and then the meta-package for your desktop environment (e.g., kde, gnome3, or xfce).

Each desktop environment installs under /usr/local/bin/ a wrapper script that can be used to launch the desktop.

GNOME: /usr/local/bin/gnome-session

KDE: /usr/local/bin/startkde

Xfce: /usr/local/bin/startxfce

As a normal user (not as root, as a matter of fact), you cannot execute the wrapper script directly. Instead, what you have to do is create a ~/.xinitrc file, which contains just one line:

```
exec <wrapper>    # <wrapper> is a placeholder for the path of the wrapper
                    script
```

That done, you can use the command startx to start your desktop. The wrapper will first start the X server in the background, and then your desktop environment which is hooked into the X server.

The root user may decide to start X at boot time automatically. For GNOME and KDE, this is straightforward: just enable the associated and built-in login manager (also known as the display manager) in /etc/rc.conf:

```
gnome_enable="YES"        # starts GDM
kdm4_enable="YES"         # starts KDM
```

Desktops that do not have a built-in login manager—Xfce for instance—can use the services of a generic login manager like XDM, SLiM, or LightDM.

Under FreeBSD, most display managers and desktop environments currently need the following services to be enabled as well in /etc/rc.conf:

```
hald_enable="YES"
dbus_enable="YES"
```

7.5 Applications in the Desktop Environment

The rest of this chapter is a discussion of commonly used desktop applications. From hereon, the term *desktop environment* is used to mean whatever graphical environment the reader is using. This could be as big as the KDE desktop environment, or as small as the Awesome window manager. It is assumed that the reader can perform common operations in a graphical environment.

7.5.1 Terminal Emulators

Since console-mode usage of a Unix box allows multiple terminals (which you can open with Alt + F2 , Alt + F3 and so on), you would dearly like to have them in X sessions too. That is not just possible, it is the *de facto* norm: Unix programmers typically need X for opening up a large number of terminal emulator windows.

Each desktop environment has a pre-packaged terminal emulator: for example, GNOME has gnome-terminal, KDE has Konsole, and MATE has mate-terminal.

The most generic (i.e., not associated with any desktop environment) X terminal emulator is xterm, which has significantly fewer features and often gets packaged into the base X.org distribution.

All X terminal emulators, including xterm, offer support for colored output. You can customize the colors using the menus (non-xterm emulators), or using command-line arguments with xterm:

```
xterm -title "Terminal" -bg black -fg grey
```

To copy text from an xterm window (or any terminal application window), you need to select that text by clicking and dragging it using the mouse's left button. The text automatically gets copied. You can paste that text later with a middle-click (or wheel-down), into xterm itself or a text editor.

This method of yanking text works in pure console mode too (when there is no X).

Note   All X clients (not just terminal emulators) implement text yanking: copy-by-highlighting (with mouse) and paste-with-middle-click.

Make sure you try out yank-copy and yank-paste in a terminal window (or in a text editor). It is a very useful technique to remember.

Once you have become familiar with yanking, you can take your skills up a notch by remembering additional tricks:

- Left double-click on a word: the word is selected

- Left triple-click on a line: the whole line is selected

- Left single-click on a position, right single-click on another position: the range between those positions is selected, and it can span multiple lines

The yanking procedure is distinct from traditional copy-and-paste, which can be implemented only in non-xterm windows with right-click operations or keyboard shortcuts. Those shortcuts—specific for terminal emulator applications—are as follows:

Copy: typically `Ctrl` + `Shift` + `C`
Paste: typically `Ctrl` + `Shift` + `V`

For other X applications (those that are not terminal emulators), the keyboard shortcuts are the long-respected text manipulation techniques that were (and still are) followed in Microsoft Windows too, and are recapped here for convenient reference:

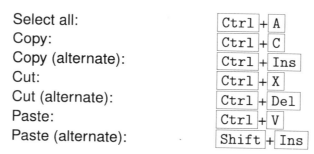

Select all: `Ctrl` + `A`
Copy: `Ctrl` + `C`
Copy (alternate):   `Ctrl` + `Ins`
Cut: `Ctrl` + `X`
Cut (alternate):   `Ctrl` + `Del`
Paste: `Ctrl` + `V`
Paste (alternate):   `Shift` + `Ins`

You might have already guessed that since yanking and traditional copy-and-paste work differently (as well as independently), they use their own separate buffers inside main memory. If you yank-copy, you cannot traditional-paste, and if you traditional-copy, you cannot yank-paste.

7.5.2 Web Browsers

The two most heavily-used web browsers in the GNU world are, quite unsurprisingly, Mozilla Firefox and Google's Chromium. Both are equally good, but Firefox always seems a touch more stable under Unix.

Whichever of the two you use, do not forget the add-on LastPass. LastPass takes care of the excruciating need to save all your web login credentials (i.e., passwords), and then fill them out when the time arrives, which is about a few dozen times every day. LastPass also has one feature that not many people use or are even aware of—it is a brilliant form-filler, although it takes a bit of time to set it up to work in that role.

LastPass also has one feature that not many people use or are even aware of - it is a brilliant form-filler, although it takes a bit of time to set it up to work in that role. Figure 7-4 below shows a LastPass form-fill profile named vb being a) created; b) activated; and c) utilized to fill up a couple of form entries - Contact::Email address and Custom Fields::Password.

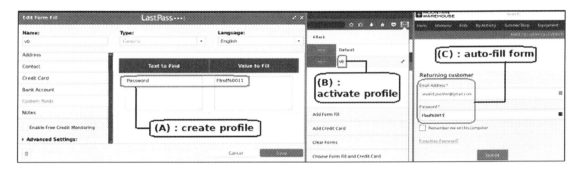

Figure 7-4. *Using LastPass as form filler*

Both Firefox and Chromium have internal sync capabilities that let you save and sync passwords. But if you use LastPass, you have the additional capability to sync from Firefox to Chromium, and the other way round.

LastPass had an associate add-on XMarks, which would let you store and then sync your bookmarks, the heart of the web-browsing experience, with the XMarks server.

Late-breaking news on the XMarks front suggests that add-on is being discontinued, so you have to use your browser's internal sync functions for syncing bookmarks.

One Firefox nicety is that you can download the .xpi add-on files from the Mozilla website to store them locally. Another nicety is an extension that its rival Chromium lacks—the add-on InformEnter. If you use InformEnter, you likely will soon get hooked to the convenience it offers for filling in forms with just a right-click. Under FreeBSD, you can install InformEnter not as an add-on, but as the package xpi-informenter.

Which brings me to ESR—Extended Service Releases—that Mozilla offers for Firefox. A few Firefox add-ons, for a variety of reasons, are banished from regular releases, one of the condemned ones being InformEnter. To install such add-ons, you need to use the ESR version of Firefox, typically with the key `xpinstall.signatures.required` set to `false` in Firefox's registry, which you can open by typing `about:config` into the address bar.

Open-source Chromium—which forms the base of the closed-source Chrome browser with some additional, minor features and a different license—is definitely a good choice for folks who use Google Hangouts for video chat. Unlike Firefox, Chromium installs extensions without a restart. You can access your Chromium extensions via the URL `chrome://extensions/` and Chromium settings via `chrome://settings/`.

If neither Firefox nor Chromium suits you, there is Opera, which has a smaller bunch of die-hard fans. Opera does not have the same razzmatazz of themes and add-ons though. But it has good speed and stability. FreeBSD users can additionally install the package `opera-linuxplugins`, which gets access to natively-Linux plugins, chiefly Adobe Flash and Acrobat Reader.

All the browsers above innately support JavaScript and HTML5 (the latest version of HTML with its own alternative Flash technology), besides a wide variety of multimedia content that can be played in the browser.

7.5.3 Email Clients

Just as a web browser has to understand many protocols (HTTP, HTTPS, and FTP, for example), an email client has to negotiate a couple—one for outgoing emails, one for incoming:

- SMTP (Simple Mail Transfer Protocol) sends out messages from your email client using a remote server (e.g., Hotmail).

- POP3 (Post Office Protocol) lets you retrieve your email from a remote server, which typically—but not necessarily—deletes the email that has been popped.

The alternative to POP3+SMTP is IMAP4 (Internet Message Access Protocol), a newer mail protocol that can handle both send and receive functions. Whether using POP3 or IMAP4, the client always hands over outgoing mail to the SMTP server.

The three protocols understood by the email client have to be implemented at the server. So Hotmail is not one, but actually three, servers—SMTP, POP3, and IMAP4. To configure an email account in the client, you must have the SMTP server address and the address for the service you will use to fetch email: POP3 or IMAP4.

It will be good to note the behavior of an IMAP4 account, which quite correctly is given the nickname "remote folders". The initial folder layout in an IMAP4 account—as shown by the email client—is just a mirror of the layout at the server. Any operations then performed in the email client are actually executed at the server. So if you create a subfolder called JohnDoe in your Inbox and then move all messages from john.doe@example.com to Inbox/JohnDoe/ in your email client, those actions will be executed first at the server.

Among email clients, Mozilla Thunderbird is the leviathan. Like its cousin Firefox, it uses the Mozilla add-ons infrastructure. One such add-on is Lightening, an integrated calendar that often gets bundled into a standard Thunderbird installation.

Thunderbird supports every single standard mail protocol and email function. One particularly useful function is message filtering. If the user chooses to, Thunderbird can set up rule-based filters to move incoming/outgoing messages into some other folder(s), or even trash them. The filters work in automatic as well as manual mode.

Figure 7-5 below shows a filter named *amazon* being setup to move all messages from ship-*confirm@amazon.com* and *order-update@amazon.com* from Inbox to a folder named *amazon*.

Figure 7-5. *Thunderbird mail filters*

Thunderbird is not alone in its league, by any means. In fact, there is an equally good full-fledged client that has many devotees both under Unix and Windows: Sylpheed. Like Thunderbird, Sylpheed has its own address book, message filtering support, and can work together with spam/junk markers.

Another full-fledged client is Evolution, which has a clean-looking interface and its own calendar. Among X email programs, Evolution—originally created at Novell—is the oldest one and has a dedicated bunch of followers. When used alongside the `evolution-ews` package, Evolution can also connect to Microsoft Exchange servers.

There are lightweight email clients too. I would not like to bother with yet another list, but the one lightweight client I do recommend to readers to try is Geary. Among Unix applications I have seen, Geary has the most visually stunning interface.

Geary has much of the functionality of Thunderbird, but nowhere near all: it cannot, for example, filter messages (yet) based on user-defined rules. Since Geary—which has been written in a new programming language Vala—is still relatively an infant, we can expect the infant to cut a tooth every once in a while.

I would be disappointing you if I were to leave you without a peek at the Geary interface. Figure 7-6 provides a glimpse.

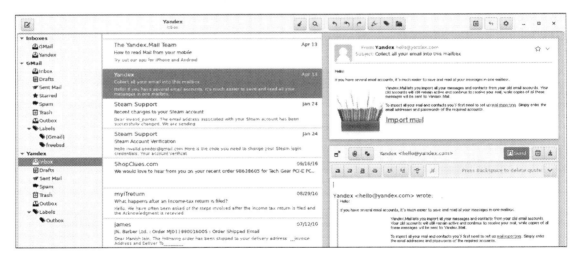

Figure 7-6. *The Geary email client*

Since Geary tries to be lightweight, it relies on the system for external functions like spell-checking. If spell-checking is not working in your Geary installation, your box might be missing one or both of these packages:

```
en-aspell; en-hunspell
```

Geary also has a dependency on an external package that does not get installed by itself, `gnome-keyring`, which stores all your passwords. After installing Geary, it is a good idea to install `gnome-keyring` too.

7.5.4 Accessing and Downloading Remote Data

For data that lies in FTP or SMB (Samba) shares, you can always use command-line tools. But I often find it more convenient to use graphical tools.

KDE provides the Net Attach tool KNetAttach (under my box it's `/usr/local/lib/kde4/libexec/knetattach`) which makes that very simple—and the tool remembers its usage history, complete with logon credentials. Not surprisingly, KNetAttach opens the remote directory in KDE's file manager Dolphin.

Figure 7-7 is a patchwork screenshot of opening the Heanet FTP directory `/pub/cygwin/x86_64/release/` hosted at `ftp.heanet.ie` (anonymous FTP service) with just a couple of clicks, with KNetAttach and Dolphin working in cahoots.

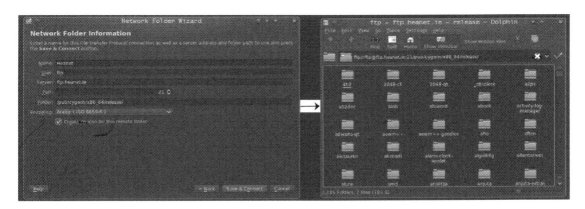

Figure 7-7. *KDE network folder attachment wizard*

If a network attachment tool is not available under your desktop environment, it's not a serious problem—you can open FTP/SMB shares in your web browser too. Browsers understand those protocols.

For downloading large files from the web (via HTTP/HTTPS or FTP), you want to stick with the command-line tool `wget`. That is supremely reliable, and it offers support for continuing partial downloads. It is the most complete download manager.

Quite a lot of the data that is available for download on the web nowadays is via the BitTorrent protocol.

Downloading via BitTorrent is a two-step process. First you get the `.torrent` file, which has the description (metadata) of the big file it would download. Once you have the `.torrent` file, you feed to it a BitTorrent client, which goes ahead and performs the actual download to your box.

We'll first deal with BitTorrent clients, which there are quite a few. Two of the full-fledged variety are Transmission and qBitTorrent. Both provide support for BitTorrent techniques like DHT (Dynamic Host Tracking) and Magnet links (support for opening .torrent files with a double-click in your X file manager).

Transmission has support for scripting too. This Transmission script writes out a message upon completion of each download and moves the download to the $HOME/tor directory.

```
#!/bin/sh
DEST=$HOME/tor
# set DEST above to the path of an existing, writeable directory

[ -n "$DEST" ] || { echo "$DEST is null !" 1>&2; exit 1; }
[ -d "$DEST" ] || { echo "$DEST not a directory !" 1>&2; exit 1; }
[ -w "$DEST" ] || { echo "$DEST not writeable !" 1>&2; exit 1; }

echo "From ${TR_TORRENT_DIR}:
Completed    TR_TORRENT_NAME=${TR_TORRENT_NAME} (TR_TORRENT_ID=${TR_
TORRENT_ID})" >> $HOME/tor-messages

mv "${TR_TORRENT_NAME}" "$DEST"
exit $?
```

Save this as posttor.sh. Then set the executable bit for the script with:

```
chmod +x posttor.sh
```

In the Transmission window, open the dialog for download preferences (choose Edit ➤ Preferences ➤ Downloading).

Check the box for Call Script When Torrent Is Completed, and then browse to locate posttor.sh.

The following shell variables are filled by Transmission automatically each time the posttor.sh script is invoked:

- $TR_TORRENT_DIR is the path of the downloads directory in your filesystem.

- $TR_TORRENT_NAME is the name of the download.

- $TR_TORRENT_ID is the original serial number allotted to $TR_TORRENT_NAME in your Transmission queue.

If you need to download via BitTorrent on the command line, that is eminently possible and the easiest way to do that is with `ctorrent`. I will leave command-line BitTorrent download to you to play with, as and when you find the time and the appetite.

An interesting go-between BitTorrent client is the "no X" version of qBitTorrent, called `qbittorrent-nox`, which is fired up on the command line and then uses a web interface for further interaction with the user.

`qbittorrent-nox` (issued in a terminal window) runs a web service on the port 8080 accessible as the user `admin` and the default password `adminadmin`.

Figure 7-8 shows the terminal interaction on the left, and a web browser window opened at the qBitTorrent admin site on the right, with an ISO download just flagged off.

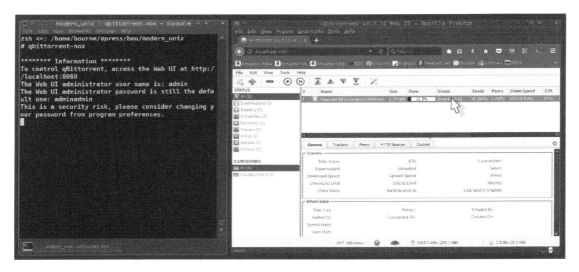

Figure 7-8. *The qBitTorrent web interface*

We'll now take up the question of how to get the `.torrent` files, which we should have taken up in the first place, but I decided to delay for a good reason. In some countries, downloading via BitTorrent is legally frowned upon and could get you into trouble. If you decide to download via BitTorrent, it is at your own discretion.

We'll take our torrent download site as Pirate Bay (`www.thepiratebay.org/`), but you can adjust that as needed.

In most locations, you should be able to open Pirate Bay (or whatever is your download site) in your web browser.

Pirate Bay itself faced a legal (and existential) crisis a few years back in its host country Sweden, until it managed to convince Swedish legal authorities that nothing it was doing contravened Swedish law. But some countries—UK and India, for example— keep in place (on-and-off) legal challenges that prevent you from accessing sites like Pirate Bay in a web browser.

For such locations, you have to use a modified version of Firefox that can circumvent the sniffers. That version is called the Tor browser. You can download Tor at `https://` `www.torproject.org/download/download-easy.html.en`.

At the time of this writing, Tor was natively available for Linux, while a FreeBSD port is under development. For the moment and until the port becomes available, FreeBSD users can run a Linux virtual machine that can do the job needed. We'll broach this subject in-depth in Chapter 9 (Virtualization).

Downloading with Tor is as easy as downloading with your web browser. Tor ultimately is just a portable version of a popular web browser (Firefox). The only problem could be that Magnet links don't work—which is not such a serious problem. You can simply right-click to copy the location, and then open that location as a download target in your BitTorrent client. Transmission does that automatically once you have copied the URL.

Tor downloads work on a packet-based approach. A large file is typically broken into a large numbers (millions) of packets hosted by multiple hosts on the web (seeds and peers). When you fetch a large file via BitTorrent, it is possible that a few thousand hosts sent you the packets—you as the downloader never control where the packets get picked from.

Using the Tor browser might not be enough to keep the "legal" hounds out of your backyard. Occasionally, you might even need VPN (Virtual Private Networking) to convince others to keep away from prying on your download agenda. Setting up VPN is a fairly technical business, and we will keep it out of the scope of this book.

7.5.5 Playing Multimedia Content

Playing multimedia content is usually not a legal concern—or so we must hope.

Audio waves are best played under X with XMMS, which has—among many other features—a graphic equalizer. Figure 7-9 below bears testimony to those goodies. A couple of good alternatives are Sonata, which uses the MPD (Music Player Daemon) application to play audio, and Audacious, which has a library organization that can be managed with the filesystem.

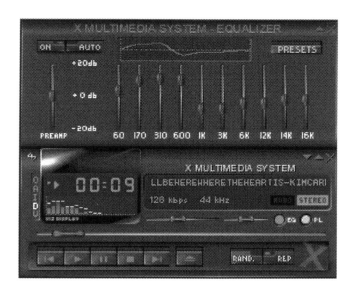

Figure 7-9. *The XMMS audio player*

Playing audio files—but not audio+video files—is possible without X too. Still under the XMMS umbrella, you can get the package `xmms-curses` to play audio files in console mode. There are a few options that I would not like to go ignored: `cmus`, `mp3blaster`, and `mpg123`. That last one even has an equalizer that you can tweak and use in pure text mode. It has a successor too: `madplay`.

Now onto the video section. All video players under Unix offer the great facility of system-managed codec setup. I have never faced a situation under FreeBSD or Linux where a file could not be played because of a missing-codec issue. Most codecs get installed when the system is set up: `gstreamer ffmpeg` contains all popular codecs. When you install a video player, the package contains any additional codecs needed.

Video support under GNU has always been remarkably touché.

Still in its early days, Linux scored a direct hit under the Hollywood banner with the smash hit *Titanic* (1997), which turned the haunting voice of Sissel Kyrkjebo into every lover's inspiration worldwide and was rendered using Linux. Figure 7-10 freeze-frames the moment.

Figure 7-10.   *Linux for lovers (Titanic, 1997)*

You can read more about the Titanic story at this URL:

```
http://www.linuxjournal.com/article/2494
```

As for video players, there is a whole gang of them. We focus on three widely used ones: MPlayer, Videolan (VLC), and Xine.

7.5.5.1 The mplayer Cult

The mplayer application is not really a player. It is a video-rendering engine that's used by a family of mplayer-based frontends: SMPlayer and GMPlayer.

I use the SMPlayer frontend, which offers support for using other video-rendering engines too, `mpv` for instance. Using SMPlayer is as easy as it could possibly get—SMPlayer has the simplest user interface (UI) among all video players. If mplayer's volume is not loud enough for you, try a mixer application like `aumix`.

Figure 7-11 shows often-used keyboard shortcuts on the left and a snapshot of SMPlayer's ultra-simplistic UI on the right.

Figure 7-11. *Getting across closed-source (Midnight Express, 1978)*

7.5.5.2 VideoLAN/VLC

VideoLAN is probably the most complete video player ever developed. It even plays the VOB files in video DVDs with perfect smoothness. An additional nicety is a built-in pre-amplifier, which can jack up the media's audio volume a fair bit.

While using VideoLAN client is as easy as using any X application, there is one problem users often face: when you set the equalizer bands in VLC to custom values, those settings do not get saved when VLC is shut down. The rest of this subsection deals with making VLC equalizer settings persistent.

The first thing you need to do is open the Equalizer dialog (choose Tools ➤ Effects and Filters). Now tweak the bands to suit your auditory senses. Refer to Figure 7-12.

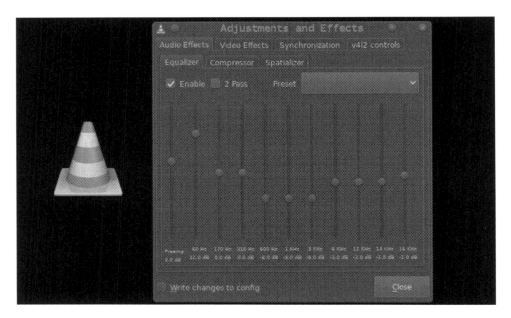

Figure 7-12. *VLC equalizer gains*

For simplicity, we have tweaked the custom values to end with `.0`, which can be ignored. Save the gains in a text file, which—for Figure 7-12—must hold the text: 3 12 0 0 -8 -8 -8 -3 -3 -3 -1.

The left-most number (3 in our tweaked settings) is for the pre-amplifier gain, and the remaining ten correspond to the equalizer bands.

Once you have saved the gains in a text file, close the Equalizer dialog.

Choose Tools ➤ Preferences.

Change the Show Settings layout (bottom-left corner) from Simple to All and THEN Navigate to Audio ➤ Filters and ensure that the box for Equalizer with 10 bands is ticked.

Expand Filters and click on Equalizer. Paste the bands gain settings in the text box to the right of Bands gain (circled in Figure 7-13).

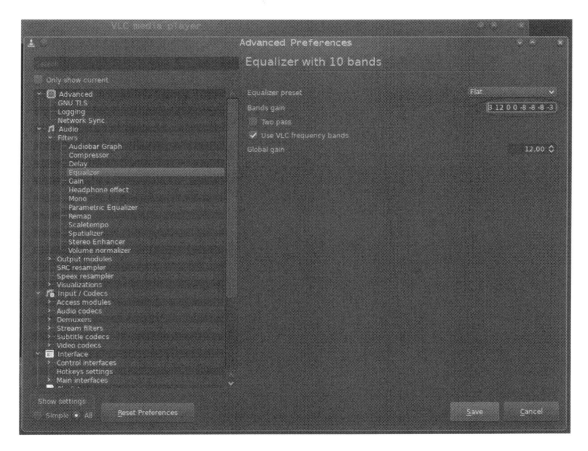

Figure 7-13. *VLC bands settings*

Finally, click Save at the bottom. The next time you start VideoLAN, your saved settings will be used for equalizer gains.

7.5.5.3 Xine

One of the X applications with a very different look and feel is Xine, the interface of which has become pretty famous in itself as the Xine UI.

Figure 7-14 shows the Xine UI.

Figure 7-14. *The widget toolbox that underpins the unique Xine UI*

Figure 7-14 is a frame of the ill-fated bus 2525 a few seconds after the last time it stopped at any bus stop. You perhaps already know the movie name.

That screenshot also shows the Xine UI in action. The centerpiece of the Xine UI is the widget-toolbox (shown at the top in the image). You can hide it whenever you don't need it, and then when you need it again, just right-click and select Show Controls (or press $\boxed{g}$).

Xine has support for VOB files too: this screenshot was taken with a VOB file.

Besides its UI, Xine flaunts another peculiarity: it is a Unix-only program, not available under Windows.

7.5.6 Paint Programs

Painting under GNU in the early days was performed by three applications still in use: XPaint, XFig, and Gimp. Gimp is the powerhouse that can do anything that any other paint program can do. On the flip side, Gimp has a learning curve of its own.

Perhaps the most widely used paint program today is Pinta, which is a queer fish in the Unix world. Despite being a Unix application, it uses the Microsoft .NET framework for its build. That might make it sound like Pinta runs under Windows only. But the truth is the other way round: Unix has ported the .NET framework too, letting applications that use the .NET framework run as Unix applications. In case you are curious, the ET port to Unix is named Mono.

With FreeBSD, there is yet another kink: Pinta has to run as a Windows application under the Windows emulation subsystem (Wine). This is so because a native port or package for Pinta is not available. We'll look at Pinta installation under FreeBSD in the next chapter when we set up Wine.

KDE, as always, has a few applications of its own. The two entries relevant to the realm of paint are KolourPaint and Krita, which have pretty much the same capabilities as Pinta.

No discussion about Unix paint programs would be complete without a mention of Inkscape. Inkscape can do everything that other paint programs can do, and a few things that most other paint programs cannot do.

One fairly unique Inkscape ability is to render calligraphic strokes, like the freeform arrows and the glyphs shown in Figure 7-15.

Figure 7-15. *Inkscape calligraphic strokes*

Another fantastic Inkscape ability is to draw straight lines with arrowheads at either of or both endpoints. See Figure 7-16 for what is often desired.

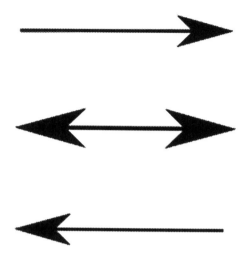

Figure 7-16. *Inkscape arrow-headed lines*

Drawing arrow-headed lines is an often-needed skill, and folks keep searching for how to do this on the web. So we'll take up a small Inkscape exercise specifically for this.

1. Open a new blank document in Inkscape.

2. Press `Shift`+`F6` to select the line-drawing tool.

3. Click in the document to start a line and drag with the mouse to the right until the ending point. Be careful not to move the mouse at the point of release. Then double-click to tell Inkscape that the line has been finalized. Otherwise, Inkscape will try the extend the curve as a set of connected lines.

4. Press `Ctrl`+`Shift`+`F` to bring up the Fill-and-Stroke dialog and open the right-most Stroke Style tab.

5. Set the line width. For starters, a 2mm thickness should be good enough.

6. Click the left Marker drop-down, and select an arrowhead.

7. Click the right Marker drop-down, and select an arrowhead.

Your arrowhead line is ready. You can save it in any of the popular graphics formats, although Inkscape's preferred format is Scalable Vector Graphics.

For still more painting, you could try the powerhouse Gimp. That suite has capabilities similar to what you get with Adobe Photoshop under a Mac.

7.5.7 LibreOffice: The New and Better Office

One of the great additions to the Unix world of late has been LibreOffice, the emergence and evolution of which has essentially eclipsed Microsoft's cash cow.

From a puritan viewpoint, the Office situation is a bit of a riddle. Unix approves just one kind of document for communication, which is the revered plain text. So why exactly has so much effort gone into the creation of LibreOffice?

There are multiple reasons:

- Folks migrating to Unix from Windows have a fair bit of their old data in formatted text documents created with Microsoft Office. It would be a buzz-killer if they were to lose the ability to open those documents.

- LibreOffice gives the Unix world a chance to beckon with confidence that we can do better than what Microsoft did, inside Microsoft's own backyard—and for free. To put the icing on the cake, LibreOffice can open even those old documents that Microsoft Office once created and that Microsoft Office now refuses to open.

- Typesetting documents with LaTex can be too much of an ask when you need to quickly create something as trivial as a one-page letter or report.

So while your ultimate goal for future would be plain-text-only (with formatted text restricted to PDF rendered with LaTex), you can take your time adapting to the Unix way of life with the ease of opening old Office documents with LibreOffice.

I will generally presume that you can work with Office and therefore LibreOffice applications. But there is one tool that Office users often ignore: macros for repetitive tasks. LibreOffice Writer has great support for macros that work in pretty much the same spirit we saw in Chapter 1 with the Vim and Joe text editors.

One fantastic utility that comes with LibreOffice is unoconv. This utility is a Swiss Army knife for dealing with Microsoft Word and LibreOffice Writer documents on the command line. It can freely convert among all supported formats—DOC[X], RTF, ODT, PDF, and TXT. You need to install unoconv separately once LibreOffice itself has been installed.

199

LibreOffice is not just the writer application—Calc is the spreadsheet solution; Base is the database application; Impress is for presentation slides; and Draw is a very handy paint program. That I suppose is pretty much all that you could ask of a full-fledged Office suite.

I would like to note about LibreOffice Draw that it has the very useful add-on ability of being able to spell check a PDF document. It can also, like Inkscape, draw arrowhead lines, with significantly less fuss too.

7.5.8 PDF Viewers

In the Unix world, the standard document type for formatted text is the Portable Document Format, engineered principally at Adobe Systems. Microsoft's DOC ideas are seriously frowned upon—with good reason. While you can continue to use Office or LibreOffice products as you transition fully to Unix, your final aim should be to whittle down to just two document types:

- Plain text. This is what you want to use 99% of the time.

- PDF. This is what you use when working on a professional publication. This is also increasingly becoming the default format expected to be fed to the printer for any printouts.

Although there are quite a few PDF viewer programs under Unix now, the only ones I can readily recommend to the reader are Xpdf and Okular, a KDE application that can work under any desktop environment.

Okular is a complete PDF viewer with an interface that is easy-to-use and highly functional. A couple of useful Okular features are:

- *Bookmarks*: These let you navigate a large PDF file with ease.

- *Review mode:* The Review mode is Okular's ability to to annotate a PDF. So if you want to quickly insert a comment in the PDF somewhere, use the Review mode, triggered by F6 .

There are a couple of features as yet missing in Okular.

One is a hook into the spell checker. To spell check a PDF, you can use LibreOffice Draw—which was noted in the previous section.

Another function not yet implemented in Okular is comparing two PDF documents. That job can be done by DiffPDF (`diffpdf`), a handy utility that you can read about at `http://www.qtrac.eu/diffpdf-foss.html`. While that URL indicates that `diffpdf` has been superseded by a commercial version, it happily continues to be available as a port under FreeBSD (`/usr/ports/graphics/diffpdf`).

An associate PDF viewer is Xpdf, which is blazing fast and thus can be used for slideshows, and which comes with the utility `pdftotext` for converting PDF to plain text. Xpdf shares a fantastic feature with Okular—both applications can pick up any changes in the background (triggered, for example, by recompiling LaTex sources) and reload a PDF file in real time with no user intervention.

7.5.9 PDF Creation

The other half of the PDF story is how to create a PDF. For quick PDF generation, LibreOffice Writer is a good solution.

For professional publications that need proper typesetting, you will need a more elaborate setup, with LaTex in the backend. One cog in the LaTex wheel is `pdflatex`, which can use the LaTex engine to compile a PDF on-the-fly. Although LaTex is not difficult to learn or use, it has a stiff learning curve—but then online documentation is available in the tons, and is always accessible easily through your best friend, Google.

The next battle in the PDF realm might be encryption and decryption with a password. There are quite a few of tools that do the job: `mupdf`, `pdftk`, and `qpdf`.

`qpdf` is more widely available, and probably is a touch easier to use. So that's what we will document.

To encrypt with the password `abc123` and 128-bit strength, you can use:

```
qpdf --encrypt --options "abc123" 128 -- input.pdf encrypted.pdf
```

The user who receives the encrypted PDF can decrypt:

```
qpdf --password="abc123" --decrypt encrypted.pdf output.pdf
```

Essentially, the file `input.pdf` at the sender's end becomes `output.pdf` at the end of the receiver.

There are still more PDF tools. You might like to extract the images in a PDF—which is done with `pdfimages`, a part of the `poppler-utils` package on my system. Then someday sooner or later, you would feel like grepping for some text in your PDF files. A `pdfgrep` is available.

This seems to be going overboard, but there is something in the nature of sed too: PDFedit. I should warn you that this tool is highly rough at the edges: it may do a good job, or it may do a bad job, or it may fail entirely, or it may just core dump. This application is not a command but a bunch of them, a few of them mentioned here:

```
add_image
add_text
replace_text
```

For example, to replace the text abc with xyz in myfile.pdf, you can use:

```
replace_text --file=myfile.pdf --what=abc --with=xyz
```

If it works for you, that's your good luck.

7.5.10   CD/DVD Writing Frontends

I usually prefer to do things from the command line. But for burning stuff to CDs and DVDs, my preference is the other way round—do it from a graphical frontend, at least when one is available.

CD/DVD writing frontends afford a happy convenience: verifying that the optical medium was burnt correctly. This, for some reason, is not possible with the cdrecord command as yet.

The two chief CD/DVD writing frontends are Brasero and K3b. I will focus on K3b, the KDE application that comes with my desktop.

K3b can burn audio CDs and data CD/DVDs. When used to write data, K3b becomes your frontend not just to cdrecord, but mkisofs too. This adds to the convenience. You can simply open a new data project and drag-and-drop data to be burnt into the compilation.

When you burn the CD/DVD, you can optionally have verification results delivered to you in a message box.

While Linux sets up K3b to work out of the box, FreeBSD needs the root user to open access to the /dev/cd*, /dev/pass*, and /dev/xpt* device nodes.

This is straightforward.

1. First make sure your normal user account is added to the group operator. For this, you can use this command:

    ```
    pw groupmod operator -m <normal>
    # <normal> is a placeholder for your normal user account
    ```

2. Then append the following lines to /etc/devfs.conf:

```
Own   /dev/pass0   root:operator   # % This configuration
                                     is for: %

perm  /dev/pass0   0664            # % CD/DVD drive + 1
                                     hard disk %

                                   # If you have 2 hard-
                                     disks,

Own   /dev/pass1   root:operator   # repeat the 2 lines
                                     above to

perm  /dev/pass1   0664            # add settings for /
                                     dev/pass2

Own   /dev/cd0     root:operator

perm  /dev/cd0     0664

Own   /dev/xpt0    root:operator

perm  /dev/xpt0    0664
```

To get this to work as intended, you can either reboot (preferred, because a system group modification is involved) or restart the devfs service:

```
/etc/rc.d/devfs restart  -OR-  service devfs  restart
```

7.5.11 Internet Messaging and Chat Clients

The easiest-to-use chat application under X is Pidgin. Pidgin works with a variety of protocols, AIM and ICQ included. But the one used most frequently nowadays is XMPP, which hooks up with Google accounts.

To set up an XMPP (Google) chat account under Pidgin, you will likely need to authenticate Pidgin in your Google account settings. For that, you must sign in to your Google account in your web browser and open the account settings. Then you need to enable Pidgin among the applications that can access your account.

The easy way to do that is to attempt to create an account in Pidgin. This would fire up notifications into your Google account settings panel about an application requesting authentication access. You might also get an email from Google about this.

This is how you fill the Pidgin account details.

First initiate addition of an XMPP account.

Then, presuming your Gmail address is `invalid.pointer@gmail.com,` fill the account details, as shown in Figure 7-17.

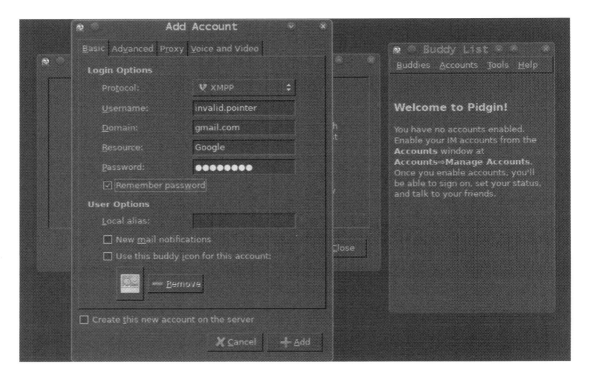

Figure 7-17. *Pidgin account setup with XMPP*

Once you click the Add button, Pidgin would likely report failure. You need to log in to your Google account settings panel and enable Pidgin.

If you cannot find the link for enabling Pidgin access, you can use the hack of turning on Allow Less Secure Apps in your Google account settings—this is as per your own discretion.

Once Pidgin has been granted access, you can chat with other Google users in your Buddy List.

Pidgin supports voice and video-chat too, but this is currently limited to the XMPP protocol.

If you need to video-chat with some other protocol, you can try Empathy, which supports a few more protocols like SIP and MSN.

The pinnacle among video-conferencing and video-bridging solutions is perhaps the Java application Jitsi, which supports almost every popular protocol for video-chat.

Using video-chat under FreeBSD requires you to enable the webcamd daemon. As root, you can add this to /etc/rc.conf:

```
webcamd_enable="YES"
```

You can then, still as root, start the service immediately:

```
service webcamd start
```

7.5.12 Multimedia Editing Software

Multimedia editing under Unix has become increasingly mainstream, but it will be a while before the top Hollywood production houses start trusting Linux as a mainline for video-rendering and soundtrack-recording. There's a tankful of functionality being served by commercial applications that will first need to be rendered in Linux in toto. Linux still has a lead—FreeBSD is a non-player in those circles as yet.

But you can turn your Unix box into a personal multimedia studio, although this is fairly niche subject and I will have to leave it with just an introductory word.

The two primary applications you can work with are Audacity and Handbrake. Audacity is an audio editor suite while Handbrake is a video encoding application. While both applications are available under all Linux distros as well as FreeBSD, Parrot Linux (Studio) bundles them in the distribution.

I have used both of these programs myself with ease as a novice—Audacity to extract a clip of movie soundtrack and remove noise from the clip, and Handbrake to re-encode a .MP4 file in .AVI format.

I presume that, if you are interested in multimedia editing, the combination of Audacity and Handbrake should give you a good platform for a homemade studio. You might also like to try out Avidemux, a video editor.

One great addition of late to the Unix multimedia family that I must not forget to mention is Blender, one of the most sophisticated animation, 3D modeling, and gaming suites in the business today. Blender is big-and-complex software, with a Python API and with a user manual that you can contribute to online.

Figure 7-18 shows a dazzling screenshot of the Blender interface, with two 3D objects (cubes) created as linked entities.

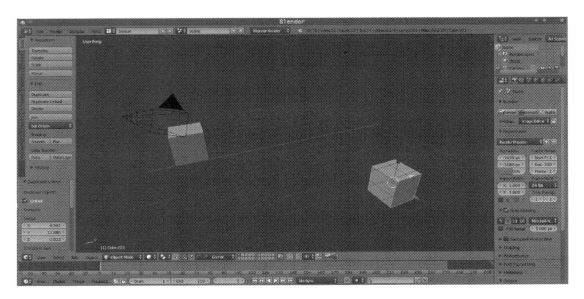

Figure 7-18. *Blender cubes*

7.5.13 Fun Stuff: Games and Blogging

Games had traditionally not been a high priority in the Unix world. This is one area where Unix still lags behind Windows. Things are looking up though. Beginning with Windows 8, Microsoft has started losing its foothold in the gaming sector—with Linux increasingly taking command of the center stage. Valve Corporation—the makers of the Steam gaming platform—made it clear that Linux will here onward be a mainstream distribution outlet for its games. It even has created its own Linux distro, aptly named SteamOS.

Among the current genre of games, chess works best. If you are a chess player, you might like to install the XBoard frontend—with many engines available in the backend—crafty, fairymax, and phalanx.

Figure 7-19 below uses XBoard analysis and the XBoard-quintessence interface Xaw to step back into 1956, when Robert James (Bobby) Fischer proved he could play chess with the move *17...Be6* in what is fondly remembered as The Game of the Century by everyone, except the unfortunate opponent, David Byrne.

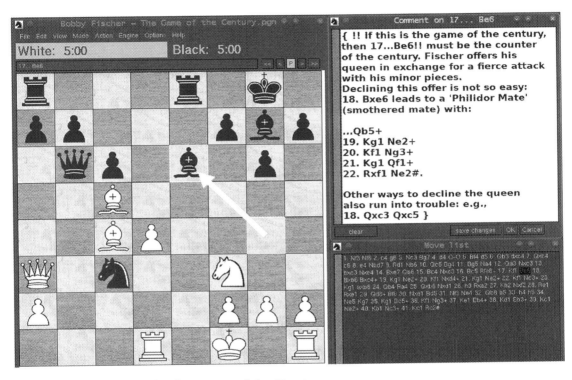

Figure 7-19. Xboard: The Move of the Century

There are a few others, mostly under the GNOME umbrella: Sudoku, Solitaire/Freecell (in the suite AisleRiot), and Minesweeper are the ones I can suggest.

Emlith, Yutaka Emura's Tetris implementation—sometimes considered the best Tetris game ever created—works like a charm under the 32-bit version of Wine (Windows emulation).

Being a Tetris player myself, I would like to pay homage to Emlith with a screenshot, shown in Figure 7-20.

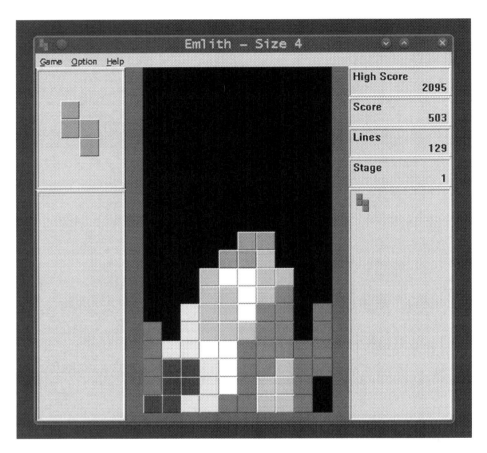

Figure 7-20. *The Tetris game Emlith running under 32-bit Wine*

A few shooting games work too: Quake 4, DooM 3, and Jedi Knight. But they often require significant backstage work and often need an emulation layer.

Don't look for anything much beyond this right now—until Steam actually goes full steam ahead, which luckily is already happening.

As for blogging, there is a cute, little application that has popped up on the radar called Choqok. This buddy can tweet for you, complete with attachment. All you need is a good Twitter handle.

Figure 7-21 is a testimony to Choqok's talents.

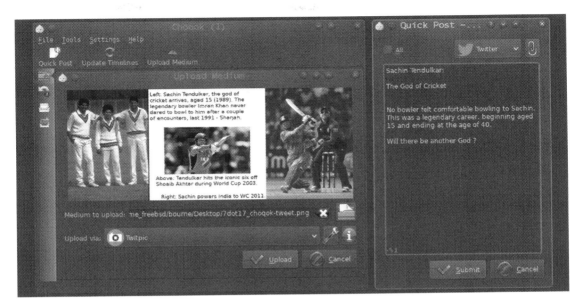

Figure 7-21. *Tweeting with Choqok*

Not to disappoint you with his (or her?) looks, Choqok comes with an adorable icon reminiscent of Angry Birds: 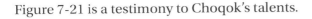.

7.5.14 The Question of a Graphical Integrated Development Environment

Everyone fresh into the Unix bloodstream, at some point or other, feels like posing the question of an Integrated Development Environment, much in the lineage of Visual Studio under Microsoft Windows.

Everyone is given the answer: it is not possible under Unix. Because Unix is vast and supremely modular, integrating all necessary tools under a single umbrella is not possible. In fact, for a developer, Unix is the IDE. You can use a text editor of your choice with syntax highlighting support to write your code and compile your code with the right tool: gcc, `valac`, `javac`, or perhaps something else.

About the closest thing to what could be called IDE is Geany. Geany supports a plethora of languages—C, C++, Java, Latex, Vala, Go, Haskell, Lua, Lisp, and SQL. It was used to write the L^A^T~E~X source code for this book.

Geany has buttons to set, and then fire up, the build functions—this works for small projects. When your project grows big, you'll need to write your own makefile.

A very nice Geany plug-in is the Scope Debugger (which is distinct from the Debugger plug-in). The Scope Debugger lets you set breakpoints and debug from the Geany interface itself—harnessing much of the power of the Visual Studio IDE.

Unfortunately, at the time of this writing, because of a bug in the `glib` library, using Scope freezes Geany. But a workaround is reportedly ready for shipment soon.

Figure 7-22 is an image of Geany with the Scope plugin in action. This is an image of Geany plus Scope working on `wget`'s C code—contributed by Scope's maintainer, Dimitar Zhekov, who had a version of `glib` that still works with Scope.

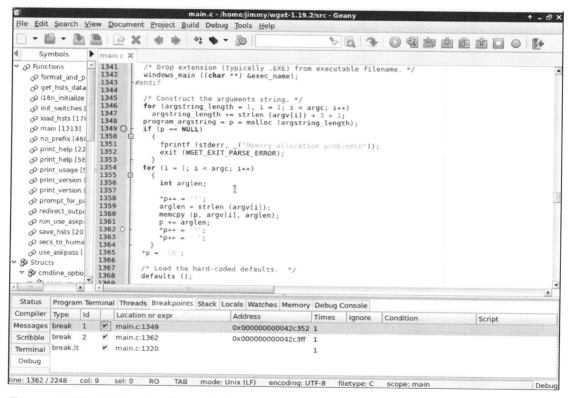

Figure 7-22. *Using the Scope Debugger in Geany*

You can hope the `glib`-bug problem has been solved by the time you are reading this, and that you can use Geany and its Scope Debugger plug-in readily.

For full-fledged debugging, you would like to be conversant with the command-line tool gdb. The gdb debugger has an X frontend that works very well——it's called DDD (Data Display Debugger).

Figure 7-23 is a screenshot of ddd breaking into a block of C++ code.

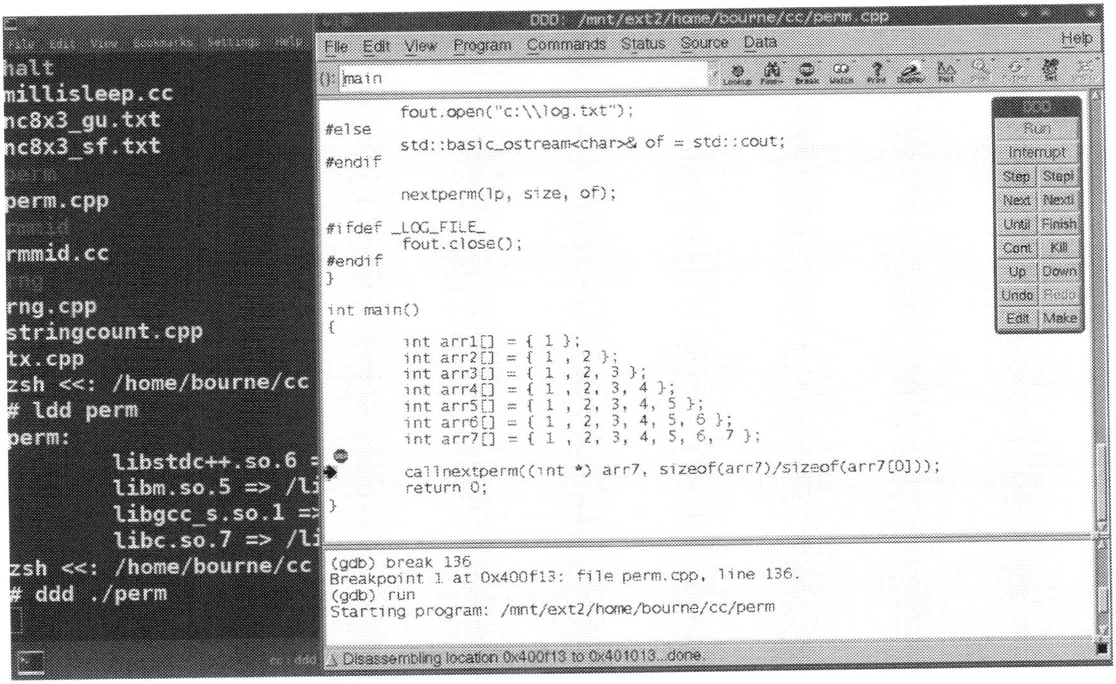

Figure 7-23. *Debugging with ddd*

Ultimately, you must remember that Unix development is a command-line process. The text editor and the shell are what you need to develop, not an all-serving powerbroker that mistakenly goes under the brand name IDE. Any X interface you get is actually a frontend for what can be done on the command line.

7.6 Summary

There was a time when there was a bedeviling dearth of applications under Unix. Programmers preferred to develop applications for DOS and its successor, Windows, which had a wider outreach among users.

Ever since the mantle passed from AT&T to GNU (which broke away from the spirit of commercial Unix with its crafty and recursive acronym—GNU's Not Unix), that scenario has been changing for the better. For any serious application development nowadays, the platform of first choice for the programming community is either Linux or FreeBSD.

The only applications nowadays available under Windows are those that are ported from the world of Unix. And that story will continue.

To make it easier for programmers to develop graphical applications under Unix, a whole—and very impressive—range of toolkits is now available, most prominently GTK and Qt. Transmission, the BitTorrent client, is a GTK application, while HPLIP (the HP Linux Imaging and Printing suite) has been created with Qt. Actually, the whole of GNOME is GTK, and the whole of KDE is Qt.

A new set of programming languages (Vala for instance) have emerged too. These languages make it very easy to develop X applications. We will write some rudimentary GUI applications with Vala in the final chapter of this book.

In short, the graphical outlook of Unix has never been any better than it is right now—and it will get even better in the days to come.

CHAPTER 8

Emulation Layers: Wine and Linuxulator

One of the things you must admire about Unix ever since GNU steered into its vanguard is that it tries hard to be complete and inter-operable. Unix as the operating system is always the hub. But there are important spokes that connect it in a variety of ways to the user. Users of Cygwin/Babun would recognize how important those tools are for Windows users in need of a programmable environment which is so sorely missing in Microsoft platforms.

But the Unix effort does not stop at providing Unix emulation to Windows. It works the other way too: emulating Windows under Unix. And then it goes further: emulating a different Unix flavor under yours. Essentially a rule of the Unix world is: if a platform becomes big and important, emulate it. Emulating Windows is a significant project just because of the huge numbers of existing Windows users and binaries, as well as the resulting improvement in the (poor) documentation of a closed-source system.

Linux has always had the ability to emulate a range of other Unix flavors (all of them effectively deceased by now): System V and SCO, for example. Now that Linux is itself big and important, it fits the Unix paradigm for host emulation. FreeBSD throws in that piece called the *Linuxulator*.

8.1 Wine HQ: Attacking Redmond

There are two distinct ways to run Windows binaries under Unix. One is running Windows as a virtual machine. If you have a multitude of Windows binaries, this should be the preferred way.

© Manish Jain 2018
M. Jain, *Beginning Modern Unix*, https://doi.org/10.1007/978-1-4842-3528-7_8

But virtualization has its problems: it is resource-hungry and it preempts the possibility of integrating individual binaries in a virtual machine (as shortcuts) in the host desktop environment. If you were to launch an entire virtual machine just to run Mozilla Sunbird (a fine calendar application no longer under active development now), it would seem like using a grindwheel to break a butterfly.

That's where Wine (a software layer for WINdows Emulation) comes in. I can just tell my FreeBSD box:

```
wine sunbird.exe
```

And I get a cool set of Mozilla Sunbird windows that show upcoming cricket events—imported from an ICS file (.ics) downloaded at ESPN's popular Cricinfo website (http://www.espncricinfo.com/). See Figure 8-1.

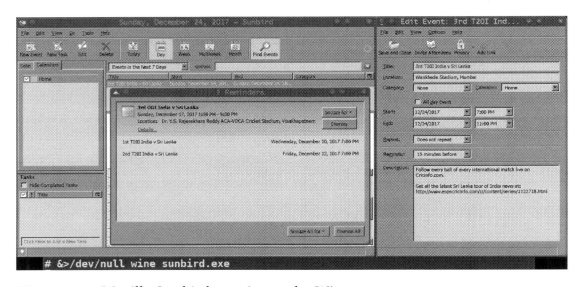

Figure 8-1. *Mozilla Sunbird running under Wine*

I assume that you agree it is useful to learn how to work with Wine: it runs whole application suites flawlessly, including Microsoft Office (32-bit versions) and many 3D games.

But I must also note that support for Windows binaries is nowhere near 100%.

- There are many Windows applications you cannot yet install under Wine. For instance, Adobe Acrobat Reader.

- Wine support for 64-bit applications is almost entirely a developer's world. They just do not run well under the current state of Wine. On the other hand, 32-bit applications often and usually do work well.

It might seem like I am trying to suggest Wine is currently a usable project only for 32-bit binaries from Windows 9x/NT/2000/XP. The impression is right on the nail's head. 64-bit support is still entirely experimental, with the experiments being conducted not just by developers, but by users too—starting right at first-blood.

8.2 Installing Wine

The first step is to get Wine working under your box. While you are at installing Wine, you also want to get a couple of useful associates: Wine Mono and Wine Gecko.

Wine Mono is an open-source implementation of the .NET framework. Wine can use a Windows build of Mono to run .NET applications—we'll do just that to run Pinta, a fine paint program not available natively under FreeBSD (my primary system).

Wine Gecko implements a sham version of Microsoft's Internet Explorer web browser—for the benefit of any applications that want IE functionality.

Under Linux, you do not have to worry about choosing between 32-bit Wine and 64-bit Wine. Wine installation automatically sets up both emulation layers, with the 32-bit version executable as /usr/bin/wine, and the 64-bit version executable as /usr/bin/wine64.

Installation should be straightforward:

```
apt-get install wine wine-mono wine-gecko     # Ubuntu
pacman -S wine wine-mono wine_gecko      # Arch
```

Note that Arch uses an underscore in the Wine Gecko package name.

Things are a bit different in FreeBSD wherein you can install only one version: either 32-bit (i386-wine) or 64-bit (wine). This may change in the days to come.

If the binaries you intend to run are sourced from Windows 9x/XP, you want to be running Wine32. If instead you want to use binaries from Windows 7/10, you likely want

Wine64. If you are undecided which one to opt for, Wine32 is almost certainly what you want. Wine64 is largely unusable as of right now anyway.

```
pkg install i386-wine wine-mono wine-gecko      # 32-bit version of wine
pkg install wine wine-mono wine-gecko      # 64-bit version of wine
```

One nicety applies to both Linux and FreeBSD. If you don't install Wine Mono and/ or Wine Gecko, there are no penalties: upon first run, Wine will automatically download and install them. But doing this yourself on the command line is a good idea so that you are aware of precisely what you need for your setup.

Linux flaunts another nicety (which can be expected under FreeBSD too in the coming days)—support for WoW64 (Windows 32-bit on Windows 64-bit). WoW64 is a subsystem of 64-bit Windows capable of running 32-bit applications. Wine under Linux has moved to a stage where installing Wine gets you both Wine32 and Wine64. And then you can execute a Windows binary with wine or wine64 as you like—the system will itself figure out its "bitness" and use the right subsystem internally.

The rest of this documentation has been compiled with the 32-bit version of Wine. If you use the 64-bit version of Wine, you can adjust mostly by just substituting wine64 in place of wine and then bracing up for the stormy season that possibly lies ahead.

8.3 The Filesystem Hierarchy of Wine

The first time you run a wine command, the system will create your Wine environment— which is a .wine subdirectory under your $HOME. Besides other weaponry, that subdirectory contains the Windows registry implemented by Wine and contained in three plain-text files: system.reg, user.reg< and userdef.reg. (Unlike Windows, Wine uses plain-text files for the registry. But still, do not modify these files in your text editor. We'll discuss registry manipulation a while later.) When populated by the system itself, $HOME/.wine is dubbed your Wine prefix.

$HOME/.wine also contains two subdirectories: dosdevices and drive_c.

The foregoing mix makes for a $HOME/.wine hierarchy that looks like this:

```
|-- dosdevices
|   |-- c: -> ../drive_c
|   |-- z: -> /
|-- drive_c
```

```
|    |-- Program Files
|    |-- users
|    |-- windows
|-- system.reg
|-- user.reg
|-- userdef.reg
```

If you are familiar with Windows filesystem hierarchy, this would already have struck a note in your mind, with a broad picture of how it all works.

drive_c/Program Files is the directory where your installed programs reside.

drive_c/windows is the Windows directory containing the system32 subdirectory (which in turn contains Wine's version of the Windows kernel ntoskrnl.exe, apart from all system libraries).

dosdevices/c: and dosdevices/z: are clever symbolic links that lend you read+write access to your Wine environment and read-only access to the entire system:

dosdevices/c: points to $HOME/.wine/drive_c.

dosdevices/z: points to the system root directory /.

I should expressly note that Wine, just like Windows, is case-insensitive in its treatment of file paths. So c: is taken to be same as C:. I should also note that Wine fully understands Unix paths too, in addition to its Windows-style paths.

8.4 Running Windows Applications Under Wine

Windows applications come in two flavors: those that have an installer, and those that can be executed directly with no install regimen.

Applications like Alexander Davidson's Metapad (a Notepad replacement available for download at http://liquidninja.com/metapad/) do not need installation. They just work straightaway:

```
wine metapad &
```

If a nice editor window pops up on the screen, you are good to go. (The & at the end of that command tells the shell to run Wine and its surrogate Metapad window in the background, letting you regain control of the command-line immediately.)

A couple of optional morsels were omitted in the foregoing Wine command:

- *The ./ path specification:* Wine is smart enough to search for the executable first in the current directory, before scouring other paths.

- *The .exe suffix:* If you don't supply the suffix, Wine will append it by itself.

Bigger applications like Mozilla Sunbird, Microsoft Office, and Pinta need to be installed. Any programs you install under Wine are local to your Wine environment. If some other user logs on to the system, he/she will have to install them as needed afresh in his/her own environment.

8.5 Running Pinta as a Windows Application

While Pinta is always available under Linux, FreeBSD users have to hack their way in. But this section is still useful for Linux readers—it documents installation and usage of programs under Wine, along with handling of the `.msi` packages.

As already noted in the previous chapter, Pinta uses the .NET framework for its build, which leaves it standing with one leg in the Windows world and the other leg in Unix. Luckily, Wine (to be specific, the `wine-mono` project) takes care of bridging issues.

You can download the Windows release of Pinta from the official releases URL, which is `https://pinta-project.com/pintaproject/pinta/releases`.

At the time of this writing, version 1.6 was the latest Windows release, available via this link:

`https://github.com/PintaProject/Pinta/releases/download/1.6/pinta-1.6.exe`

Pinta setup needs a GTK-Sharp already installed (Otherwise the setup will itself download a GTK-Sharp module for you. This is okay, but then you won't be able to save the module's installer locally in your system for future use.)

You can use the following MSI module, which works cleanly with Pinta version 1.6:

`http://download.xamarin.com/GTKforWindows/Windows/gtk-sharp-2.12.26.msi`

Once you have downloaded the files (most conveniently with `wget`), things are easy. First install the `.msi` package for GTK-Sharp:

`wine msiexec /i ./gtk-sharp-2.12.26.msi`

This is the standard methodology for dealing with `.msi` packages.

Once GTK-Sharp is installed, you can run Pinta's setup: `wine ./pinta-1.6.exe`

When setup finishes, move over to `~/.wine/"Program Files"/Pinta` to run the newly installed program:

```
cd $HOME/.wine/"Program Files"/Pinta
wine Pinta.exe &
```

Note that we are having to cater to the embedded space in the name of the directory `Program Files` with the use of quotes. You can, if you want, put the entire path under double-quotes: `"$HOME/.wine/Program Files/Pinta"`

While Pinta setup usually would create a shortcut merged into your Applications Menu somewhere under the Wine category, it is good to know how to launch applications yourself. If needed, you can create `.desktop` shortcuts too.

Here is a `Pinta.desktop`:

```
[Desktop Entry]
Exec=wine "$HOME/.wine/drive_c/Program Files/Pinta/Pinta.exe"
Icon=FC42_Pinta.0
Name=Pinta
Path="$HOME/.wine/drive_c/Program Files/Pinta"
StartupNotify=true
Type=Application
```

You may need to fix the `Icon` setting in this shortcut. If so, you can use the path of any PNG file in your box.

The `Path` setting in a `.desktop`/Applications Menu launcher for Wine applications is often optional. But if the Wine application links to a DLL in its own directory, Wine could run into an error trying to launch the program (when the `Path` cue is missing).

8.6 Maintaining Your Wine Environment

Most of the time, the foregoing discussion is all that you need to use Wine comfortably. The rest of the discussion is for digging into Wine a few inches below ground level.

Here are a few things to do to keep your Wine headquarters in good health:

- If you want to look up the broad configuration of your Wine environment, use the command:

  `winecfg`

The window popped up by that command (`winecfg`) shows, most prominently, the version of Windows your Wine maps to. If you are using 32-bit Wine, this would typically be Windows XP. 64-bit Wine usually maps to Windows 7.

- Uninstalling software is simple. Just use the command:

```
wine uninstaller
```

That will give the Windows Add/Remove Programs applet, which you can use as usual.

- Editing Wine's registry is simple too. You can use either of these commands:

```
wine regedit
```

or simply

```
regedit
```

That will give you the Registry Editor window that you would have probably encountered some time or the other.

Since you cannot set one $PATH for your Unix shell and another one for Wine, if you want to tell Wine about a default directory for looking up executables and/or DLLs (in addition to the standard Wine paths), you need to use the Registry Editor.

Figure 8-2 shows PATH, a new string variable (REG_SZ) being created under the registry key HKEY_CURRENT_USER/Environment and modified to hold the path C:\Program Files\Mozilla Sunbird. (Path strings in the registry must not be quoted.

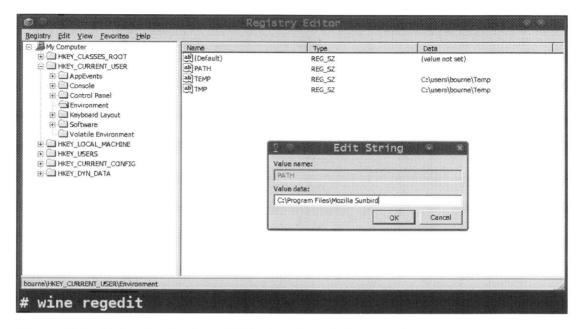

Figure 8-2. *Using the Registry Editor to add a default path*

With a PATH value set as in the last image under the key HKEY_CURRENT_USER/
Environment in Wine's registry, I can invoke the binary sunbird.exe (which is present in
the directory C:\Program Files\Mozilla Sunbird) from any location in my Unix shell:

```
cd /tmp
wine sunbird
# And I get the Sunbird window
```

Looking at that last screenshot, you ought to admire how closely Wine mimics
native Windows functionality—it is almost impossible to spot any difference. The only
difference I could spot is an extra registry branch HKEY_DYN_DATA, which I have never
seen in Windows XP.

Note   If you make a mess of your Wine, it's not a big deal.

Just delete $HOME/.wine and run winecfg again: that will initialize a new Wine
environment, and you can then install programs afresh.

In Wine jargon, this is stated as *creating a new prefix.* Recreating your prefix is the
Wine equivalent to reinstalling Windows.

8.7 Wine Patches

Wine is one Unix component that is heavily doctored at all levels—developers provide sets of patches to run atop regular Wine, and then users tweak at their own level.

If regular Wine does not serve you well, you can try a patched version. Once any of the patches under a patchset become generally accepted, they get merged into the mainstream Wine distribution. So you might like to keep in mind that patchsets, even the popular ones, are experimental code not considered "fit-as-yet" for regular distribution.

Two fairly popular patchsets are Staging and Gallium Nine. These are so well-nurtured in the community that they have their own packages: `wine-staging` (available under both FreeBSD and Linux) and `wine-staging-nine` (available under Linux only at this moment).

While I have nothing against patches and patchsets at a personal level, I would like to admonish you from using them unless you really need them (which essentially means "if regular Wine does not work well for you").

One thing that bears a mention is that you cannot install a patched version of Wine alongside regular Wine. If you try to install `wine-staging` or `wine-staging-nine` with Wine already installed, the package manager will first delete the regular Wine package.

8.8 Version Mimicking Under Wine

You can use the Applications tab of `winecfg` to instruct Wine to run a different Windows flavor for a specific executable. Figure 8-3 shows the `metapad.exe` being configured to run as a Windows 98 application (in a Windows XP prefix).

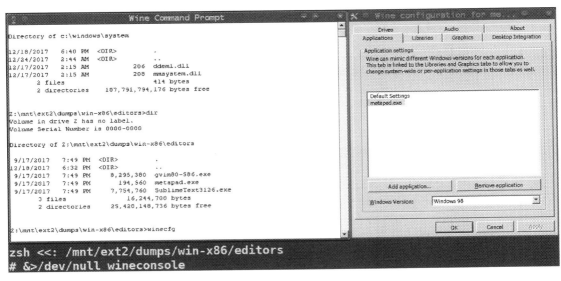

Figure 8-3. *Getting a Wine application to use a different Windows flavor*

There are a couple of things to note about Figure 8-3. The `winecfg` command was issued not from the Unix terminal directly, but from a Wine built-in utility: `wineconsole`, which occupies almost all of the left-side real estate in the image.

The `wineconsole` command mimics Windows `cmd.exe`, and—quite helpfully—starts off in the Unix directory from which it was invoked:

/mnt/ext2/dumps/win-x86/editors
↓ which in Wine notation becomes ↓
Z:\mnt\ext2\dumps\win-x86\editors

I would like to remind you that Wine's Z: is a link to/of your Unix filesystem.

If you need to convert between Unix and Wine paths yourself, use `winepath`:

```
winepath -w /mnt/ext2/dumps/win-x86/editors
# Gives the output: Z:\mnt\ext2\dumps\win-x86\editors
```

Keep in mind though that a single backslash in the output becomes two for you when feeding input—in other words, your \\ translates as a single backslash for the system.

8.9 Wine Libraries (DLLs)

The way Wine organizes libraries for the user is by creating a system-wide library directory at the time of installation. On my box, that directory is /usr/local/lib32/wine.

Whenever a new Wine prefix is created, Wine uses the system-wide libraries to populate the prefix with DLL stubs at the path $HOME/.wine/drive_c/windows/system32. This closely mimics Windows filesystem layout. Those DLLs are classed as built-in: shipped with the Wine distribution.

You can extend Wine DLL resources by copying DLLs from Windows. If you run into a missing DLL error, such as err:module:import_dll Library MFC42u.dll, just copy the missing DLL (MFC42u.dll) from Windows under Wine's system32/. That should fix things. (Section 8.12 offers tips on skirting such Microsoft-licensed DLLs.)

Built-in DLLs in your prefix can be replaced with native (original Windows) versions: this too is largely supported by Wine. To override a built-in DLL, perform two steps:

1. Copy the native DLL at the location $HOME/.wine/drive_c/
    windows/system32.

2. Run winecfg and specify a loading order for the DLL under the
    Libraries tab.

Figure 8-4 shows a screenshot of winecfg telling Wine to use the native version of comdlg32.dll ahead of the built-in version.

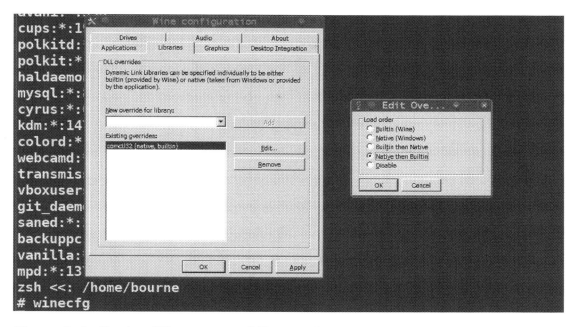

Figure 8-4. *Getting Wine to use a different DLL*

If you intend the DLL override to not be global, and instead be application-specific, you cannot do that with `winecfg`. But you can do it on the command-line using the `WINEDLLOVERRIDES` environment variable to set the DLL loading order:

```
WINEDLLOVERRIDES="comdlg32=n,b" wine ./mspaint.exe
# Load comdlg32 as native first; if failure, fall back on built-in

WINEDLLOVERRIDES="comctl32=b" wine ./mspaint.exe
# Load comctl32 as built-in only

WINEDLLOVERRIDES="oleaut32="  wine  ./mspaint.exe
# Disable oleaut32 entirely
```

While Wine, at least on paper, mostly supports mixing DLLs, this is deprecated. Using native DLLs breaks the freedom from Microsoft licensing, and still more importantly results in unpredictable behavior, with the system significantly more prone to crashes.

But there are times when using a native DLL could lead to a performance benefit, or a Wine version of the DLL is not available, which is why the DLL override facility exists in the first place.

225

A few critical DLLs must always be built-in and never replaced/overridden with natives:

```
kernel32.dll
gdi32.dll
user32.dll
ntdll.dll
```

The DLLs need low-level Windows kernel access not implemented in Wine.

While replacement of built-in DLLs is largely supported by Wine, replacement of built-in executables is not. So do not try to copy Windows' `regedit.exe` over the `regedit.exe` that exists in your Wine prefix. The prefix may soon cease to exist.

8.10 Tweaking Wine Still Further

One tweak I do recommend for Wine users, particularly the gamers, is to enable Emulate a Virtual Desktop under the Graphics tab of the `winecfg` window. Some applications, most prominently games, try to change the screen resolution—often making a mess of the desktop. If you check Emulate a Virtual Desktop, Wine will run every program in a separate, new window environment—essentially creating a virtual desktop for every application launched. If the application tries to do something nasty—like mess up the screen resolution—the effects are limited to its own desktop.

Gamers might like to tweak Wine's audio, which can be done under the Audio tab of `winecfg`, as well as on the command line using environment variables:

```
AUDIODEV=/dev/dsp1 MIXERDEV=/dev/mixer1 MIDIDEV=/dev/midi1 wine <Program>
```

Keep in mind that Wine uses its own audio driver, typically `system32/wineoss.drv`.

8.11 Wine Uses a Client-Server Model Too

You might be taken aback by this, but—just like X.org—Wine uses a client-server model too. All Wine applications you launch from the command line or via shortcuts are, in truth, Wine clients.

You can't have clients without having a server in the first place, which is just what the situation is. If you fire up `winecfg &` (or any other Wine command that persists for a while), you can then run `ps -x | grep -i wine` to list all Wine processes:

```
> winecfg &
[1] 3432
> ps -x | grep -i wine | grep -v -w grep
3438  -  SNs   0:00.36 /usr/local/bin32/wineserver
3444  -  SNs   0:00.01 C:\\windows\\system32\\services.exe (wine)
3446  -  SN    0:00.01 C:\\windows\\system32\\winedevice.exe (wine)
3448  -  SN    0:00.01 C:\\windows\\system32\\plugplay.exe (wine)
3450  -  SNs   0:00.07 C:\\windows\\system32\\explorer.exe (wine)
3432  5  SN    0:00.07 winecfg.exe (wine)
```

There it is: `wineserver` (PID 3438) at the top of the listing.

`wineserver` is a daemon that provides to Wine clients the same services that the Windows kernel provides to Windows applications. It gets launched automatically when you invoke any Wine client—which is the reason not many people notice it.

It shuts down automatically too. If you close the `winecfg` window, `ps -x | grep -i wine` will report no `wineserver` process running. This usually is the desired behavior, since the invocation was auto, the shutdown must by default be auto too.

But `wineserver` invocation demands its own CPU time and other resources, which is why at times you might want it not to exit automatically. That is possible—and perhaps a good idea if you use Wine applications a lot.

If you run `wineserver` with the argument -p, it will persist, waiting for Wine clients until kingdom come:

```
wineserver -p && pgrep -x wineserver # prints PID of wineserver
```

Using the PID, you can shut down the server when it suits you with the `kill` command (`killall wineserver` works too), or else, just let it get killed with a system halt.

8.12 Graphical Tools for Wine Administration

There are two nice tools for Wine administration—`winetricks` and `q4wine`.

`winetricks`, at its heart, is intended to work around commonly-encountered Wine problems. But it can be used as a graphical frontend for Wine administration too.

`winetricks --gui` provides ways to tweak Wine as well as download and install fonts, games, DLLs, and applications. If you select Install an Application, `winetricks` will display a list of programs that it can install. Very few of those programs install correctly and then work well—as of date.

One `winetricks`-listed program that does install smoothly and then work well (at least on my box) is Adobe Digital Editions version 1.7. I would be doing serious injustice to `winetricks` and Adobe if I do not post proof of success with ADE; see Figure 8-5.

Figure 8-5 has deliberately not been cropped so that it shows ADE running in a virtual desktop (the window with the blue background on the left side in the image)—a feat accomplished by checking Emulate a Virtual Desktop under the Graphics tab of the `winecfg` window.

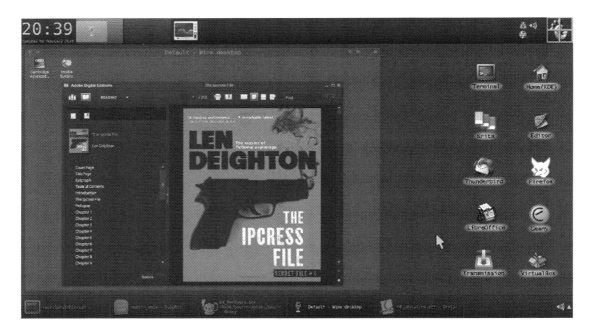

Figure 8-5. *winetricks booty: Adobe Digital Editions version 1.7*

Despite its (limited) goodness, `winetricks` is a fairly crude application in terms of its interface. Much slicker is the full-fledged Wine administration suite `q4wine`—a Qt application that can efficiently use the services of `winetricks`.

For a start, `q4wine` can create and manage multiple Wine prefixes for you—with a mix of 32-bit and 64-bit Wine permitted.

The left half of Figure 8-6 shows an additional prefix named `wine32` being created under `q4wine` at the path `$HOME/wine32`. This second, `q4wine`-created Wine prefix is intended—as its name suggests—to be 32-bit Wine always. The `wine`-created prefix that lies in `$HOME/.wine` (and referred as `Default` in the left half of the image) can be either 32-bit or 64-bit as per user need.

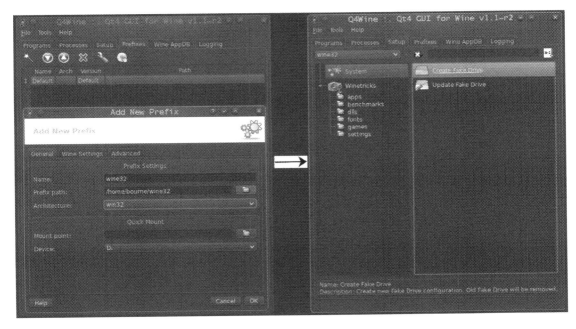

Figure 8-6. *Creating a new Wine prefix with q4wine*

Prefixes can be managed under the Prefixes tab.

If you then—once a new prefix has been created—move over to the Setup tab, you can create a `C:` drive for the new prefix by choosing System ➤ Create Fake Drive. Refer the right half of Figure 8-6 for illustration.

You can use the Programs tab of `q4wine` to launch a host of Wine tasks from inside the new prefix: `winecfg`, `uninstaller`, `taskmgr` (task manager), and `control` (control panel). If you run (i.e., double-click) the Uninstaller right now under wine32, you will get an empty programs list, because the wine32 prefix is brand new. See Figure 8-7.

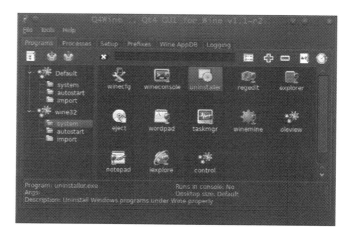

Figure 8-7. *System applications in a Wine prefix*

One thing you might like to do whenever you create a new prefix is to pull in winetricks into the prefix. Just move over to the Setup tab, click Winetricks, and double-click Install or Update Winetricks Script. See Figure 8-8.

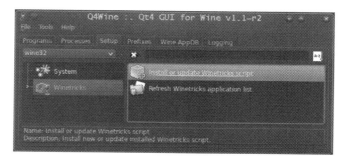

Figure 8-8. *Installing winetricks via q4wine*

You can now put the combination of q4wine and winetricks to good effect—pulling in those MFC42* DLLs, which many Wine applications seem to need, into the new prefix.

Just double-click on mfc42 under Winetricks ➤ dlls, and you should be good on the MFC42 front. Of course, the same idea applies to any missing DLLs that you might need: always check q4wine ➤ Setup ➤ Winetricks ➤ dlls first. These DLLs are not Microsoft-licensed. See Figure 8-9.

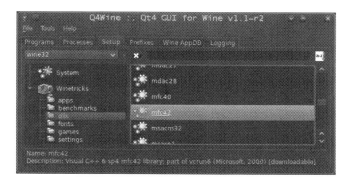

Figure 8-9. *Using q4wine to get DLLs*

As for browsing applications available at Wine HQ, you can use the Wine AppDB tab—which, as of this moment, only lets you browse, with no support for installing applications from within q4wine. The way Wine works, it is pretty much impossible to get one single graphical frontend to install from among the million applications lying in store at https://appdb.winehq.org/.

8.13 Developing Applications for Wine

This section is intended to be just a pointer. For developers, Wine is, quite unsurprisingly, a great playground. A standard Wine installation has quite a few tools that are developer-oriented: winegcc, wineg++, winebuild, winemaker, and even a debugger called winegdb.

While you can always read the man pages for more information, I would like to refer to winemaker, the heart of a library of tools called Winelib—which facilitates conversion of an existing Win32 project to Unix.

winemaker is a fine and dandy Perl script which, among many other things, takes care of case-conversion (unlike Windows, Unix filenames are case-sensitive) and newline conversion (Windows CRLF ➤ Unix LF). Upon success, it generates a GNU makefile.

For illustration purposes, I used winemaker to generate a Wine executable for a C source file halt.c—a Win32 shutdown initiator that takes a positive integer n as argument. If n is between 1 and 24, halt.exe powers off the system at [0]n:00 hours (24-hour format). If the argument is more than 24, halt.exe shuts the system down when the process with the PID n exits. The sources for halt.c are available in the appendix.

231

All that I had to do to make `halt.exe` work as a Wine application was create a project directory called `halt` and copy `halt.c` therein. After that, `winemaker` and `make` did the rest with the following commands issued under my Linux installation:

```
winemaker --lower-uppercase .
make # Use 'gmake' under FreeBSD, wherein 'make' is a different system
```

`winemaker` churned out a GNU makefile, which `make` used to invoke `winegcc`, which in turn spewed out `halt.exe` and `halt.exe.so`.

Wine's `halt.exe` is actually a Bourne script that just feeds the binary `halt.exe.so` to Wine's loader—the `wine` command itself. I can thus execute `halt.exe` in two ways:

```
./halt.exe     -OR-     wine ./halt.exe.so
# Ignoring the numeric argument  halt.exe itself needs
```

As you can see, converting Win32 projects to Wine is easy.

`winemaker` supports not just single-source-file projects, but entire Win32 projects (`.vcproj`/`.dsw`/`.sln`). You can read more about `winemaker` at `https://wiki.winehq.org/Winelib_User%27s_Guide`.

8.14 The 64-Bit Mess

Speaking objectively, the 64-bit situation with Wine is nowhere near bearing fruits for the user yet. Any success you get from Wine64 needs the right combination of luck and system configuration—what runs on somebody else's box might (and often would) conk out under yours. Very limited success is reported anyway.

Under FreeBSD on my box, Wine64 is a complete fiasco: I have not yet managed to get any 64-bit binary to run under Wine. With Linux (particularly Arch/Manjaro), I have had some success—getting 64-bit PuTTY and a new web browser Pale Moon to execute nicely. But even Manjaro Linux is unable to run `Notepad.exe` and `mspaint.exe` from Windows 7—which seems, and actually is—a bit counterintuitive. `Notepad.exe` would be the first thing the user might expect to run under Wine. Note that the reference here is to Windows' native Notepad, not Wine's own Notepad (`wine64 notepad`). Which, of course, runs flawlessly.

The problem with Wine64 is not that there is a lack of effort. The problem has more to do with the following factors:

- 64-bit Windows is a huge platform. While 32-bit Windows is itself substantial in its scope, 64-bit does not just double the scope. It more like multiplies it a couple of dozen times.

- With virtualization having matured well enough to run 64-bit Windows seamlessly, the need to make the labyrinthine Windows projects (Office 2013 and Visual Studio 2015, for instance) run under Wine64 does not fit anyone's bill any longer.

- 32-bit executables are frequently misidentified as 64-bit. That rot started with Windows XP 64-bit, in which perhaps the only 64-bit executable was the kernel itself—almost everything else was compiled as 32-bit. There are plenty of `.exe`/`.msi` binaries on the web that identify themselves as 64-bit, but in truth are 32-bit. The only way to be sure is to feed them as arguments to the `file` command, which reports PE32 executable/80386 for 32-bit Windows binaries, and PE32+ executable/x86-64 for 64-bit ones.

Is there a positive side to all this? Yes. Microsoft is finding it increasingly difficult to get its releases adopted by users worldwide. Despite a massive marketing campaign, Windows 10 is still outnumbered, positively by Windows 7 and perhaps by Windows XP too. Windows 10 has still been relatively lucky—Windows 8 almost did not sell at all, while Windows 9 had to be entirely cancelled in the boardroom.

Considering its waning revenues in the face of soaring business effort, Microsoft may well decide to stabilize with what has already been delivered to the markets—with fewer OS releases and updates in future. If that happens, it would give GNU developers the breathing space to spruce up Wine64 into a working platform. But don't expect miracles any time soon—GNU has already been something like a decade into the Wine64 essay. This suggests that the pace of evolution is not going to be frenetic in the future as well.

There is an interesting way in which Wine influences Windows market dynamics. Since 64-bit applications largely do not work well under Wine, they usually get facilitated in Unix via virtualization. Wine itself thus keeps the interest in and the need for 32-bit Windows alive and kicking, contributing to the "immortalization" of Windows XP—much to the chagrin of Microsoft, who would obviously want old versions of Windows swept under the carpet by its new releases.

8.15 Yet Another Imitation Game: Linuxulator

Just as one cannot dream of being in America while one is in America, one cannot emulate Linux while in Linux. This section is thus of less import to Linux users and more geared to FreeBSD users.

One facet of the Unix situation is that Linux is more widely used than the BSDs. Most developers develop for Linux. While almost all of these applications get ported to FreeBSD sooner or later, some don't. FreeBSD therefore hosts a special platform within itself that caters to Linux applications not yet ported to FreeBSD. And it works remarkably well—although, in most cases, some (often significant amount of) preliminary work is required. But that work tends to be simple enough—mostly copying libraries from a Linux installation.

Like Wine, Linuxulator is not a 100%, sure-bet agent—a few applications (TeamViewer, for instance) need so much work that they are beyond the practical limits of the average reader. Such an application must simply wait until either the authors port their software for FreeBSD, or the FreeBSD development team itself makes a concerted porting effort.

Unlike Wine—which is a pure user-space suite—Linuxulator is a kernel-space emulation layer. What this means is that to use the Linuxulator, certain bits in the FreeBSD kernel have to be activated:

```
kldload linux     # FreeBSD i386
kldload linux linux64    # FreeBSD amd64
```

While it is perfectly acceptable to manually `kldload` Linux support into the FreeBSD kernel, the better way to do it is simply put the following line in /etc/rc.conf and reboot the system:

```
linux_enable=YES
```

At this stage (post-reboot), you have to make a key choice.

At the time of this writing, FreeBSD supports two versions of Linux for the Linuxulator middleware: CentOS 6 and CentOS 7. The corresponding Linuxulators are nicknamed c6 and c7. You can't have both—installing c7 with c6 already installed will compel the package manager to first delete c6, and vice versa.

The two Linuxulators—c6 and c7—share certain characteristics:

- The Linuxulator root directory is always /compat/linux.

- The FreeBSD kernel automatically prefixes the Linuxulator root directory path to Linux application binary interface (ABI) paths.

  So when a Linux ABI application uses the path /usr/bin, the FreeBSD kernel will prefix the path with /compat/linux, and consider the actual filesystem path /compat/linux/usr/bin.

- Similarly, when a Linux ABI program needs a library under /lib, the FreeBSD kernel will look up under /compat/linux/lib.

- Under FreeBSD i386, c6 and c7 are 32-bit, whereas under AMD64, the Linuxulators support both 32-bit and 64-bit applications. 32-bit applications have their libraries located under /compat/linux/lib, while 64-bit libraries go under /compat/linux/lib64.

  The FreeBSD kernel distinguishes between 32-bit libraries and 64-bit libraries on its own, which means libXYZ.so under /compat/linux/lib is distinct from libXYZ.so under /compat/linux/lib64.

Despite being close relatives, c6 and c7 have contrasting social acceptance profiles. CentOS 6 support in the Linux world has nose-dived, with users encouraged to switch to the newer CentOS 7, which— unlike CentOS 6 (and unlike c7 too)—is 64-bit only. You might, for a moment, be inclined to think that c7 is the better choice for a Linuxulator, at least so on an AMD64 box. But then FreeBSD's own application ports, which makes those applications a snap to install and use, are still largely based on c6.

If you want to set up your own Linux applications under FreeBSD, you will have a better shot with c7, because CentOS 7 is actively supported by the Linux community. But then most of the userspace work for tweaking the application(s) to work under a c7 Linuxulator would have to be done by you yourself.

I won't try to coax you into choosing c6 over c7, or the other way around. Instead, I will furnish two subsections—one targeting c6 and the other c7. The c6 subsection assumes you want to use pre-existing ports, while c7 assumes you want to play with the Linux ABI yourself.

Both subsections require you to put the following into /etc/fstab:

```
Tmpfs      /compat/linux/dev/shm   tmpfs       rw,mode=1777,size=1g  0  0
linprocfs /compat/linux/proc       linprocfs   rw                    0  0
linsysfs   /compat/linux/sys       linsysfs    rw                    0  0
```

You also need to put the following in /etc/devfs.conf:

```
link /compat/linux/dev/shm shm
```

I also encourage you to create a couple of aliases in the root user account's .cshrc for mounting/unmounting your Linuxulator's virtual filesystems:

```
alias linmount "mount tmpfs; mount linprocfs; mount linsysfs"
alias linumount "umount tmpfs; umount linprocfs; umount linsysfs"
```

Unlike the Bourne shell, C shell aliases do not use = following the alias identifier.

Note   Under FreeBSD, the root user's default shell is the C shell, and FreeBSD does not recommend using Bash/Zsh as the root user's login shell. That disrupts the predefined system defaults—interfering, for instance, with `chroot` environments.

If you want to use `bash` or `zsh` for the system administrator account, there is a "mirror" of root—very nicely named toor—under whose account you can use the shell of your choice. The toor user has all the privileges of the root user.

8.15.1 Using c6 Linuxulator

Installing the c6 Linuxulator middleware is simple:

```
pkg install linux_base-c6
```

You need to then put the following lines into /etc/sysctl.conf:

```
compat.linux.osrelease=2.6.32
kern.ipc.shm_allow_removed=1
```

And then you need to reboot, or else issue the following commands:

```
ROOT#    service sysctl restart
ROOT#    service devfs restart
ROOT#    linmount      # Or else:  mount tmpfs; mount linprocfs; mount
                            linsysfs
```

You can now readily install any of the Linux programs that have been tweaked by developers to work with the FreeBSD kernel using Linux ABI, such as the Opera (Linux version) web browser (linux-opera), which automatically bundles in all the natively-Linux plugins, or Sublime Text (linux-sublime3), the very nifty (albeit commercially-licensed) text editor available as freeware for personal use.

The next (intentionally uncropped) screenshot, Figure 8-10, shows both Opera (Linux version) and Sublime Text literally running side-by-side under my FreeBSD desktop.

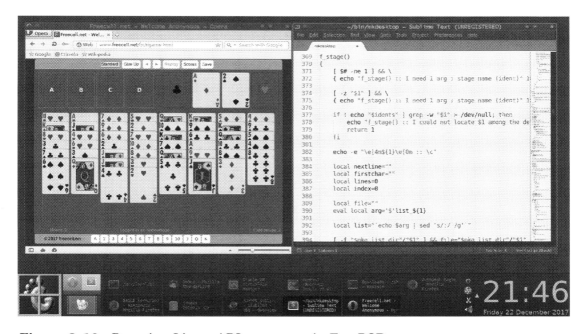

Figure 8-10. *Running Linux ABI programs in FreeBSD*

You can use either packages or ports to install most Linux ABI programs:

```
pkg install linux-opera
# or else: cd /usr/ports/www/linux-opera; make install clean
```

```
pkg install linux-sublime3
# or else: cd /usr/ports/editors/linux-sublime3; make install clean
```

Of course, building a port requires significantly more time compared to installing the corresponding precompiled package.

Linuxulator is not limited to web browsers and text editors. Some pretty fancy, highly technical suites work flawlessly under the Linux ABI. For instance, Maplesoft's Maple, the scientific/mathematical computing and analysis suite; and Autodesk's Eagle, the top-ranked CAD software for electronic circuit board designers.

Installing and running Eagle under FreeBSD is a simple matter of building the port `/usr/ports/cad/linux-eagle5`. (A package was not available at the time this book went into print.)

Figure 8-11 is a screenshot from my desktop that shows an Eagle printed circuit board (PCB) layout getting ready to receive a Toshiba fiber optic device.

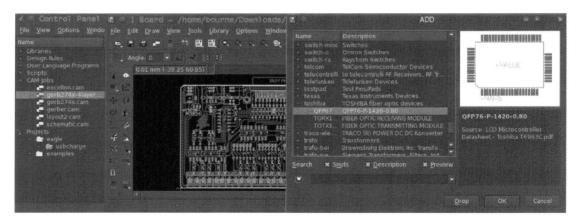

Figure 8-11. *Autodesk's Eagle CAD software running under Linux ABI*

If you want to list all FreeBSD ports that use the Linuxulator, it is quite straightforward:

```
cd /usr/ports
make fetchindex
grep linux_base INDEX-* | less -S
```

If you are a gamer, you'll happily find quite a few games, particularly of the 3D shooting ilk, in that listing. Of those, Doom3 (demo) works so well that I feel inclined to post a patched screenshot as proof—see Figure 8-12.

Figure 8-12. *Using the Linux ABI to play Doom3*

3D games such as Doom3 have the uncanny habit of rearranging desktop icons, which is something you should get used to if you are a gamer—gaming companies would rather take up agriculture than mend their ways.

8.15.2 Using c7 Linuxulator

Installing the c7 Linuxulator middleware is simple too:

```
pkg install linux_base-c7
```

You need to then put the following lines into /etc/sysctl.conf:

```
compat.linux.osrelease=3.10.0
kern.ipc.shm_allow_removed=1
```

And then you need to reboot, or else issue the following commands:

```
ROOT#    service sysctl restart
ROOT#    service devfs restart
ROOT#    linmount      # Or else: mount tmpfs; mount linprocfs; mount
                              linsysfs
```

Since you'll be using the Linuxulator mostly for your own program installations (at least so for the time being), it is a good idea to install the Qt ports for the Linux ABI, because a high percentage of graphical applications nowadays use Qt widgets:

```
pkg install linux-c7-qt linux-c7-qtwebkit linux-c7-qt-x11
```

This is also a good time to become familiar with a few commands relevant for managing a Linuxulator:

- `ldd <exe>` prints the list of dynamic libraries (`.so` files) that the binary executable `<exe>` links to (i.e., needs for its execution).

- `strings <file>` prints the strings of printable characters embedded in `<file>`, which could be a binary executable or a library.

- `brandelf <exe>` brands the binary executable `<exe>` as a particular type, with our chief concern being the Linux type: `brandelf -t Linux <exe>`. The `brandelf` executable exists because binary executables under FreeBSD can be of native type (FreeBSD) or non-native (Linux).

We'll take up a fancy, gee-whiz development environment called SlickEdit (64-bit) for our c7 exercise. SlickEdit is not available natively under FreeBSD as yet.

A 15-day trial version of SlickEdit is available at `https://www.slickedit.com/trial/slickedit`.

At the time of this writing, the following command was good for fetching the 64-bit Linux installer of SlickEdit:

```
wget https://customer.slickedit.com/assets/trial/se_22000100_linux64.tar.gz
```

You can download the tarball and unpack it with `tar -xvzf se_22000100_linux64.tar.gz`. Upon unpacking, the archive would reveal the installer executable `vsinst`. The very first thing to do is brand it using `brandelf -t Linux vsinst`.

Next up, find the dynamic libraries `vsinst` needs and not present in your box:

```
ldd -a vsinst | grep "not found" | sort | uniq
```

The list of missing libraries I pieced together using the pipeline was:

```
libICE.so.6; libSM.so.6; libX11.so.6; libXt.so.6; libxcb.so.1; libXau.so.6
```

Note that the (six) entities in the `ldd` generated list are symbolic links that point to the actual libraries. For instance, `libxcb.so.1` points to `libxcb.so.1.1.0` (as I found soon afterward).

You now have to get down to copying out the missing `.so` files from a CentOS 7 machine into your box's `/compat/linux/lib64`. Note that `ldd` does not reveal all missing `.so` dependencies in one shot—each time you copy a few libraries, you have run to `ldd` again, until it stops listing any missing dependencies. For every library copied, you also have to create a symbolic link with the name reported by `ldd` (under the same path `/compat/linux/lib64`).

When you're done, run the installer:

```
chmod +x vsinst
./vsinst
```

You can use the default installation path under `/opt`, which magically translates, courtesy of the Linux ABI, as `/compat/linux/opt`.

When installation finishes, you need to carry out the two-stage operation (`brandelf` + `ldd`) upon each executable under SlickEdit's `bin` directory `/compat/linux/opt/slickedit-pro2017/bin`. Most importantly on `vs_exe`. With each file reported as executable by the `file` command, any library reported as missing by `ldd` has to be copied under `/compat/linux/lib64` from a Linux (preferably CentOS 7) system, and its referred symbolic link created under the same directory.

When the entire operation finished on my box, `ldd` issued this warning message for `assistant_exe`:

```
/lib64/libcrypto.so.10: version 'OPENSSL_1.0.2' not found (required by /
lib64/libQtNetwork.so.4)
```

Minor mismatch in versions most of the times is not a showstopper, but this depends on a few things. So I ran `strings` to discover what OpenSSL versions the available `libcrypto.so.10` can support:

```
strings /compat/linux/lib64/libcrypto.so.10 | grep OPENSSL_1
```

The preceding `strings` command reported the following:

```
OPENSSL_1.0.1
OPENSSL_1.0.1_EC
```

This is just a minor version glitch (`1.0.1` almost equals `1.0.2`). Plus, this is with a secondary executable, not the main executable `vs_exe`. So things should be okay.

So I finally tried running SlickEdit:

```
chmod +x vs_exe
./vs_exe
```

Whoa! SlickEdit popped up, guided me through a trial license installation, and garnered me this chapter's final screenshot—Figure 8-13—generated with a GNU C project.

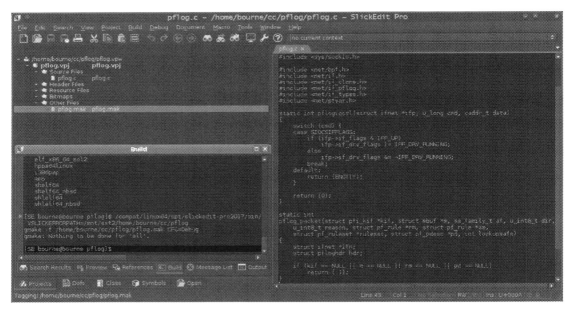

Figure 8-13. *The SlickEdit development environment under Linux ABI*

Among its many, many bells and whistles, SlickEdit can build your project with a self created and self-managed makefile. The `.mak` file selected with a mouse click in the previous screenshot is one such makefile.

SlickEdit also lets you use the debugger, record/execute macros, evaluate regular expressions, generate GUIDs—all from within its interface.

A SlickEdit license is not cheap by any means—a Pro license will set you back a cool US $300. This is all the more reason for you to finish your c7 Linuxulator skills acquisition enterprise before the trial license elapses.

8.15.3 Installing Linux ABI Applications via rpm

You will often come across Linux applications available as RPM (Red Hat Package Manager) archives. You cannot install RPMs under FreeBSD the Linux way (which first checks on dependencies). But you can extract the RPM contents and merge them into your Linuxulator. For that, you need to first install the rpm4 package, which has a bundled utility rpm2cpio.

Once rpm4 is installed, you can extract from a .rpm file:

```
cd /compat/linux
rpm2cpio < /path/to/rpm | cpio -id
```

No dependency checks are carried out in this command sequence.

For reasons unknown to me, some RPM extract operations run into rough weather with symbolic links: bin, sbin, lib, and lib64 under /compat/linux are actually symbolic links to directories with the same names under /compat/linux/usr. One (tedious) workaround is to repack the .rpm as a .tar archive, and then extract with the tar command.

For each binary executable extracted from the .rpm file, you need to carry out the same two-stage operation that we performed on vsinst while installing SlickEdit in the c7 exercise: brandelf + ldd. Any missing libraries have to be copied over from Linux and symlink'ed as indicated by ldd. When copying libraries, it's best to get them from the same Linux distribution as the Linuxulator's base.

Once this is done, you have performed the equivalent of installing the RPM under FreeBSD—and the application should work just as under Linux.

One day in the times to come, Linuxulator might advance to the stage where you can use the rpm -Uvh command under FreeBSD to directly install a .rpm file into the Linuxulator. But that perhaps is thinking a bit too far ahead for the time being.

8.16 Summary

In this chapter, we saw the power of being someone else, which sounds a bit shady in linguistic terms, but in programming terms is a boon as well as a skill to build on. If native tools are not sufficient for the job at hand, there is absolutely no sin in bringing in emulation software. On the contrary, it is a necessity. Even for non-programmers, emulation brings so much to the table that if not a matter of technical expertise, it ushers in a lot of interesting, educative fun. Wine and Linuxulator are thus here for good—and for everyone's good too.

The next chapter—Virtualization—takes emulation to a higher level of gamesmanship. Therein we will use emulation to launch not individual programs from a foreign operating system, but the foreign operating system itself.

## CHAPTER 9

Virtualization: The New Buzzword

Until just a few years back, using virtualization software was almost entirely a corporate-world phenomenon, with almost all the activity being staged under the VMware banner which was, is, and will remain closed-source and commercial.

Open-source software has now leap-frogged ahead of the rest of the pack. VirtualBox, an open-source virtualization product created by Germany's Innotek GmbH—acquired in 2008 by Sun Microsystems (which in turn was acquired by Oracle a couple of years later), now has the pole position on the virtualization grid. And it has a few other open-source applications catching up fast—KVM under Linux and BHyVe under FreeBSD. We'll start our charter with VirtualBox, and then look closely at KVM and BHyVe too.

Quite mercifully, even though virtualization is complex, state-of-the-art technology crafted by brilliant folks, using VirtualBox, KVM, and BHyVe is easy enough, as we are about to see.

9.1 What Is Virtualization (And Why Is It Important)?

Virtualization is pure emulation, which is one reason why this chapter follows immediately in the footsteps of Chapter 8, which discussed emulation.

Emulation layers like Wine and Linuxulator can launch foreign binary executables as processes using the host computer's native operating system. Executing `Notepad.exe` under Wine lends it resources like CPU time, RAM and file handles, just as for any other Unix process.

What if you wanted to execute `ntoskrnl.exe`, the Windows kernel, under Wine?

245

© Manish Jain 2018
M. Jain, *Beginning Modern Unix*, https://doi.org/10.1007/978-1-4842-3528-7_9

That sounds ridiculous: `ntoskrnl.exe` is not a normal, run-of-the-mill binary. It's a whole freaking operating system.

At second thought, why not? If you as the user are willing to dedicate all needed resources: CPU, RAM, a hard disk, serial/parallel/USB ports, and anything else needed, it should be possible to run `ntoskrnl.exe` as a subsystem of the host.

Which is precisely the situation. But since launching a foreign operating system under the host requires dedicated hardware resources at a level entirely different from emulated processes, emulation layers like Wine and Linuxulator are not enough for the mission. What we need for this is software that can do (hardware-provisioning) pure emulation, aka virtualization.

Using virtualization, you can turn your Unix box into a multi-OS system, capable of running any or all of Windows, FreeBSD, and Linux as windowed applications (or virtual machines) under the host operating system. All of them simultaneously, if you want. Figure 9-1 is proof, captured under the hood of my FreeBSD box.

Figure 9-1. *Windows, FreeBSD, and Linux running in parallel as virtual machines*

9.2 Storage for Virtual Machines

One common hardware-provisioning necessity for virtual machines is the hard disk—every operating system needs a hard disk for its installation.

The universal approach for this is to create a file a few GB in size, and then the file is presented to the virtual machine (VM in short) as a virtual hard disk. The VM considers the file as a real hard disk, partitions it accordingly, and then creates its root filesystem somewhere therein. Quite notably, the VM cannot access any other part of the host system's storage. Similarly, the host cannot access any files in the virtual hard disk.

This gets us into an important question—how do we exchange data between the VM and the host? If you need to pass in an important file from the host to the VM, or pass out a file from the VM back to the host, your virtualization software will not help you.

Networking will. If you run an FTP/SMB server on the host, the VM can download files from and upload files to the server. VirtualBox builds on the SMB server idea with its Guest Additions (GA) extension.

We'll look at VirtualBox Guest Additions too, but we'll ourselves adopt a technique that caters to all needs and situations: an anonymous FTP service, courtesy vsftpd, on the FreeBSD/Linux host. We'll tackle the FTP server first so that you can exchange data readily when you launch your first virtual machine.

9.3 Running an Anonymous FTP Server
Under FreeBSD/Linux

You can install the vsftpd package as usual. Note that under FreeBSD, you will likely need to install its extended version vsftpd-ext with the package manager, or else build the port /usr/ports/ftp/vsftpd (which means run make install therein).

Before we continue with vsftpd configuration, there's one point to note. When you have a path like /a/b/c.txt, the file c.txt is, obviously enough, located in the b directory. Another way to say the same thing is that c.txt is located in the root of the b directory. Similarly, b is located in the root of the a directory, which itself is located in the root of the / filesystem. All in all, you would now know what is meant when I say that c.txt is located in (the hierarchy of) the a directory, but not in its root.

This terminology is important because vsftpd insists that the root of its home directory, as configured in vsftpd.conf (not in /etc/passwd), must not be writeable. For example, if /usr/local/vsftp is configured in vsftpd.conf as vsftpd's home directory (which corresponds to the local_root directive), it must not be writeable. Instead, the superuser must create a subdirectory under /usr/local/vsftp and then lock the home directory itself as read-only (mode 555). The subdirectory, which is writeable, can then be used for downloads and uploads. Failure to imbibe this key concept causes acute and widespread grief, which a Google search would provide ample evidence of.

vsftpd actually needs two users and two root directories. One user is the standard user ftp (which would likely exist in your system already). The other is an unprivileged user (whom we will call ftpdummy), with a read-only and empty home directory.

We won't bother ourselves with why vsftpd needs two users and two root directories. Instead, we'll just create the layout this daemon needs, centered around a read-only home at /usr/local/ftproot, with a writeable subdirectory xfer.

We start by adding the ftpdummy user:

```
pw useradd ftpdummy -d /var/ftpdummy -s /sbin/nologin     # FreeBSD
useradd -d  /var/ftpdummy -s /usr/bin/nologin ftpdummy    # Linux
```

Continue with the following:

```
mkdir -p  /usr/local/ftproot/xfer
chown -R ftp:ftp /usr/local/ftproot
chmod 777 /usr/local/ftproot/xfer
chmod 555   /usr/local/ftproot

mkdir /var/ftpdummy 2> /dev/null
rm  -rf /var/ftpdummy/* 2> /dev/null
rm  -rf  /var/ftpdummy/.* 2> /dev/null
chown ftpdummy:ftpdummy /var/ftpdummy
chmod 555 /var/ftpdummy
```

Now, you can delete the existing contents of vsftpd.conf (which would be located under /etc or /usr/local/etc), and then put the following therein:

```
background=YES                     # For Linux, you will likely need NO
allow_writeable_chroot=YES
listen=YES
listen_ipv6=NO
anonymous_enable=YES
local_enable=YES
```

```
write_enable=YES
anon_upload_enable=YES
anon_mkdir_write_enable=YES
dirmessage_enable=YES
xferlog_enable=YES
connect_from_port_20=YES
chown_uploads=YES
chown_username=ftp
nopriv_user=ftpdummy
secure_chroot_dir=/var/ftpdummy
chroot_local_user=YES
chroot_list_enable=YES
chroot_list_file=/etc/chroot_list
anon_root=/usr/local/ftproot
local_root=/usr/local/ftproot
```

It's time to start the service.

Under FreeBSD, you can do that with:

```
echo 'vsftpd_enable=YES' >> /etc/rc.conf
service vsftpd start
```

Under Linux, you can use the command chain underneath:

```
systemctl enable vsftpd && systemctl start vsftpd
```

If pgrep -x vsftpd now prints a PID, your anonymous FTP service is up and running. If not, try flipping the background setting from YES to NO, or the other way round.

From the client side, wget and wput will log in automatically when downloading/uploading respectively. If you need to log in to and browse the FTP site hierarchy, use these credentials:

```
username=anonymous     # you can also username=ftp and password=@
password=X@Y.Z         # where X, Y, Z could be anything you like
```

You can download from the server with wget, upload with wput, and browse the FTP site hierarchy with ncftp, or any FTP client of your choice.

Do not place any downloadable data in the root of /usr/local/ftproot. Instead, place it in the xfer subdirectory (and chown it over to the ftp user immediately; otherwise clients won't be able to download it). If and when needed, you can create additional subdirectories under /usr/local/ftproot, although this book will assume that xfer is the only one.

If your box's IP address is 192.168.1.3, wget on the client side should download from ftp://192.168.1.3/xfer/, and wput should upload to that URL as well.

One caveat here is that a VM running under your host might not see the pristine host IP address if the VM gets subnetted by the virtualization software differently, which happens with VirtualBox as well as KVM.

If you use VirtualBox, the application would convert your host IP address, 192.168.1.3 for example, to a default router/gateway address, usually 10.0.2.2, and the VM itself would have an IP in the 10.0.2.* range. In such a case, wget and wput can exchange data with the host's vsftpd via the default router IP address (10.0.2.2), and not the pristine host IP (192.168.1.3).

The following shell functions, which use the default VirtualBox host gateway address 10.0.2.2, are a great convenience when inside a VM:

```
pull()
{
        [ -n "$1" ] && wget ftp://10.0.2.2/xfer/"$1"
}

push()
{
        [ -f "$1" ] && wput "$1" ftp://10.0.2.2/xfer/
}
```

For BHyVe, use the host IP address as it is in place of 10.0.2.2.

9.4 VirtualBox

9.4.1 Installing VirtualBox

Although VirtualBox usage is exactly the same across the Unixes, installation methodology varies owing to differences in how the product is packaged.

9.4.1.1 Installing Under FreeBSD

Installing VirtualBox under FreeBSD couldn't be easier:

```
pkg install virtualbox-ose
```

Add the following line to /boot/loader.conf:

```
vboxdrv_load=YES
```

Add the following line to /etc/rc.conf:

```
vboxnet_enable=YES
```

The loader.conf entry is optional if the rc.conf entry is in place. Once the install finishes, add your normal user account to the vboxusers group:

```
pw groupmod vboxusers -m <normal>
```

Reboot the system. Upon reboot, run this command to determine whether VirtualBox kernel modules have been loaded correctly:

```
kldstat | grep vbox
```

If you get three lines (something like this), your VirtualBox enterprise is ready:

15	3	0xffffffff81c62000	4e760	vboxdrv.ko
16	2	0xffffffff81cb1000	2a02	vboxnetflt.ko
19	1	0xffffffff81cc5000	3f64	vboxnetadp.ko

9.4.1.2 Installing Under Ubuntu

For Ubuntu Linux, VirtualBox installation needs a bit more work. Recommending the default VirtualBox pre-packaged in Ubuntu is less than ideal: it tends to be fairly out-of-date. If you use the following steps, you'll get a newer version of VirtualBox (5.2 at the time of this writing, compared to 5.0 available right now in the Ubuntu repositories).

First add this line to /etc/apt/sources.list:

```
deb http://download.virtualbox.org/virtualbox/debian <dist> contrib
```

Replace <dist> to match your Ubuntu version (check it via uname -a):

Ubuntu 17.04 → zesty

Ubuntu 17.10 → artful

Ubuntu 16.10 → yakkety

Ubuntu 16.04 → xenial

You can continue with VirtualBox installation as follows:

```
wget -q https://www.virtualbox.org/download/oracle_vbox_2016.asc -O- | \
sudo apt-key add -


wget -q https://www.virtualbox.org/download/oracle_vbox.asc -O- | \
sudo apt-key add -

sudo apt update
sudo apt upgrade                    # Very important for VirtualBox
```

Reboot. Don't forget to reboot at this point.

Upon reboot, search for the highest VirtualBox version available with:

```
apt search virtualbox | grep "Oracle VM VirtualBox"
```

(When this chapter was being written, 5.2 was the highest version available).

You can now install VirtualBox with:

```
sudo apt-get install virtualbox-5.2 virtualbox-dkms
# Replace 5.2 with the highest version you got with 'apt search'
```

Reboot again.

9.4.1.3 Installing Under Arch Linux

For Arch Linux, first update/upgrade the system with: pacman -Syyu

A system-wide upgrade is very important for a good VirtualBox installation. Then you must reboot. Some folks take reboots lightly. Some folks then ask wonderful questions at VirtualBox/Unix user forums. The answer always is: after a system upgrade, kindly reboot.

Next up, you'll need to get the supporting setup for your kernel version:

```
ver='uname -r | sed 's/\.//' | sed 's/\..*//''      # Got me 49
pacman -S linux${ver}-headers linux${ver}-virtualbox-host-modules
```

You are now ready to install VirtualBox:

```
pacman  -S  virtualbox-host-dkms  virtualbox
```

Reboot the system again. Under Linux (any), after you have rebooted the system (post VirtualBox-installation), check the output of: `lsmod | grep 'ˆvbox'`

You should get at least four lines, something like this:

```
Vboxpci        24576     0
Vboxnetflt     28672     0
Vboxnetadp     28672     0
Vboxdrv       393216     3     vboxnetadp,vboxnetflt,vboxpci
```

If the modules are loaded correctly (as per the `lsmod` output), add your normal user account to the `vboxusers` group: `usermod -a -G vboxusers <normal>`.

You can now happily use VirtualBox (as the normal user).

9.4.2 Hosting Your First VirtualBox Virtual Machine

We'll take up the exercise of creating a Linux Mint VM—or *guest*, as VirtualBox prefers to call it. You can use any Linux distribution for the guest—Linux Mint (in its Cinnamon incarnation) just happens to be a personal favorite of mine.

You can also use any operating system as the host, although I will be using FreeBSD that enables me to follow up on my promise in Chapter 7 ("The Best of the Graphical Unix World") where I obliged myself to elucidate using the Tor browser with FreeBSD, which does not yet have a native Tor port and must therefore use Linux services for BitTorrent fishing.

The first thing to do is get the ISO for the latest Linux Mint installer. At the time of this writing, 18.3 was the freshest release available at Linux Mint's downloads page: `https://linuxmint.com/download.php`.

Click the Verify Your ISO link and save the file `sha256sum.txt` so that you can later verify your ISO download. Then copy the link for the ISO, and fire up `wget -c <iso>`, where `<iso>` is the URL copied. If 18.3 Cinnamon (64-bit) is just what you need, you can use this direct link which delves into Manitoba User Group repository:

```
http://muug.ca/mirror/linuxmint/iso/stable/18.3/linuxmint-18.3-cinnamon-
64bit.iso
```

Once you have a good ISO (cross-checked via its sha256 sum), click New at the top-left corner of the VirtualBox window. Enter mint in the Name field and then click Next.

Refer to Figure 9-2, where the buttons you need to click are circled.

Figure 9-2. *New virtual machine: Step 1*

The name you choose for the VM plays a role in itself. VirtualBox has smart type-deduction heuristics based on the name: the software automatically adjusts the Type and Version of the VM accordingly. If the heuristics don't work well for you, you can choose the Type (operating system type: Windows or Linux or BSD, and a few more choices) and the Version (bitness and flavor) yourself from the drop-down lists.

The next screen is for the amount of RAM to be allocated to the VM. Figure 9-3 furnishes the relevant illustration.

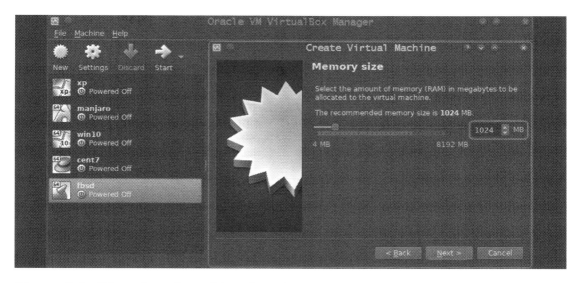

Figure 9-3. *New virtual machine: Step 2*

I have some notes here.

- In general, if you are using virtualization software, your host system must have at least 8GB of physical memory. With 4GB, you can make do if you have a swap partition and you don't try to set up memory hoggers (e.g., Windows 10).

- You should limit any VM to a cap of 25% of the system's total physical RAM. With 8GB RAM in the host, any VM should thus get a maximum of 2GB. An exception is Windows 10, a VM of which demands 3GB+ for smooth running.

- VirtualBox default RAM allocation is usually fine—just a bit on the conservative side. You can, if you want, add a few more megabytes to the default RAM value, keeping the preceding couple of points in mind.

- Unlike the virtual disk image size, the RAM allocation for a VM can be increased (or decreased) later too.

Tune the RAM setting for the guest as it suits you and then click Next.

Figure 9-4 starts to tackle the file that will be fed to the VM as its hard disk.

Figure 9-4. *New virtual machine: Step 3*

Since this is your first VM, you must use the default, which says Create a Virtual Hard Disk Now. But as you start using VirtualBox regularly, you will adapt to reusing existing images. For the moment, we must simply choose to create a new disk and then click Create.

The next three screens are for the disk file's format, storage type, and finally its size.

On the first screen—refer to Figure 9-5—the default selection VDI usually is just right for VirtualBox. So we'll just use that and click Next here.

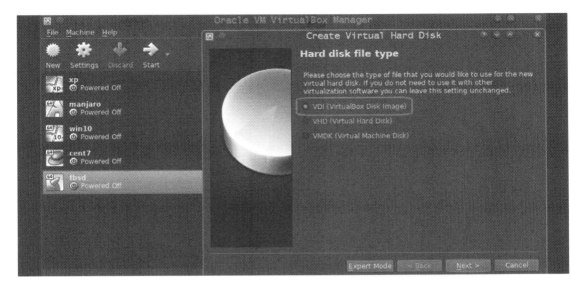

Figure 9-5. *New virtual machine: Step 4*

The second screen is a significant one: should VirtualBox immediately eat up all of the disk space allocated (Fixed Size), or should VirtualBox allocate disk space for the VM incrementally and only as needed (dynamically allocated)? See Figure 9-6.

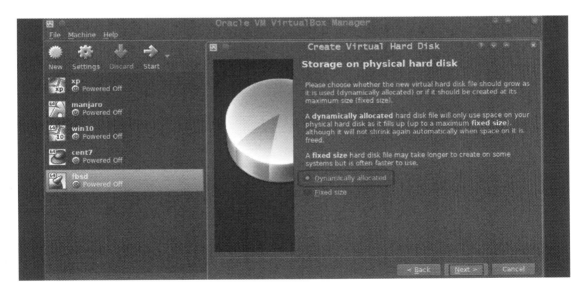

Figure 9-6. *New virtual machine: Step 5*

There are advantages as well disadvantages to both. For the moment, we'll play along with the default choice for dynamic allocation (which allocates only a few MB upfront for a virtual hard disk image sized 10GB or even more) and then click Next.

The final screen, Figure 9-7, is for the maximum disk size.

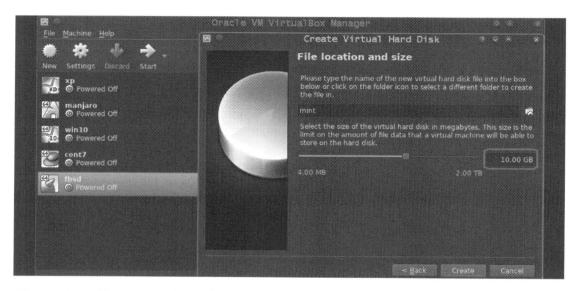

Figure 9-7. *New virtual machine: Step 6*

The size mandated in the previous step is the maximum allocation. Even if the VDI is dynamically allocated, you cannot get anything beyond this limit. The point is most significant for VM types (e.g., Windows 10) which hog disk space. A Windows 10 C: drive needs at least 50GB in production usage. So be careful when setting the VDI size. VirtualBox's default value for maximum disk size suits an experimental VM.

When you click Create (see Figure 9-7), a new VM disk will hit your filesystem headlines.

Refer to Figure 9-8. With the new VM (mint) selected in the list of guests (extreme left), click Settings ➤ Storage. Under the Controller: IDE section, you will find a CD icon labeled Empty. This device will be passed to the VM as its optical drive. Click Empty and then use the CD icon (extreme right) to browse for the ISO downloaded.

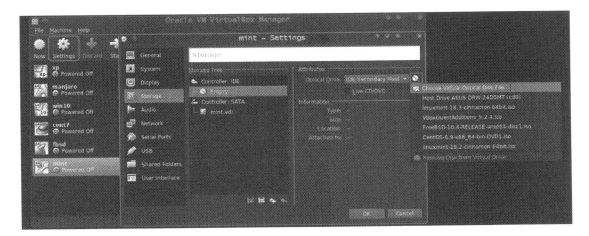

Figure 9-8. *New virtual machine: Step 7*

When Empty changes to the ISO's name, you are ready to flag off the VM. With all due respect to Figure 9-9, all you need to do for that is click the Start button (left), and Mint greetings will pop up in a new window (right).

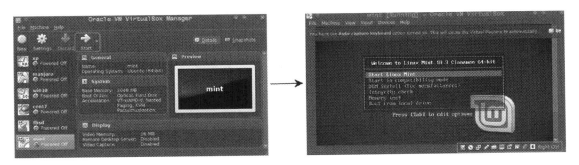

Figure 9-9. *New virtual machine: Step 8*

Just click Start Linux Mint and install Linux as usual.

The bottom bar of the VM window contains a control toolbox (the circled rectangle in the previous image). You don't need to be familiar with the toolbox immediately, but just remember that a toolbox exists for controlling and getting information about many VM parameters, for example, its Ethernet interface's IP address, or settings for capturing its video in a file on the host.

Complete the installation in the virtual machine. Then, upon the VM's reboot, we immediately delve into our Tor mission. In the Linux VM, you can use Firefox to open Tor's download URL: `https://www.torproject.org/download/download.html.en`

At the time of this writing, 7.0.11 was the newest version, which you can `wget` with this link: `https://www.torproject.org/dist/torbrowser/7.0.11/tor-browser-linux64-7.0.11_en-US.tar.xz`

It's embarrassingly simple hereon:

```
unxz tor-browser-linux64-7.0.11_en-US.tar.xz
tar xf tor-browser-linux64-7.0.11_en-US.tar
mv tor-browser_en-US ~/Desktop/
```

Open `~/Desktop/tor-browser_en-US` in Nemo (or any file browser) and double-click the Setup link. Tor will ask you to connect to the Tor network. All that you have to do for that is click Connect.

When you're connected, you can type `https://thepiratebay.org` into Tor's address bar, press Enter and there you are, where Figure 9-10 suggests you ought to be now.

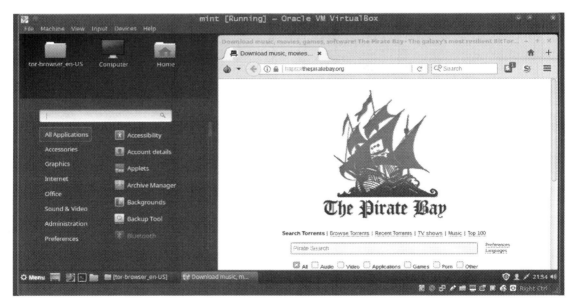

Figure 9-10. *Pirate Bay visited in a Linux virtual machine*

9.4.3 Exchanging Files with the VirtualBox Host

VirtualBox acts as a DHCP server for any of its virtual machines. The application converts your host IP address, `192.168.1.3` for example, to a default router/gateway address. That address typically is `10.0.2.2`, and the VM itself would have an IP in the `10.0.2.*` subnet.

If you are unsure of what IP address denotes the host inside a VM, use the following command (in the VM) to get the default router IP:

```
ipconfig    # Windows VM
ip route show    # Linux VM
bsdconfig  networking → Default  Router/Gateway    # FreeBSD VM
```

Once you have the default router IP address, ping it:

```
ping 10.0.2.2
```

If ping succeeds and your host's `vsftpd` server is up, you can download files to the VM with `wget` and upload to the host with `wput`:

```
wget ftp://10.0.2.2/xfer/.bashrc    # works only if a .bashrc lies under
                                           xfer/
wput tor-browser-linux64-7.0.11_en-US.tar ftp://10.0.2.2/xfer/
```

9.4.4 VirtualBox Extensions

Installing VirtualBox extensions is entirely optional. Extensions don't affect essential VirtualBox usage in any way, which is why this discussion was deferred.

While USB mouse and keyboard work out-of-the-box (as OHCI, aka USB1, devices) under the basic VirtualBox suite, other devices don't. Nor can you use EHCI (USB2) or XHCI (USB3) modes for any USB devices.

If you need to pass other USB devices (i.e., other than mouse and keyboard) to your virtual machines, or use EHCI/XHCI functionality in VirtualBox, you need to install the VirtualBox USB extension pack, which is closed-source.

The extension pack can be downloaded at the URL:

```
https://www.virtualbox.org/wiki/Downloads
```

The VirtualBox USB extension pack does not yet work under FreeBSD hosts. This is a fairly sore sticking point that Oracle has not yet addressed. It can reasonably be hoped that Oracle will enable the extension pack for FreeBSD too in the days to come, just as reasonably as can be feared that Oracle never will.

The USB extension pack version must match the VirtualBox version installed on your box. If your VirtualBox is 5.2.* (5 = major version; 2 = minor release; * = patch level), the USB extension pack version too must be 5.2.something (otherwise, VirtualBox will abort the extension pack installation). The patch level usually does not matter.

Double-click on the extension pack (.vbox-extpack) file to install it. With the USB extension pack installed, you can pass in sundry USB devices from the host to any VirtualBox guest, whereupon the device becomes unavailable in the host until detached from the guest.

Figure 9-11 shows a USB pen drive (HP) being passed to the Linux Mint VM.

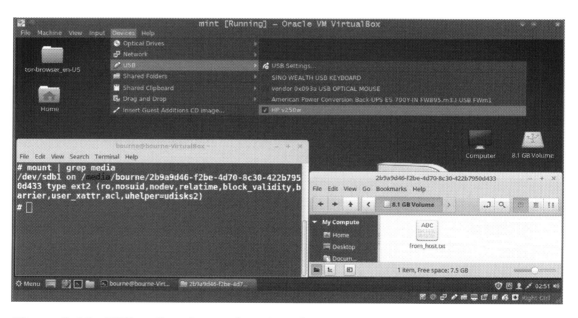

Figure 9-11. *USB redirection under VirtualBox*

Perhaps the greatest use of the extension pack would be to pass a USB device not yet supported under Unix to a Windows VM via VirtualBox USB redirection. Printers and scanners can work in that fashion.

Another closed-source extension pack is the Guest Additions (GA) ISO. Among other benefits it begets, GA enables VirtualBox hosts to pass part of their filesystems as SMB shares, wherein the guest can copy/paste files.

To download the ISO image, visit VirtualBox's download URL in your browser:
`http://download.virtualbox.org/virtualbox/`

Navigate into the directory for the highest release available, wherein you will find the Guest Additions ISO.

If it suits you, you can directly `wget` the following link:

`http://download.virtualbox.org/virtualbox/5.2.4/VBoxGuestAdditions_5.2.4.iso`

This link should work well for everyone (at least so for a while) because the GA version can be different from the version of the host's VirtualBox installation.

Linux distributions often make the Guest Additions ISO, and occasionally the USB extension pack too, available as packages. If so, you can choose either way to get them: directly from VirtualBox website or from your distribution's repositories.

Once you have the Guest Additions ISO, you need to pass it in to each VirtualBox VM that you would like to use the GA for. Passing in the ISO to a VM is the same as passing in an ISO image for any OS installer. Refer to the next image, Figure 9-12.

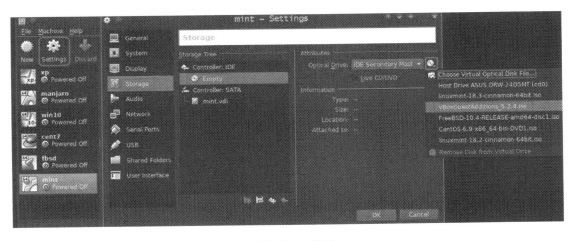

Figure 9-12. *Passing in the Guest Additions ISO to a guest*

(Note that you cannot pass the Guest Additions ISO in any meaningful way to FreeBSD guests.)

You then need to start the VM, upon which a Windows VM would mount the ISO automatically. A Linux VM usually would auto-mount it as well, or otherwise you can mount `/dev/sr0` yourself somewhere (as a device of type `iso9660`).

Finally, execute from the mount's root:

```
VBoxWindowsAdditions-x86.exe    # Windows 32-bit VM
VBoxWindowsAdditions-amd64.exe   # Windows 64-bit VM
Sh ./VBoxLinuxAdditions.run    # Linux VM
```

With Guest Additions installed in a virtual machine, VirtualBox will act as an SMB server for the guest while it is running.

You can navigate to the VM's settings in VirtualBox on the host, choose Shared Folders and browse to add a share-able directory path. That directory will become an SMB share for the VM.

The next screenshot, Figure 9-13, illustrates a directory /mnt/ext2/dumps being shared with the Linux Mint guest.

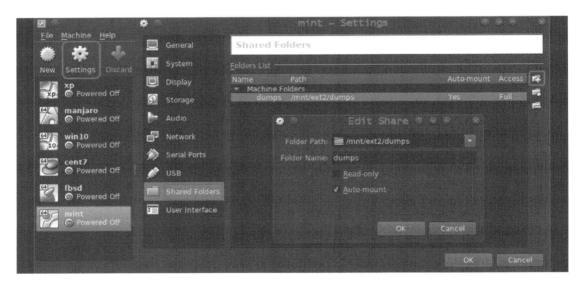

Figure 9-13. *Adding a new VirtualBox shared folder*

Figure 9-13 also flaunts an inset properties window for the directory dumps shared in the main window. As the inset shows, each share has a few options—Name, Read-only (default is read+write), and Auto-mount (default is manual mount).

A Windows VM will automatically pick up a share (as drive D: or E:) if you choose auto-mounting, while Linux would usually auto-mount it somewhere under /media.

If auto-mounting is not available, you can mount the SMB share yourself in Windows as well as in Linux:

```
net use x: \\vboxsvr\dumps        # Windows VM
mount -t vboxsf dumps /mnt/something       # Linux VM

# Note that dumps is the Folder Name of the directory shared in the last
image
```

Under a Linux VM, you can make things a touch easier for yourself by adding your normal user account to the vboxsf group: usermod -a -G vboxsf <normal>

Since we can already exchange files with the host via FTP, the more important aspect of GA is sharing clipboard buffers between host and guest. You can enable clipboard sharing under the Settings ➤ General ➤ Advanced tab. See Figure 9-14.

Figure 9-14. *Sharing the clipboard in VirtualBox*

You can tweak any of the numerous settings VirtualBox makes available. The USB and Shared Folders settings are relevant only with the USB extension pack installed on the host and Guest Additions installed in the guest, respectively.

9.5 KVM

KVM, short for Kernel-based Virtual Machine, is an offshoot of the long-standing virtualization suite qemu. While qemu is largely distribution-independent, KVM is almost entirely a Linux phenomenon with hooks into the Linux kernel that go deep.

This section is being written under a Linux AMD64 (Mint Cinnamon) host, which we will use to illustrate KVM usage. We'll fire up the old workhorse, Windows XP (i386), as a virtual machine. If you don't have the Windows XP installer ISO, you can use something else and then adjust accordingly.

KVM uses a graphics system named Spice, which has a server of its own and many client applications. Currently, KVM and Spice are both under intense development, so you may need to improvise on the following steps, mostly when you run into errors launching the VM. (I'll later mention a couple of errors I got with two KVM runs, each upon a clean, new install.) If you run into errors, Google is your best friend.

The first thing to do is get KVM, along with the widely needed associate packages. You can install the following list with your distribution's package manager:

```
qemu-kvm qemu-utils virt-manager spice-client-gtk spice-vdagent
```

The `qemu-utils` package contains a utility `qemu-img`, which you can use to create a fully pre-allocated virtual hard disk file:

```
qemu-img create -o size=6G -o preallocation=full xp.qcow2
```

That creates a disk file of size 6GB. For production, at least triple that size.

Next up, start `virt-manager` from the Applications menu or from the shell. From the manager's menus, choose File ➤ New Virtual Machine.

The following screenshots, cobbled up as the patchwork image in Figure 9-15, and the ensuing notes should now be good enough.

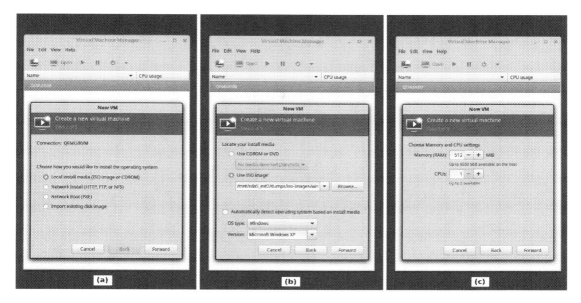

Figure 9-15. *Creating a new virtual machine in KVM: screens a through c*

(a)   Local install media is just what we want.

(b)   Choose Use ISO Image. Then choose Browse, and Browse Local, and then browse for the Windows XP installer ISO. Turn off Automatically Detect Operating System Based On Install Media, and choose Windows and Microsoft Windows XP from the drop-down lists.

(c)   The defaults are fine.

Refer to Figure 9-16 for the next few steps.

(d)   Choose Select or create custom storage. Then click Manage and
then Browse local. Browse to locate the `xp.qcow2` virtual hard disk
we created previously.

(e)   The defaults are fine. Take a deep breath and click Finish,
whereupon a new window with Windows XP setup running will
hopefully greet you, as shown in Figure 9-16(f).

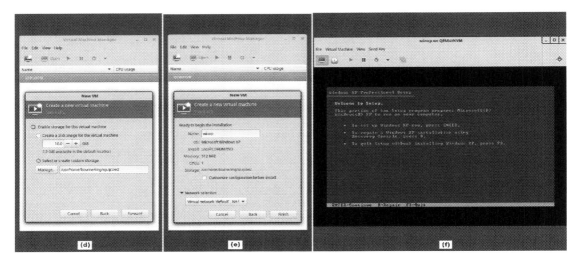

Figure 9-16.   *Creating a new virtual machine in KVM: d through f*

Figure 9-16(e) is the stage where things can go wrong— when you click Finish. I had
to solve the following in two separate KVM runs:

```
Error opening Spice console: SpiceClientGtk missing
Error connecting to graphical console: could not get a reference to type
class
```

Solving such problems calls upon you to search for and install any Spice packages
that you think might help. It further helps if you, after installing a few packages, restart
KVM or even reboot.

When you get the Windows XP setup window, you can go through the Windows
installation procedure as usual. Once the installation finishes, reboot the virtual
machine.

Note   Clipboard sharing between the Linux host and the new VM will not work until you download and install (in the virtual machine) the Spice Guest Tools executable from `https://www.spice-space.org/download/binaries/spice-guest-tools/`.

The Windows link for the latest Guest Tools executable is `https://www.spice-space.org/download/binaries/spice-guest-tools/spice-guest-tools-latest.exe`.

Upon VM reboot, open a command prompt (in Windows) to check your VM's IP configuration and your connectivity with the `vsftpd` server on the host, accessible at the Default Gateway IP address reported by `ipconfig`. Refer to Figure 9-17.

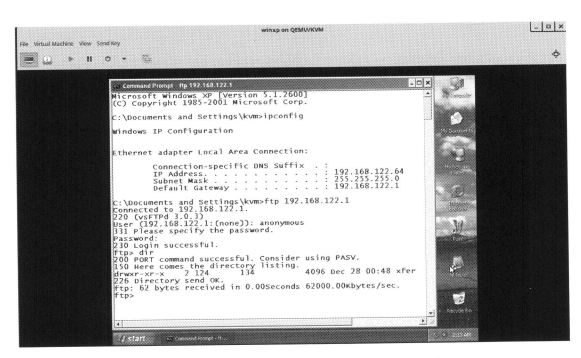

Figure 9-17. *Checking IP configuration in a KVM virtual machine*

If you need to redirect a USB device to the VM, choose Virtual Machine → Redirect USB Device and then select the device to be redirected. Refer to Figure 9-18.

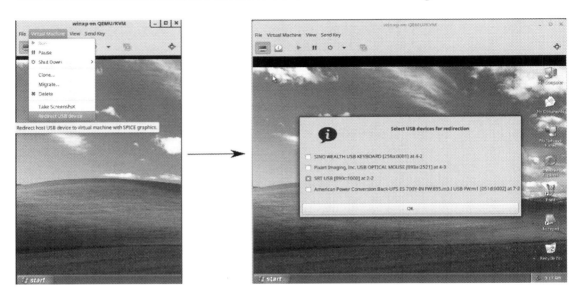

Figure 9-18.   *USB redirection in KVM*

9.6 BHyVe

Just as KVM is largely specific to Linux, BHyVe is specific to FreeBSD. Not surprising at all because BHyVe stands for BSD Hypervisor, which—a bit surprisingly—was created not by FreeBSD, but at NetApp Inc. Its authors were Peter Grehan `<grehan@ FreeBSD.org>` and Neel Natu `<neel@FreeBSD.org>`, both NetApp developers.

BHyVe is a command-line oriented virtualization product, bundled with the FreeBSD distribution. As BHyVe's popularity with users grows, FreeBSD might create X frontends for it. Until such time, users will have to rely on the shell for VM invocation, which actually makes scripting as well as documenting BHyVe much easier.

BHyVe's VM itself can be graphical. We'll be setting up a Windows 10 virtual machine for illustration. To go through this exercise, you need to have a Windows 10 installer ISO along with its product keys.

Since BHyVe does not have a graphics system, the user has to plug into the virtual machine's graphics with RDP (Remote Desktop Protocol) or with a VNC (Virtual Network Computing) client. We will use TigerVNC for this discussion.

To make good use of BHyVe, you need to be on FreeBSD 11.0 or better. (Under FreeBSD 10.x, you will be limited to console-mode virtual machines.) You might even consider running FreeBSD-CURRENT to get the best of BHyVe.

Even more importantly for running BHyVe, your CPU and motherboard must be fairly recent (manufactured 2012 or later) with support for virtualization technologies like Extended Page Tables (EPT). There's a couple of things to do to determine if BHyVe will work well for you:

1. `dmesg | grep POPCNT` should get you a line, something like this:

   ```
   Features2=0x802009<SSE3,MON,CX16,POPCNT>
   ```

If it does, you CPU seems to be good for BHyVe.

2. `kldload vmm; kldstat -n vmm` should get a couple of lines, something like this:

   ```
   Id Refs Address              Size   Name

   38     1 0xffffffff81f4d000 1b0c17 vmm.ko
   ```

If so, your motherboard has virtualization features enabled.

vmm—short for Virtual Machine Management—is the single most important kernel module when virtualizing with BHyVe under FreeBSD.

Note   FreeBSD 11.0 and up can be expected to have graphics support bundled in for bhyve as shipped with the base distribution. In case graphics support is missing, you can install BHyVe graphics support with:

```
svnlite co http://svn.freebsd.org/base/projects/bhyve_graphics
```

```
cd bhyve_graphics
make BHYVE_SYSDIR=/usr/src/ -m /usr/src/share/mk
```

Copy the bhyve executable over the one shipped under `/usr/sbin`.

The first thing to do is create the tap0 device and insert it into a bridge that will provide networking to the VM:

```
kldload vmm
kldload nmdm
kldload if_bridge
kldload   if_tap

ifconfig tap0 create
sysctl net.link.tap.up_on_open=1
echo 'net.link.tap.up_on_open=1' >> /etc/sysctl.conf
ifconfig bridge0 create
ifconfig bridge0 addm re0 addm tap0 # Change re0 to your NIC's name
ifconfig   bridge0   up
```

Append the following lines to /boot/loader.conf:

```
vmm_load=YES
nmdm_load=YES
if_bridge_load=YES
if_tap_load=YES
```

Append the following lines to /etc/rc.conf:

```
cloned_interfaces="bridge0 tap0"
ifconfig_bridge0="addm re0 addm tap0" # Change re0 to your NIC's name
```

Reboot.

Upon reboot, you need to get the version (118) of virtio (a library for a virtual machine's input-output and networking functions) that works well with Windows 10. The virtio URL is so long that it has to be broken up over three lines:

```
FEDGROUPS=https://fedorapeople.org/groups
V118DIR=virt/virtio-win/direct-downloads/archive-virtio/virtio-
win-0.1.118-2 V118FILE=virtio-win-0.1.118.iso

V118URL=${FEDGROUPS}/${V118DIR}/${V118FILE}
```

You can now run wget $V118URL.

You next need to get BHyVe UEFI/firmware packages. It does not hurt to get some additional packages: vm-bhyve (a BHyVe VM manager) and grub2-bhyve (for booting a Linux VM):

```
pkg install uefi-edk2-bhyve bhyve-firmware vm-bhyve grub2-bhyve
```

The final package to get is TigerVNC, which will get us a view of the Windows 10 VM:

```
pkg install tigervnc
```

We can now flag off our VM with:

```
truncate -s 15G bhyve.img
```

This creates a virtual hard disk that is 15GB in size. For production usage, a Windows 10 VM should be at least 50GB.

We'll need to boot the VM (named win10 in our commands below) four times—once for Windows installation, once (and another time because of a reboot that happens automatically) for virtio installation, and once is the normal boot-off-hard-disk-only.

BOOT 1:

```
bhyve -c 1 -m 4G -H -w \
  -s 0,hostbridge \
  -s 3,ahci-cd,win10.iso \
  -s 4,ahci-hd,bhyve.img \
  -s 5,virtio-net,tap0 \
  -s 29,fbuf,tcp=0.0.0.0:5900,wait \
  -s 30,xhci,tablet \
  -s 31,lpc \
  -l com1,stdio \
  -l  bootrom,/usr/local/share/uefi-firmware/BHYVE_UEFI.fd  \
  win10
```

In a separate terminal, run the command vncviewer. Put your host's IP address in the VNC Server field, and then click Connect. (This is something you have to do each time you launch the BHyVe VM.) Figure 9-19 illustrates the step.

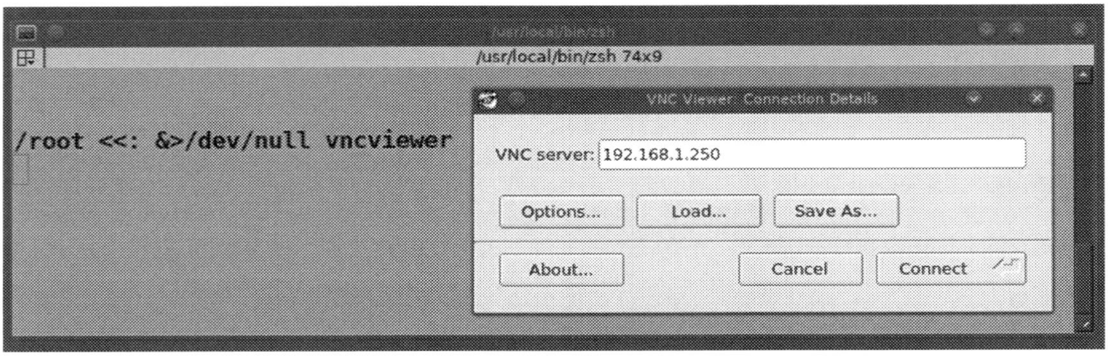

Figure 9-19. *Connecting to a graphical virtual machine with TigerVNC*

Then in the VNC window, go through the complete Windows 10 installation and let the TigerVNC window close by itself once installation completes.

We will now replace the Windows ISO with the virtio ISO to install network drivers in the virtual machine.

BOOT 2 (and 3, because 2 will reboot on its own after a while):

```
bhyve -c 1 -m 4G -H -w \
  -s 0,hostbridge \
  -s 3,ahci-cd,virtio-win-0.1.118.iso \
  -s 4,ahci-hd,bhyve.img \
  -s 5,virtio-net,tap0 \
  -s 29,fbuf,tcp=0.0.0.0:5900,wait \
  -s 30,xhci,tablet \
  -s 31,lpc \
  -l com1,stdio \
  -l  bootrom,/usr/local/share/uefi-firmware/BHYVE_UEFI.fd  \
  win10
```

Log in using TigerVNC. Then open the CD drive in Windows Explorer, go into the NetKVM/w10/amd64 directory, right-click on netkvm[.inf] and select Install. This should install the Ethernet drivers that can use the host system's bridge and bring your Windows networking up (possibly after a couple of minutes).

Once the network icon in the Windows taskbar changes to a "good" one (meaning you're connected), you need to shut down the VM.

There are two ways you can shut down a BHyVe VM:

- Power off the VM using the VM's own shutdown function. For our exercise, this means powering off using the Start menu of Windows 10.

- Close the VNC window and then run the following commands:

```
kill -9 'pgrep -x bhyve'
bhyvectl --destroy --vm=win10
```

The first one should be your preferred way to shut the VM down. Also note that VM destruction with bhyvectl is not needed if the host itself shuts down (or reboots).

We are now ready for the final launch.

BOOT 4:

```
bhyve -c 1 -m 4G -H -w \
  -s 0,hostbridge \
  -s 4,ahci-hd,bhyve.img \
  -s 5,virtio-net,tap0 \
  -s 29,fbuf,tcp=0.0.0.0:5900,wait \
  -s 30,xhci,tablet \
  -s 31,lpc \
  -l com1,stdio \
  -l  bootrom,/usr/local/share/uefi-firmware/BHYVE_UEFI.fd  \
  win10
```

This is the stage where we would like to be absolutely sure that Windows' network works flawlessly: Internet connectivity and connectivity with the host's anonymous FTP server (vsftpd).

The next, unadulterated, screenshot allays all fears.

- BBC's homepage opens in a flash in Microsoft Edge.

- ipconfig shows that the VM has an IP address in the host system's subnet as it is. This means that the vsftpd service should be accessible at the pristine host IP address.

- Windows' ftp command sees the xfer subdirectory of the FTP server after logging in anonymously at the host IP address (unaltered).

Figure 9-20 captures Windows 10 under sail, with BHyVe at the rudder.

Figure 9-20. *Windows 10 virtual machine running under BHyVe*

There's one point you might like to note about our list of arguments for the bhyve command:

```
-s 29,fbuf,tcp=0.0.0.0:5900,wait
```

The point of interest is the wait option utilized at the end. What this option means is that the VM will wait for a VNC connection to be established before kicking off its booting sequence. This is optional. You can, when sure that your virtual machine is running flawlessly, change that part of the argument list to:

```
-s 29,fbuf,tcp=0.0.0.0:5900
```

One area where BHyVe lags behind both VirtualBox and KVM is USB redirection, which currently is not implemented. But this is under active and intense development. It can be hoped that by the time FreeBSD 12 graduates from CURRENT to RELEASE, USB redirection under BHyVe would work at a par with its peers.

Clipboard sharing can be made to work for the BHyVe VM. In theory this should be possible with VNC itself, but I could never get clipboard sharing to work under VNC. The solid way to do this is RDP (Remote Desktop Protocol).

To use RDP for the Windows 10 VM, start it under TigerVNC one final time. In the VM, right-click Windows' Start menu and choose System ➤ Remote settings. Under the Remote Desktop section, tick the box for Allow remote connections to this computer, and then click Apply. Figure 9-21 illustrates what is to be done.

Figure 9-21. *Enabling Windows 10 RDP*

Also note the IP address of the VM with the `ipconfig` command. This IP will serve as the RDP server in our RDP connection.

Power off the VM. You can next install Remmina, the bellwether RDP application, with:

```
pkg install remmina freerdp remmina-plugin-rdp
```

Start the VM with the `wait` option removed. Here is the entire `bhyve` command for ease of reference:

```
bhyve -c 1 -m 4G -H -w \
  -s 0,hostbridge \
  -s 4,ahci-hd,bhyve.img \
```

```
-s 5,virtio-net,tap0 \
-s 29,fbuf,tcp=0.0.0.0:5900 \
-s 30,xhci,tablet \
-s 31,lpc \
-l com1,stdio \
-l bootrom,/usr/local/share/uefi-firmware/BHYVE_UEFI.fd  \
win10
```

You can now invoke `remmina` and click the + sign at the top-left corner (with RDP selected as the protocol).

Figure 9-22 shows the fields being filled in as needed.

Figure 9-22. *Using Remmina to create an RDP connection*

Use the Windows 10 VM's IP address in the Server field, and Protocol must be RDP. The User Name and User Password are your Windows 10 login credentials. Domain should be `WORKGROUP`, unless you changed the VM's domain configuration.

When you log in with RDP, clipboard sharing will work.

9.7 Summary

The world of computers has long been fettered by commercial giants whose chief purpose is maximization of revenue. AT&T, Microsoft, and Apple have all tried to exploit their hold on computer users in various, often ludicrously petty, ways that never targeted the broader interests: growth and spread of computing fundamentals and technologies.

As the power of open-source shows, top-flight technologies like virtualization need a sound foundation, and then a go-together spirit with the masses to succeed. Developers create and users use—and then earnestly report back problems and feature requests. And this happens.

VirtualBox, KVM, and BHyVe will all live in the annals as virtualization pioneers. It actually suits the user to have so many high-quality products to choose from. If one does not work well for a given need, something else will.

PART 3

Preparing for Part III

To proceed further into the last phase of your Unix essay—programming with Unix—you need three commands in your system: c++, dialog, and valac.

Note the following:

- Yes, we'll be using the C++ compiler (c++/g++), not cc or gcc.

- FreeBSD always has dialog as well as c++ in its base system.

- All commands are available (either already installed or can be downloaded) under Unix as well the Unix emulator Cygwin (and its fork Babun too).

Here are notes for installation (if and as needed) of c++, dialog, and valac:

- The dialog command always corresponds to the package dialog. If your box is missing the dialog command, just install the package with the same name.

- The C++ compiler is typically available under FreeBSD as well as Linux. It might be a command named c++ or g++.

- If there is no C++ compiler in your system, you can try the package names: (in order of package name to be tried first) clang, g++, gcc-g++, and gcc.

- The valac command is in a package named either vala or valac.

Here's a quick reminder of package search-and-install functions under Unix.

To search for a package named foo:		To install the package foo:	
pkg search foo	# FreeBSD	pkg install foo	# FreeBSD
apt search foo	# Linux (Ubuntu)	apt install foo	# Linux (Ubuntu)
pacman -Ss foo	# Linux (Arch)		
pact find foo	# Babun	pacman -S foo	# Linux (Arch)
		pact install foo	# Babun

## CHAPTER 10

Advanced Techniques in Shell Scripting

The title of this chapter is misleading—by design, too. The word "advanced" usually is taken to mean "difficult to understand" and/or "not essential". This chapter is neither of those—the whole chapter is easy to understand, and the first half is essential to understand as well.

While you can write elementary scripts with the material presented in Chapter 2 ("Essential Unix Commands and Terminology") and Chapter 3 ("Bourne Shell Scripting"), sooner than later you will find your code becoming inelegant, or you might even hit a roadblock. This chapter gives you the remaining ammunition needed to deal with those kinds of problems.

10.1 The here-doc Tool

The following looks like a good way of getting help from the computer in remembering weekdays:

```
echo 1 = Monday
echo 2 = Tuesday
echo 3 = Wednesday
echo 4 = Thursday
echo 5 = Friday
echo 6 = Saturday
echo 7 = Sunday
```

© Manish Jain 2018
M. Jain, *Beginning Modern Unix*, https://doi.org/10.1007/978-1-4842-3528-7_10

But seven echo commands to print this table looks a bit of an overkill. Unix has the perfect tool to print multiple lines with a single command. It is called the here-doc.

```
cat << Weekdays
1 = Monday
2 = Tuesday
3 = Wednesday
4 = Thursday
5 = Friday
6 = Saturday
7 = Sunday
Weekdays
```

All the text between the opening limit string (Weekdays after <<) and the closing limit (Weekdays on its own line) is echoed in a single shot. Although you can choose any name as the limit string, the clockwork-like regular is EOF—short for End-Of-File.

Here-docs have excellent understanding of shell variables, command substitution, and even arithmetic expansion.

For example, let's put the following in a script.

```
num=67

cat << EOF
'df -h /'
Inside heredoc, the value of num = $num
EOF
```

If you run this code, you will get something like:

```
Filesystem      Size      Used    Avail    Capacity    Mounted on
/dev/ada1s3a     54G       22G      28G        44%        /
Inside heredoc, the value   of num  = 67
```

So the back-quotes got expanded via command substitution and $num was dereferenced.

You can turn off command substitution, shell variable dereference, and arithmetic expansion by putting the opening limit string within quotes (double or single).

```
num=67

cat << "EOF"
'df -h /'
Inside heredoc, the value of num = $num
EOF
```

If you run the preceding code (with quoted opening limit string "EOF"), you will now get this output:

```
'df -h /'
Inside heredoc, the value of num = $num
```

So, if you put the opening limit string in quotes, the shell will perform no substitution whatever in the here-doc—pretty much like putting a shell string under single quotes.

If you use <<- instead of << as the limit operator, all leading tabs/whitespace within the here-doc (and on the closing limit line) will be stripped by the interpreter. This makes formatting of the shell script's code aesthetically superior and more readable. So generally, whenever you write a here-doc, it's best to use the <<- operator.

Here-docs can also be used to turn interactive commands like ftp into scriptable applications. The following script uses a here-doc to anonymously download a couple of files from the FreeBSD FTP server.

```
#!/bin/sh

set -e      # exit upon first command failure

SERVER="ftp.freebsd.org"
DIR="pub/FreeBSD/releases/amd64/amd64/ISO-IMAGES/10.4"
PASSWORD="me@example.com"
FILE1="CHECKSUM.SHA256-FreeBSD-10.4-RELEASE-amd64"
FILE2="FreeBSD-10.4-RELEASE-amd64-mini-memstick.img.xz"

ftp -n $SERVER <<- EOF
    quote USER anonymous
    quote PASS "$PASSWORD"

    binary
    cd $DIR
```

```
    mget $FILE1 $FILE2
    bye

EOF

set +e
exit 0
```

10.2 Variable Type Modifiers: Readonly/Local

In the early days of Unix, shell script variables had only one storage class: globally writable. So you could assign some value to a shell variable inside a function, and the script's main body would see the new value.

Let's take a small example:

```
n=2

fx()
{
    n=3
}

fx
echo $n
```

If you run this code, it will output 3.

What if we wanted to ensure the function fx() does not alter n?

The answer is readonly—which is the counterpart of const in the C/C++ world.

```
readonly n=2

fx()
{
    n=3
}

fx
echo $n
```

Running this code returns the following error message.

```
n: is read only
```

Variables of type readonly can only be assigned an initial value. The readonly modifier is available anywhere needed inside a script, but makes sense only at the global level (outside of any shell function). If you declare a shell variable readonly inside a function, you need to ensure that the function will be invoked only once. Otherwise, the second invocation will produce an error message when the shell attempts to reassign to the readonly variable.

You might at times want to ensure that each shell function in a script uses its own shell variables, so that no function alters the variables of some other function or variables at the global level. This is what the modifier local does.

```
n=2

fx()
{
    local n=3
    echo "Inside fx: n = $n"
}

fy()
{
    local n=4
    fx
    echo "Inside fy: n = $n"
}

fy

echo "Inside main: n = $n"
exit 0
```

If you run this code, you will get the following output:

```
Inside fx: n = 3
Inside fy: n = 4
Inside main: n = 2
```

As might be obvious, the storage class `local` is only applicable to variables defined inside a shell function, not in the script's main body, where variables must be global.

Since this particular point is not intuitive, it might be good to note that the Bourne shell does not permit functions to assign to a `local` variable of the same name as a global readonly. I have no idea why this is the case.

10.3 Bit-Wise Operations

The Bourne shell supports bit-wise arithmetic operations: `<<` (left shift), `>>` (right shift), `&` (bitwise AND), `|` (bitwise OR), and `^` (bitwise XOR). If you are not conversant with bit-wise operations, visit Section 11.1.12 in Chapter 11 for a primer.

The following snippet populates a bit-field of four bits, spanning the right half of a byte as per the following OS-information capture schema, depicted in Figure 10-1.

Note   Counting offsets from the smallest-value (right-most) bit, one of the three right-side bits is turned on for OS type:

bit 0 → Cygwin

bit 1 → Linux

bit 2 → FreeBSD

If the installation is further detected to be virtualized, bit 3 is turned on as well.

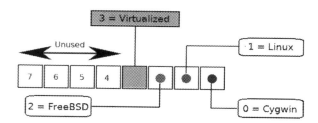

Figure 10-1. *Four-bit schema*

```
readonly UNITY=1
readonly SYSTEM_CYGWIN=$(( UNITY<<0 ))  # 1 % Exclusive bits: %
readonly SYSTEM_LINUX=$(( UNITY<<1 ))   # 2 % only one of these %
readonly SYSTEM_FREEBSD=$(( UNITY<<2 )) # 4 % three can be on %
readonly VM=$(( UNITY<<3 ))             # 8

machtype=0                              # begin with all bits off
system='uname -s'

if echo $system | grep -i Cygwin; then
    machtype=${SYSTEM_CYGWIN}

    model='systeminfo | grep -i "System Model" | \
    awk -F : '{print $2}' | sed 's/^[[:space:]][[:space:]]*//''

    [ "$model" = "VirtualBox" ] && machtype=$(( machtype | VM ))
else
    if [ $system = "Linux" ]; then
        machtype=${SYSTEM_LINUX}

        if cat /proc/cpuinfo | grep '^\<flags\>' | grep -qw hypervisor;
        then machtype=$(( machtype | VM ))
        fi
    else

        if [ $system = "FreeBSD" ]; then
            machtype=${SYSTEM_FREEBSD}

            vmode='sysctl -a | grep 'kern.vm_guest' | \
            awk -F : '{print $2}' | sed 's/^[[:space:]][[:space:]]*//''

            [ "$vmode" != "none" ] && machtype=$(( machtype | VM ))
        fi
    fi
fi
```

To find out whether the installation is virtualized, the user can now just check on machtype's bit 3 with an AND-based test: [$((machtype & VM)) -ne 0]

10.4 Trapping Signals

Shell scripts are permitted to catch and deal with signals like:

INTERRUPT ↔ (SIGINT; numeric value 2; generated by pressing `Ctrl`+`C`)

TERMINATION ↔ (SIGTERM; numeric value 15; the default signal sent by `kill`)

The only signal that that can never be caught is KILL (SIGKILL; numeric value 9), which will immediately kill the receiving process.

Here is a small script that runs an endless loop, with SIGINT and SIGTERM trapped.

```
#!/bin/sh
trap "echo Trapped and ignored INTERRUPT" SIGINT
trap "echo Trapped TERMINATION; exit 255" SIGTERM
echo "Running with PID: $$"

n=0
while true; do
    n=$(( n+1 ))
    echo $n
    sleep 1
done
exit 0
```

Whenever the user presses `Ctrl`+`C`, the script will print a diagnostic message and continue looping. If the user issues SIGTERM (with `kill <pid>` or `kill -TERM <pid>`) to the process, the script acknowledges the signal and exits.

10.5 Mixed Quotes

Most of the times, strings in a shell script are decorated as one of the following:

- Unquoted (if the string has no whitespace or special characters)

- Entirely double-quoted (if the string has special characters that need to be expanded by the shell)

- Entirely single-quoted (if the string has special characters that need to be prevented from being expanded by the shell)

There could be times when things are not so lucid. It is often needed in Unix shell scripting to have part of a string under single quotes and part in double quotes, and the double-quoted portion may have embedded back-quotes.

Let's say you have been assigned the task of writing a script to replace all occurrences of SOMETEXT with OTHERTEXT in a file called SOMEFILE. The converted text has to be printed on standard output, while SOMEFILE remains unchanged.

The script will be passed three parameters:

```
SOMETEXT OTHERTEXT SOMEFILE
```

SOMETEXT and OTHERTEXT could be any strings with any combination of characters that could be typed at the standard 101/104/105 keyboard. SOMEFILE's path has no special characters or whitespace.

The "normal" first try could be:

```
sed "s/$SOMETEXT/$OTHERTEXT/g" $SOMEFILE
```

Pretty soon, you'll realize this is not an enterprise solution. Either $SOMETEXT or $OTHERTEXT (or both) may have embedded forward slashes. If that is the case, sed will conk out immediately, citing an invalid command.

So we first write a function called escape() that takes text as input as outputs modified text with all forward slashes converted to the combo of a backslash and a forward slash.

escape() is an ugly little function to write, because the first thing it has to do is escape any embedded backslash. Then we have to remember that escapes happen twice—once when the escape() function is invoked and then when the actual call to sed in the script's main body is made. This means a literal backslash in escape() would need to be denoted as four of them: \\\\.

The following escape() looks as ugly as possible, but does a reasonable job:

```
escape()
{
    out='echo $1 | sed 's|\\\\|\\\\\\\\\\|g''      # \ becomes \\
    out='echo $out | sed 's|/|\\\\/|g''            # / becomes \/
    echo $out
}
```

Now the solution is straightforward:

```
sed 's/'"'escape $SOMETEXT'"'/'"'escape $OTHERTEXT'"'/g' $SOMEFILE
```

Purely from a technical viewpoint, single quotes are not necessary in this sed command, which could have been written entirely using double quotes only. But the use of part single and part double quotes makes it visually clear to the writer, the shell and the reader, where shell expansions are welcome and where they are not.

10.6 Recursion

Recursion happens when a script or a function calls itself. The Bourne shell supports recursion, but this is no reason for delight. If you find yourself needing recursion in your script, you probably should have written the application in C. Recursive code is fairly messy to write, and then when things go wrong, you need supreme cool inside your head and a good understanding of how stack overflow happens. The fact that variables inside shell scripts are global by default makes things trickier.

Secondly, any recursive code can be programmed normally (i.e., without recursion). Avoid recursion whenever you can, at least in shell scripting.

For times when you feel recursion must be a part of your shell life, I'll put in a small example script that uses recursion to find out the deepest sub-path in a given path that represents a symbolic link.

Let's say the given path is /home/unix/pix/tinkerbell/asleep.png. Then the script should find if /home/unix/pix/tinkerbell/asleep.png is a symbolic link. If not, then is /home/unix/pix/tinkerbell a symbolic link? Then /home/ unix/pix and then /home/unix and then /home?

If no symbolic links are found, the script exits quietly.

The following script uses recursion to do the job required:

```
#!/bin/sh

[ $# -gt 0 ] || { echo "Need path !" 1>&2; exit 1; }
[ -e "$1" ] || { echo "Need existing, valid path !" 1>&2; exit 1; }

path="$1"
counter=${2:-0}

if [ -L "$path" ]; then
    echo $path
else
    counter='expr $counter + 1'
```

```
    if [ $counter -ge 32 ]; then
        echo "Recursion too deep! (>= 32)" 1>&2
        exit 1
    fi

    if echo $path | grep -q '\/'; then
        path='echo $path | sed 's|/[^/]*$||''

        if [ -n "$path" ]; then
            'basename $0' "$path" "$counter"     # recurse here
        fi
    fi
fi

exit 0
```

10.7 Special Shell Variables: LINENO and IFS

There are a couple of special Bourne variables that are very helpful in shell scripting, and that newcomers to the world of shell—occasionally even experienced hands—are not aware of.

You might at times need to print the current line number inside a shell script. Bourne shell has a macro for that:

```
$LINENO
```

That macro, which expands as the line number in the script where it is referenced, makes diagnostic messaging much better.

If, let's say, you find an important test to fail midway through your script, you can exit the script pointing out the line number where you fell afoul, which you can pass to a helper die() function like the following one:

```
die()
{
    echo "error initiated at line $1: $2" 1>&2
    exit 1
}
```

In the script, when you decide it's time to die(), pass $LINENO as the first argument, and the reason of death as the second argument:

```
[ -f /etc/rc.conf ] || die $LINENO "/etc/rc.conf does not exist"
```

The other important shell variable is $IFS, which stands for Input Field Separator. Normally, the shell takes three characters as separators: space, tab, and newline.

There are times when you need to suppress space and tab as a field separator. This typically happens when you are recursing down a directory that contains files or subdirectories with embedded whitespace in the name. So if you want to list all the plain text files under /usr, the following code is extremely error-prone:

```
for f in '{ find /usr -type f -exec file {} \;; } | \
grep "ASCII text" | awk -F : '{print $1}''; do
    echo "$f"
done
```

The moment find hits on an entity with whitespace in the name, your script will fly off the handle. To get a good result, you need to set IFS to newline only, and then reset IFS to the earlier state when done:

```
oldifs="$IFS"
IFS=$'\n'

for f in '{ find /usr -type f -exec file {} \;; } | \
grep "ASCII text" | awk -F : '{print $1}''; do
    echo "$f"
done

IFS="$oldifs"
```

10.8 The Magic of eval

One of the most powerful tools in Unix shell is eval, which is a way of creating and populating variables dynamically via indirection.

Let's say we have this:

```
integer=99
var=integer
```

If you echo $var, you will get the output integer. Can you get the number 99 itself rather than the variable name integer?

The answer is yes:

```
integer=99
eval var='$'integer
echo $var
```

This outputs 99, just what we wanted.

We can add another level of indirection too:

```
integer=99
number=integer
eval var='$'$number
echo $var
```

This outputs 99 too.

eval leads to great convenience in looping over shell variables:

```
for var in PS1 PATH LD_LIBRARY_PATH; do
    eval val='$'$var
    [ -n "$val" ] || echo "$var is not set"
done
```

You can dynamically create a variable from an existing string (as long as the string conforms to shell variable naming rules):

```
string=xyz
eval $string="Hello World"
echo $xyz
```

This outputs our favorite greeting "Hello World".

A cool variation of this allows for the existing string to be mangled, creating an entirely new shell variable:

```
string=xyz
eval my_${string}="Hello World"
echo ${my_xyz}
```

This outputs our favorite greeting yet again.

10.9 Non-POSIX Scripting

Non-POSIX scripting is what you get when you use something other than vanilla Bourne shell as the interpreter.

This is deprecated because it makes the script non-portable. If, for example, you use zsh as the interpreter, you could run into multiple problems. The Z shell may not be available at the other end when you give your script to some other user. Or, if available, it may be wired to behave differently than the environment in which you coded the script. As an example, Zsh permits array indexing to begin at 0 (Korn emulation) as well as 1 (the default). So you might run into indexing problems if there is a difference between the array indexing environment at your end and at the end of the other user.

Still, at times, it becomes necessary to use bash or zsh as the interpreter. This happens primarily when you need to use arrays in your script. Support for arrays is not available in the Bourne shell, and it will likely remain that way forever.

We'll take bash as the fallback interpreter when vanilla Bourne is not enough for the mission, primarily because bash is more likely than zsh to be available with other users.

If you use bash as the interpreter, you can do everyone a favor by not hard-coding the path of bash into the shebang:

```
#!/bin/bash          # WRONG
```

The path of bash is not certain to be under /bin. It might be /usr/bin/bash or /usr/local/bin/bash.

The portable way of invoking bash is by using the command env, which is always available under /usr/bin:

```
#!/usr/bin/env bash         # RIGHT
```

Now that we have invoked bash, we'll take a quick look at the chief inspiration behind the invocation: arrays.

We'll create an array named unix, filling the array with the three distributions we recognize as Unix: FreeBSD, Linux, and Cygwin.

```
declare -a unix          # optional

i=0

unix[$((i++))]="FreeBSD"
unix[$((i++))]="Linux"
unix[$((i++))]="Cygwin"
```

If we want to determine the size of the Unix array, we can use ${#unix[*]} or ${#unix[@]}

```
echo ${#unix[*]}      # outputs 3
echo ${#unix[@]}      # outputs 3 too
```

Note   The Bash shell always starts array indexing at 0. The highest index in a Bash array is its size minus 1.

To access the element at index n in the array, we have to use ${unix[$n]}

```
echo ${unix[0]}          # outputs FreeBSD
echo ${unix[3]}          # outputs nothing; the highest index of unix is 2
```

Putting together all the tidbits, we can write a small script that outputs whether we are on a Unix box:

```
#!/usr/bin/env bash

dist='uname -o'

declare -a unix        # optional

i=0

unix[$((i++))]="FreeBSD"
unix[$((i++))]="Linux"
unix[$((i++))]="Cygwin"

i=0
is_unix=false

while [ $i -lt ${#unix[@]} ]; do
    if [ "$dist" = "${unix[$i]}" ]; then
        is_unix=true
        break
    fi

    ((i++))
done

echo $is_unix
exit 0
```

10.10 Scripting with ncurses

Note   This section is optional. If you do not intend to script with ncurses, you can skip this section for the time being. But remember to visit this section late—the ncurses library adds significantly to ease of interaction with the user on the command line.

Scripting with ncurses (console-mode widgets library) lets you interact with the user using widgets like message boxes, radio lists, and input boxes. The most versatile ncurses suite for scripting is `dialog`, which is always available under FreeBSD in its base system, and as a package under Linux. It's often automatically installed along with the operating system itself. In case the package is missing, you can always pull it in yourself via the package manager.

Both Cygwin and Babun (Cygwin fork with Z shell as the default login shell) provide an add-on package called `dialog`. Cygwin needs you to run its setup for installing add-ons, while under Babun you can install `dialog` with the command `pact install dialog`.

We'll look at usage of some elementary `dialog` widgets.

Remember that `dialog` writes its output to standard error by default, and whenever needed to capture the output in a result variable—we need to pass in `--stdout` to direct the output to standard output.

Also note that the numbers at / near the end of dialog commands usually indicate the desired window geometry:

```
<height> <width>            # for windows that do not use a list
```

or

```
<height> <width> <entries*>  # for windows that use a list
```

   * : suggests the number of list entries.

Note   A `dialog` command that populates an output variable returns two things: an exit code (0 if there was no error), and a string that gets trapped in the output variable. The output string is meaningful only if the exit code was 0.

10.10.1 Message Box

There are no marks for deducing what a message box does. The following command results in the message box, as shown in Figure 10-2.

```
dialog --title "Message" --msgbox "\nHello World" 8 16
```

Figure 10-2. *The dialog message box*

A related widget is `infobox`, which exits automatically after displaying the message. To persist the box on the output device for a while, the calling thread can sleep for a few seconds:

```
dialog --infobox "Please wait. Processing ..." 5 35; sleep 3
```

10.10.2 YesNo box

A YesNo box, shown in Figure 10-3, makes the user choose between Yes (exit code 0) or No (exit code non-zero). Here is the snippet used to generate the image:

```
dialog --title "Query" --yesno \
"\nAre you rich, bright and young ?" 7 37

[ $? -eq 0 ] && echo You chose Yes || echo You chose No
```

Figure 10-3. *The dialog YesNo box*

10.10.3 Input Box

An input box prompts the user to enter some text. If the user clicks Cancel, dialog returns a non-zero exit code to the shell.

```
out='dialog --stdout --title "User input needed" \
--inputbox "\nWhich city do you live in?" 9 30'

[ $? -eq 0 ] && echo You entered $out
```

These commands yield Figure 10-4.

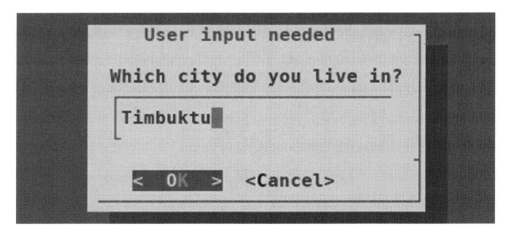

Figure 10-4. *The dialog input box*

10.10.4 Range Box

A range box lets the user select a number from a predefined range, with a default value that sets the initial position of the slider.

The user can use Page Up / Page Down (for big changes) as well as Up / Down (for small changes). The Home key immediately takes the user to the minimum value and End takes the user to the maximum.

```
out='dialog --title Range --stdout --rangebox  \
"\nSelect a number from 0 to 100" 3 36 0 100 64'

[ $? -eq 0 ] && echo You chose $out
```

The first two numeric arguments at the end (3 and 36 in the preceding code snippet) determine window geometry (height and width respectively), while the last three (0, 100, and 64) specify minimum, maximum, and initial value, respectively.

This code snippet leads to the screenshot shown in Figure 10-5.

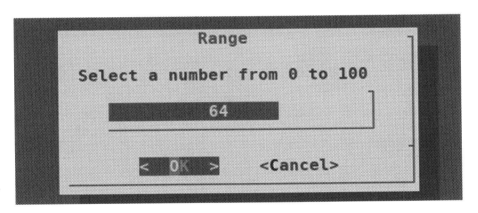

Figure 10-5. *The dialog range box*

10.10.5 Text Box

The text box widget displays the contents of a text file. The user can scroll the contents with Up, Down, Page Up, Page Down. Refer to the following command and Figure 10-6 for illustration.

```
dialog --textbox ~/.login 12 72
```

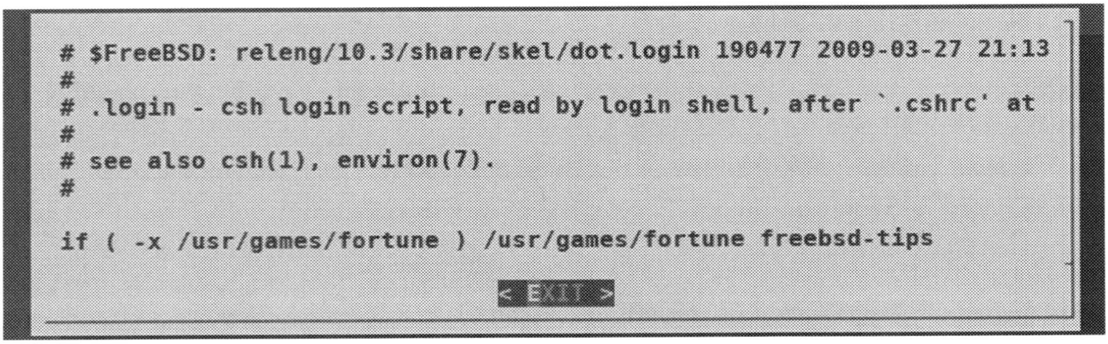

```
# $FreeBSD: releng/10.3/share/skel/dot.login 190477 2009-03-27 21:13
#
# .login - csh login script, read by login shell, after `.cshrc' at
#
# see also csh(1), environ(7).
#

if ( -x /usr/games/fortune ) /usr/games/fortune freebsd-tips

                              < EXIT >
```

Figure 10-6. *The dialog text box*

10.10.6 Program Box

A program box displays the output of a command piped in. Refer to the following command and Figure 10-7 for illustration.

```
ls -l | dialog --programbox 20 100
```

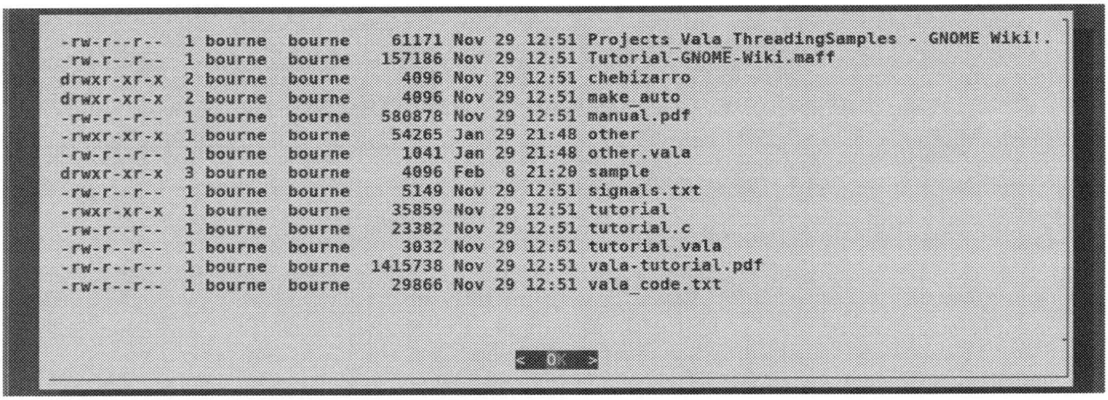

```
-rw-r--r--  1 bourne  bourne    61171 Nov 29 12:51 Projects_Vala_ThreadingSamples - GNOME Wiki!.
-rw-r--r--  1 bourne  bourne   157186 Nov 29 12:51 Tutorial-GNOME-Wiki.maff
drwxr-xr-x  2 bourne  bourne     4096 Nov 29 12:51 chebizarro
drwxr-xr-x  2 bourne  bourne     4096 Nov 29 12:51 make_auto
-rw-r--r--  1 bourne  bourne   580878 Nov 29 12:51 manual.pdf
-rwxr-xr-x  1 bourne  bourne    54265 Jan 29 21:48 other
-rw-r--r--  1 bourne  bourne     1041 Jan 29 21:48 other.vala
drwxr-xr-x  3 bourne  bourne     4096 Feb  8 21:20 sample
-rw-r--r--  1 bourne  bourne     5149 Nov 29 12:51 signals.txt
-rwxr-xr-x  1 bourne  bourne    35859 Nov 29 12:51 tutorial
-rw-r--r--  1 bourne  bourne    23382 Nov 29 12:51 tutorial.c
-rw-r--r--  1 bourne  bourne     3032 Nov 29 12:51 tutorial.vala
-rw-r--r--  1 bourne  bourne  1415738 Nov 29 12:51 vala-tutorial.pdf
-rw-r--r--  1 bourne  bourne    29866 Nov 29 12:51 vala_code.txt

                              <  OK  >
```

Figure 10-7. *The dialog program box*

A related widget is `tailbox`, which clings to the end of the output, much like `tail -f`.

10.10.7 Menu Box

A menu box presents the users with a menu of indexed choices, out of which they can select one.

The indexes can be any integers of the programmer's choice, and they need not necessarily be sequential.

When the user selects a choice from the menu, the corresponding index is returned. If the clicks hits Cancel, `dialog` returns a non-zero exit code to the shell.

This code snippet is used to generate Figure 10-8:

```
out='dialog --stdout --title "Linux filesystem format options" \
--menu "\nChoose your preferred filesystem:" 12 40 3 \
1 ext2 \
2 "ext3 (journaling)" \
3 "ext4 with discard"'

[ $? -eq 0 ] && echo "You chose $out"
```

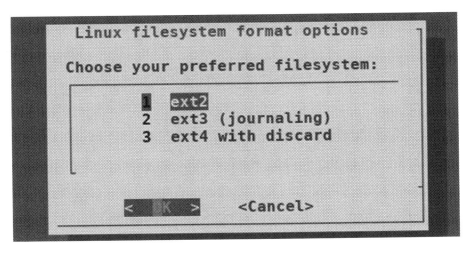

Figure 10-8. *The dialog menu box*

10.10.8 Radio List

A radio list presents a menu of indexed choices that can be toggled. The user can select any one of the choices after toggling it on by pressing the spacebar.

One of the choices may be optionally be marked as on (in which case that entry will be displayed as starred) in the initial menu. Toggling a choice on automatically toggles all others to off.

The indexes can be any integers of the programmer's choice, and they need not necessarily be sequential.

When the user selects a choice from the menu, the corresponding index is returned. If the user clicks Cancel, `dialog` returns a non-zero exit code to the shell.

Refer to the code snippet and Figure 10-9 for illustration.

```
out='dialog --stdout --radiolist "Select an OS:" 10 30 3 \
1 FreeBSD on \
2 Linux off \
3 Cygwin off'

[ $? -eq 0 ] && echo You selected $out
```

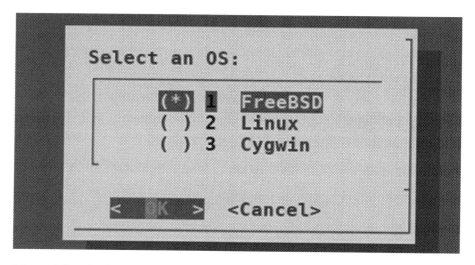

Figure 10-9. *The dialog radio list*

10.10.9 Progress Gauge

A progress gauge displays progress, with input read from standard input. No user input is needed. When the gauge reaches 100%, the window disappears.

The easy way to use the progress gauge widget is to run a loop with your shell, with the loop echoing 0 at the beginning and 100 at the end. The value echoed by the loop and piped to `dialog` is interpreted as the percentage of work done.

```
{
    n=0

    while [ $n -lt 100 ]; do
        echo $n
        n='expr $n + 20'
        sleep 1
    done
} | dialog --title "Wait" --gauge "\nProcessing ..." 8 50
```

Figure 10-10 captures the state of the `dialog` window three seconds after the loop goes into action.

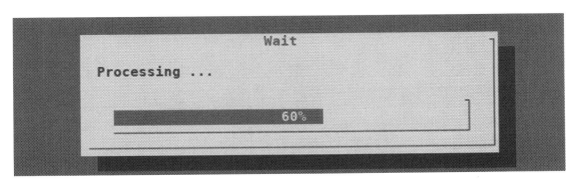

Figure 10-10. *The dialog progress gauge*

10.10.10 Check List

A checklist box presents a set of items to the users, each of which they can toggle on or off individually using the spacebar. Each item has an associated number (shown to its right). The number is a visual aid and does not affect the widget's functioning.

When the user clicks OK, all the on items are concatenated into a space-separated string, which is returned. If the user clicks Cancel, `dialog` returns a non-zero exit code.

The following code sample prompts the user for desktop environments the user likes, and Figure 10-11 shows possible usage with a user who approves of KDE and Cinnamon.

```
list=""
n=1

for de in 'cat <<-Desktop_Environments
    KDE
```

```
    GNOME
    Cinnamon
    XFCE
Desktop_Environments'; do
    list="$list $de $n off"
    n='expr $n + 1'
done

chosen='dialog --stdout --checklist \
"Choose desktops you like:" 11 36 4 $list'

if [ $? -eq 0 ]; then
    for choice in $chosen; do
        echo "You selected $choice"
    done
fi
```

If the user were to press the OK button in Figure 10-11, dialog would return 0 to the shell and populate the output string as "KDE Cinnamon".

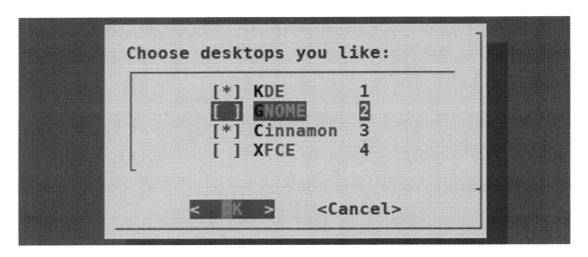

Figure 10-11. *The dialog check box*

10.10.11 Time Box

The time box lets the user choose a time, returned as hh:mm:ss (24-hour format).

The user can use Up / Down keys as well as Page Up and Page Down to set the hours, minutes, and seconds, and the Tab key to switch among the fields.

The following code sample, and Figure 10-12, is an example of the user being prompted for a time value and 14:30:00 being returned.

```
out='dialog --stdout --title "Reboot Pending" \
--timebox "\nSet the time for the system to restart:" 0 0 14 30 00'

[ $? -eq 0 ] && echo "You set the time: $out"
```

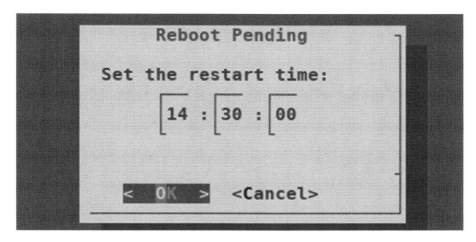

Figure 10-12.   *The dialog time box*

10.10.12 Calendar Box

The calendar box lets you choose a date, returned as DD:MM:YYYY.

As in the preceding time box, the user can use Up / Down keys as well as Page Up and Page Down keys to set the date, month, and year fields, and the Tab key to switch among the fields.

The following snippet and Figure 10-13 show an example prompting the user for a date value, for which the user selects 19-01-2038.

```
out='dialog --stdout --title "Unix Date Bomb" \
--calendar "\nWhen do you expect the next Y2K ?" 0 0 19 01 2038'
[ $? -eq 0 ] &&  echo "You set the date: $out"
```

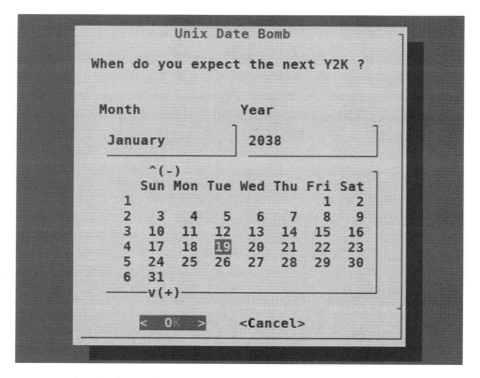

Figure 10-13. *The dialog calendar box*

10.10.13 File Selection Box

The File selection box lets you choose a file, with an optionally pre-selected file path. It is a bit tricky using the file selection widget the first couple of times. The widget presents three windows to the user: directories in the upper-left window, files in the upper-right window, and the user's selection in the lower window.

To jump from one window to another, use `Tab`.

Pressing `Up`/`Down` lets you navigate the current list in the Directories/Files windows.

Pressing `Left`/`Right` navigates the selection text.

To select a file in the Files window, you need to press the spacebar. The trick: To change into a directory, select the directory and then press `Space` twice. Here is the example code, with Figure 10-14 illustrating usage for the snippet.

```
out='dialog --stdout --fselect $HOME/tetris/tetris.xpm 4 30'
[ $? -eq 0 ] && echo "You chose: $out"
```

This command and Figure 10-14 presume `tetris/tetris.xpm` and `tetris/src/tetris.c` are existing files under $HOME. To change the selection from `tetris/tetris.xpm` (pre-selected) to `tetris/src/tetris.c`, you need to do the following:

1. At (a), tab into the Directories window. Use `Up`/`Down` to set `src` as directory.

2. Press `Space` once. The widget now appears as in (b). Files are still not refreshed.

3. Press `Space` a second time to actually navigate into that directory, whereupon the Files window will list files in `src` and the widget will appear as in (c).

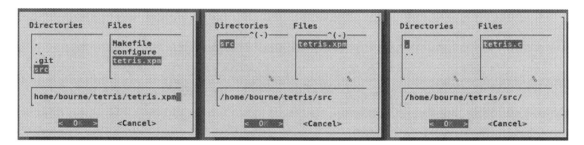

Figure 10-14. *The dialog file selection box: (a) → (b) → (c)*

If the user now clicks OK, `dialog` will return $HOME/`tetris/src/tetris.c` as output.

The selection window also plays a part in navigation: the user can type in the path, and the widget will update the contents of the other windows to match user input.

A related widget is `dselect`, which can prompt for a directory path.

10.10.14 And There Are Many More

There are a few other widgets in `dialog`—some of them variants of the widgets discussed previously (Progress Box and Password Box) and others which are fundamentally different (Form Box, Pause Box, and Treeview Box).

I will leave it to you to research the remaining widgets on your own as and when needed. For complete documentation, you can look up the man page with `man dialog`.

10.11 Scripting with GTK

Note   Reading this section is optional. If you do not intend to script with GTK, you can skip this section entirely. Scripting with GTK is not advisable as a standard course of scripting. This section therefore is just an awareness exercise.

There are many GUI toolkits that are available in Unix. `dialog` itself has an associated X sub-package called `Xdialog`, which can serve as a ready drop-in for `dialog` commands.

There are independent pure-X widget libraries too, widgets of which can be invoked from within a script. Perhaps none better than Zenity, a cross-platform suite that allows the execution of GTK+ dialog boxes from the command line (and therefore shell scripts too).

Zenity user interface is not particularly well-polished, and the suite has fewer features than more complex GUI creation suites. But it does a perfect job of enabling a shell script to interact seamlessly with an X user. To boot, Zenity usage is pretty much the same as `dialog`.

This book does not intend to provide a comprehensive discourse on Zenity. The primary reason is that scripting should usually assume that there is no X around. So scripting with GUI toolkits should never be your first choice.

We'll look at one example—the file selection widget—which shows how easy it is to invoke GTK dialogs from the command line.

If you want the user to select a file, Zenity makes it simple. Refer to the following commands and Figure 10-15:

```
FILE='zenity --file-selection --title="Select file"'
[ $? -eq 0 ] && echo "$FILE selected."
```

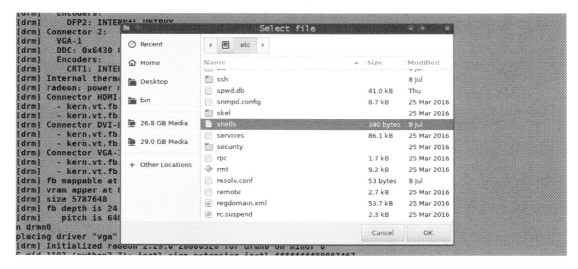

Figure 10-15. *The Zenity file selection dialog*

If the user clicks OK, Zenity will return 0 to the shell and populate the output variable FILE with /etc/shells.

The file selection dialog has a couple of noteworthy switches:

- --multiple: Allows selection of multiple files (separated by | in the output).

- --directory: Allows selection of a directory. As you would expect, Zenity has many, many widgets that you can play with. An excellent Zenity introduction and examples are available at https://linuxaria.com/howto/introduction-zenity-bash-gu.

And there is man zenity too, which always has complete documentation for your distribution.

10.12 Summary

Now that you are fully familiar with command-line interaction with Unix (at least at a beginner level—and hopefully at the intermediary level), you can utilize your skills to gain further Unix proficiency of your own rendering in the areas that interest you most: shell scripting, installation, administration, emulation, and virtualization. That's quite a strong punch already.

We'll make the punch even stronger in the next—and the final—chapter of this book, with skills for you to pick up in creating binary applications under Unix. Our primary vehicle of delivery will be the C programming language.

If you have never programmed with C before, the final chapter will possibly read like the riot act—not particularly user-friendly from the viewpoint of the newcomer. So batten down the hatches before you tune in.

CHAPTER 11

Unix Programming with C and Vala

This chapter is for readers who intend to develop binary applications under Unix. As you can imagine, this is a vast, almost limitless, area. Just the number of programming languages today is in dozens: C, C++, Go, Haskell, Java, Lisp, Swift, Vala, and quite a few more.

If you are new to programming, you want to whittle down the choice of languages to work with. C is an excellent choice to develop skills in, almost a necessity when programming with Unix. Unix kernels, device drivers, system libraries, and essential executables are all written in C—apart from most of the object-oriented compilers (`c++`, `valac`, and `javac`). That's why it is deemed first-and-foremost a systems programming language. That also means C is very well-documented: your installation will likely already have man pages for C routines (at least if gcc, the GNU compiler collection, is installed).

Because C is essentially a systems programming language, developing graphical applications with C demands a lot of work from the programmer. While many programmers do still use C for developing graphical applications, we will take up a new C derivative, Vala, for that purpose. Vala, while resembling C in its syntax, is geared to take care of all the tedious X-related work in the language itself, leaving the programmer significantly less to worry about.

This book is not intended to be a reference book for C or for Vala. The objectives of this chapter can be broken up as follows:

- The C section caters to two types of readers: Those new to C under Unix (some prior exposure to C is desirable), as well as those who think they might benefit by revisiting the language fundamentals.

313

© Manish Jain 2018
M. Jain, *Beginning Modern Unix*, https://doi.org/10.1007/978-1-4842-3528-7_11

- The Vala section is a quick-and-dirty intro for kicking off development of graphical applications under Unix. Reading this section will become significantly easier once you understand C basics.

Although in general, I do not encourage use of C++, the truth is C++ as a language brings in some much-needed improvements to C:

- A built-in `bool` type (which C does not have per se)

- Operators `new`/`delete` (which are easier and less error-prone to work with compared to the traditional C counterparts, `malloc()`/`free()`)

- A native string type `std::string`, which makes on-the-fly string manipulations possible

- Single-line comments (which the original C did not have, but most newer C compilers as well as the new C standard support)

- The keyword `struct` can optionally be omitted when declaring an instance

What I propose is a new version of C called C+, which is C with just the five improvements mentioned here, plus a couple of cutbacks in the C language itself:

- No multiple declarations are permitted within a single statement.

- A control statement (`if`/`else`/`while`/`for`) must be followed by a pair of braces, no matter whether the braces enclose zero, one, or one million statements.

The other way to look at C+ as a language is a watered-down version of C++, with almost all object-oriented features disabled. Just as C++, C+ freely uses both C-style strings (which are very important to understand) as well as C++-style strings (which are not as important to understand but easier to work with, although object-oriented—which essentially means: their internal working is not transparent). There are two reasons C-style strings are crucial to understand: C-style strings are more efficient; and, low-level API functions use C-style strings exclusively.

From hereon, I will use C to mostly mean the middle-ground language C+ (which utilizes the C++ compiler: `c++` or `g++`).

11.1 Systems Programming with C

The primary characteristic of the C programming language that makes it ideal for systems programming is a supremely barebones core that can be used to deliver incredibly complex, power-packed binaries ranging from the simple `ls` command to entire web browsers (as well as compilers written in C).

One aspect of C that is an advantage to experienced users and a disadvantage to greenhorns is that C is entirely a conceptual language—possibly the most conceptual language ever developed. Everything has to be understood—there is nothing to commit to memory raw (without comprehension).

The C section presented in this chapter is therefore mostly a compendium of the bedrock concepts that have to be understood. Given that I have just one chapter to explain C, OOP, and rudimentary Vala, quite a lot of the material presented here might be reader-unfriendly: you are told a concept, and it is assumed that you understand. Although the chapter has a generous number of examples and code snippets, you are encouraged to write code snippets of your own to test the validity of each concept as it emerges. If you find the material overly unfriendly, you perhaps need to look at an entire book on C.

Although you do not need to have an understanding of CPU architectures to program with C, there is one term you must know about: a *register*. A register is a fixed-width piece of memory inside the CPU itself. The CPU never processes what is inside system memory (RAM). When it needs to process a portion of system memory, it pulls that portion "onboard" into the CPU itself inside its registers, where the processing (and subsequent "offboarding") then takes place.

A register can hold one of two types of contents: data or instruction that acts on data. Each register's width is fixed and depends on the CPU architecture: 32 bits under i386 and 64 bits under AMD64. (There was a time half a century back when there just 8-bit registers.) The width of a CPU register is known as a *word*—a term that connotes the natural computation size for the system's architecture.

There is a ten-point charter you will have to understand and then commit to memory:

- A byte in the x86 world is equivalent to 8 bits. Note that a CPU register always holds 32 bits (i386) or 64 bits (AMD64) even when what is being processed is just an octet (8 bits), with the rest of the bits ignored.

315

- In C, before you start using a variable, you have to explicitly tell the compiler its type. Telling the compiler a variable's type ahead of time is called declaration, which can be clubbed with first-time usage:

```
int i; i = 99;

-OR-
int i = 99;
```

- As you might deduce from these statements, every statement in C sources must be terminated with a semicolon. Further, the C compiler does not care about your whitespace usage. If you prefer it this way, you could write this snippet as:

```
int i;i=99;
```

- If a line of code begins with //, the compiler treats the line as a comment. If the // occurs anywhere in the middle of a line, the only portion considered code is what lies before the first occurrence of //. The compiler considers the rest of the line a comment. Original C just had a block-oriented commenting construct: /* .. */, where .. represents the block (which can span multiple lines) to be commented. But we will stick with C++-style single-line comments.

- C considers the number 0 as equivalent to false; any non-zero number evaluates as true. Because C does not have a native bool type, true and false are keywords borrowed from C++.

- C uses the = operator for assignments only. To check for equality, use the == operator. The pseudo-test if (i = 1) will succeed even if i was originally 0.

- In C, strings are always double-quoted. Single quotes are reserved for enclosing exactly one character. So "A" and 'A' are very different things. The first one is a string of length one, while the second is just a regular uppercase character (with a numeric equivalent).

- There are multiple ways in C to print a string, let's say "Hello", on standard output. The simplest is puts("Hello"), which automatically appends a newline.

- To use input-output functions—of which `puts()` is one, you need to have this line at (or near) the very top in your source code file: `#include <stdio.h>`.

- Header files are needed because the C compilation process needs information about any external functions and macros.

- After your `#include` statements, your file must have a `main()` function (if the source code file is intended to generate an executable upon compilation). For simplicity during the introductory phase, you can put everything else other than the `#include` statements inside `main()`.

  Here is a small "Hello" sample created as `first.c`:

  ```
  #include <stdio.h>

  int main()
  {
      puts("Hello");
      return 0; // In C, returning 0 usually indicates No Error
  }
  ```

- When your source code is ready, you need to compile it into a binary. For the sample file `first.c`, you can use the following command:

  ```
  c++ -g -o first first.c
  // The -g switch (optional) pulls debug symbols into the
  executable
  ```

11.1.1 The C Compilation Process

Three different agencies are involved in the C compilation process.

- *Preprocessor* (`cpp`): Determines what finally gets compiled.

- *Compiler* (`cc`): Creates object code (machine code with unresolved placeholders for external variables/functions) for each unit compiled.

- *Linker* (ld): Resolves all the placeholder addresses to create a fully independent binary (executable or library) in pure machine code.

The following pipeline is a handy way to envisage the compilation process:

```
input -> Preprocessor -> Compiler -> Linker -> binary
```

An equivalent flowchart for the source code file xyz.c would be:

```
xyz.c -> cpp ----------> cc -------> ld -----> a.out
```

The default name a.out of the binary executable generated is a historical artifact. Modern binaries under Unix use the Executable and Linkable Format (ELF).

Although the classic C compiler under GNU is cc, we'll be using c++ since sources in this chapter use C++ features (those imbibed as C+). That does not affect the compilation process, from the user's viewpoint.

11.1.2 Data Types in C

It wouldn't be wrong to say that C has just one data type of its own: numbers. Depending on a couple of characteristics, the numbers assume different names and elicit different attitudes from the compiler.

One such characteristic is the size. The following sizes apply to 64-bit Unix.

```
Bool      :  1  byte → max value:   1
Char      :  1  byte → max value:   (2^08) - 1
Short     :  2 bytes → max value:   (2^16) - 1
wchar_t   :  4 bytes → max value:   (2^32) - 1
int       :  4 bytes → max value:   (2^32) - 1
long      :  8 bytes → max value:   (2^64) - 1
```

With a 32-bit gcc, long would drop from 8 bytes to 4 bytes. If you want to use a 64-bit integer under 32-bit gcc, you can use the type long long. If you want to force a particular size (in bits), you can use __int<N>_t: __int8_t forces a char equivalent.

A couple of noteworthy variants are the size and offset types—size_t and off_t—which must be positive integers (or else 0). Both are remembered most easily as equivalent to unsigned long.

I have left out the floating point types (`float` and `double`) because those are not often needed. All the numeric types except `bool` are available as `signed` (which is the default) as well as `unsigned` (0 or positive only).

The second distinguishing characteristic asks, is the number an ordinary integer, or is it an address of something stored in memory? If it is an address, it is called a *pointer,* which is a special subtype that corresponds most closely to the `unsigned long` type. We'll look at pointers in a dedicated subsection.

11.1.3 int

While a C `int` is a simple integer, the simplicity has its limits. First of all, 8 billion— roughly the current global human population—qualifies as an integer, but does not suit an `int` in the x86 (i.e., i386 or AMD64) world. If you assign 8 billion to an `int` and print it, you should not expect to see 8 billion in the output because x86 compilers use 4 bytes for an `int`, placing a limit of $((2^{32}) - 1 =)$ 4294967295 on an `unsigned int`. For a `signed int`—which is the default if you do not specify a signed-ness, the left-most bit serves as a metabit to interpret the other 31 bits—0 for positive `int` and 1 for negative `int`. Therefore the largest positive `signed int` is $((2^{31}) - 1 =)$2147483647. On the negative side, the limit is -2147483648.

It is unwise to compare a `signed int` to an `unsigned int`:

```
unsigned int ui = 1;
int si = -1;

if (si < ui)
{
    puts("less");
}
```

You might expect to see `less` in the output but you won't: the compiler will treat `si` as an unsigned quantity for the comparison, making its effective value wrap around to the upper limit of an `unsigned int`, which would be a few billions.

When you have to print integers like `si` from your code, you need to use `printf()` with the %d modifier (and then read `man 3 printf` for a discussion of all modifiers):

```
printf("%d\n", si);
```

To read an integer from standard input, use the `scanf()` routine:

```
scanf("%d", &si);
```

Other input-output functions are discussed in Section 11.1.18.

This is also a good stage to get familiar with operator `sizeof`, which you can use to determine how many bytes a variable or type occupies inside physical memory.

Either of the following prints 4:

```
printf("%d\n", sizeof(si));
printf("%d\n", sizeof(int));
```

11.1.4 char

The most commonly confused type among the numeric types is `char`, the smallest unit of memory allocation equivalent to at least a byte. Both C and C++ permit `char` to use more than the minimum 8 bits, but Unix C/C++ compilers stick with the minimum. This means that a `char` is only big enough to hold a maximum value of 127 (signed) or 255 (unsigned). It also means that under Unix, the terms `byte`, `char`, and `octet` are used pretty much interchangeably to signify the same idea. A set of eight contiguous bits that form the smallest possible piece of memory the operating system can allocate. You can never say "I want half a byte", nor "Give me four bits from here and four from there".

It is a common misconception that the `char` data type corresponds to characters from the English alphabet or those found on the keyboard. To stem the confusion, this book consciously uses the term "symbol" where other books use "character".

In electronic memory, a bit is a pair of points across which a voltage may have been applied (representing a value of 1) or not applied (representing a value of 0). Every bit in a byte has as increasing level of effect on the aggregated value, starting from the rightmost bit (level 0) to leftmost (level 7). The levels have a direct translation into mathematics as "2 raised to the power of". So the number 38 (i.e., $2^5 + 2^2 + 2^1$) in physical memory would correspond to the following byte layout:

```
0 0 1 0 0 1 1 0
```

If you think about it, there is no other byte layout that could represent the number 38. If any of the bits were to change its value, such as from 0 to 1 or vice versa, the number itself would change. One point from basic mathematics is worth a recall: for any integer n, (n^0) is 1 if n is non-zero, while (0^n) is 0 as long as n is positive.

It's worthwhile to note the influence of hexadecimal notation in programming. Even though you cannot split a byte into two halves when allocating memory, the hexadecimal system in computer programming is built around that very idea when denoting values. If you look again at the byte layout, you will find that it can be denoted as 0x26, with 0x standing for hexadecimal notation, 2 standing for the decimal value of the left-side four bits, and 6 standing for the decimal value of the right-side four bits.

An often misunderstood notion is what to make of a char with all bits set to 0:

```
char c = 0;
```

Some programmers complain that this statement won't even compile and that a char can only be assigned exactly one symbol (alphanumeric or punctuation, sometimes with a preceding backslash) in single quotes.

This cannot possibly be any further removed from reality: remember that a char is a small integer. There can't be any integer smaller than 0 (ignoring negative integers). So this statement will compile and will work correctly, as long as you know what "correctly" means in this context, a topic which we will discuss a few paragraphs down.

When the C language was developed, its creator Dennis Ritchie realized that the highly limited range of a char (just 256 integers) made it unusable for storing numbers for general computation. So he put the char data type (more precisely, the 0-to-127 range common to both char and unsigned char) to a special use: denoting numeric codes for letters in the English alphabet and numeric equivalents for any other symbol you could type from the standard US keyboard.

This statement is an important one. It should immediately strike a couple of chords in you:

- The computer only understands numbers: It cannot by itself make any sense out of a or $. All such, symbols have to be translated to numbers for the computer's benefit.

- When you press the key for the number 0 on a US-style keyboard, you are not typing in the number 0. Instead you are transmitting the symbol 0.

The scheme for translating a US keyboard's symbols into numbers is standard ASCII, which you are surely aware of. There is no ASCII code for the number 0 because it is already a number, but there is an ASCII code for the symbol 0—which is the number 48. If you want to look up ASCII codes, you can do so with man 7 ascii. FreeBSD also has a handy X package xascii that serves this purpose nicely.

A variant of the char type is wchar_t (wide character), which typically occupies four bytes. This is useful for localization of strings, with Unicode being the standard scheme. Luckily (or should I say, by ingenious design), the first 128 codes map to the same symbols in ASCII and Unicode.

A char that stores the number 0 (i.e., all 8 bits off) is termed as a null byte (in C, "null" is nothing but another fancy word for zero) and is taken as end-of-string marker for C-style strings, which we will discuss in a short while.

Let's go through a small piece of code:

```
#include <stdio.h>
int main()

{
    char c1 = '0';
    char c2 = 0;
    int i = '0';

    printf("%c:%c:%d\n", c1, c2, i);
    return 0;
}
```

If you run this code, you'll find the output:

```
0::48
```

By the rules of C, a null byte is considered non-printable. That explains why nothing appears in place of c2.

Both c1 and i store 48, the ASCII equivalent of 0. c1 is output as 0 (without the quotation marks) because the compiler has to check the data type of c1 before output. Since its type is char, the compiler outputs the symbol 0, which is equivalent to the ASCII code 48. Finally, the 0 of i is output as 48 because it has been declared as an int and therefore the compiler does not want to output a symbol but a number—in other words, the ASCII code itself.

Reading a char from standard input is easily done with getchar():

```
int ch = getchar();
printf("ascii code = %d; symbol = %c\n", ch, ch);
```

11.1.5 bool

The simplest data type among all is bool, not present in C *per se* but available if you #include <stdbool.h>, and always readily available in our C+ standard of C, which uses c++ as the compiler.

A bool is like a bit in that it can store only 0 (= false) or 1 (= true). It is unlike a bit in that it occupies a whole byte. Any value other than 0 is treated as 1. If you assign 29 or -29 to a bool variable and print it, you will see 1 in the output.

Since booleans are very simple, they can serve as a good launching pad to start writing optimized code.

```
if (some_bool == false)
{
    // code
}
```

Unless the compiler's optimizer kicks in, the condition's expression will trigger three operations:

- some_bool is loaded into a CPU register

- 0 (i.e., false) is loaded into another CPU register

- The CPU compares the values in the two registers

In professional code, expect the condition to be stated as:

```
if (! some_bool) // needs one register and one op less
```

11.1.6 Pointers

The next data type to discuss in this section is pointers. Some people wonder why other people have so much trouble understanding and using pointers. Other people wonder why some people do not have so much trouble understanding and using pointers.

Pointers are fundamental to C and data structures. So we look at a simple way of understanding them in x86.

```
int i = 24;
```

Let's presume that at runtime, i gets stored in four bytes starting at memory address 5000, which means that bytes 5000-to-5003 hold the bit-pattern for the number 24 (which is 27 zeroes followed by 11000). Now let's say in our code we have another int variable:

```
int j = 5000;
```

Just like four bytes were allocated for i, another four bytes get allocated for j. Those four bytes hold the bit-pattern for the number 5000. We can now say that the numeric value of j is equal to the numeric value of the address at which i is stored. In effect, j is something like a pointer. It has a value equal to the numeric address of another variable. We cannot call j a full-fledged pointer yet because of two reasons: declaration mismatch and lack of ability of being programmatically dereferenced. Further, it is only a matter of chance that j has been assigned the same value that is the numeric address of i.

What if we always want to be sure that j has the same value as the numeric address of i? We can do this:

```
int j = (int) &i;
// fetch the starting address of i, and treat it as an int
```

Closer, but not there yet. We have to specifically tell the compiler that i can be accessed indirectly via j, which is what dereferencing means.

To tell the compiler that j is intended to be a pointer holding the address of i (a variable of type int), we have to tell the compiler this:

```
int * j = &i;
```

j is now a pointer, a real pointer. To change the value of i with the help of j, we can write the following code:

```
(*j)++;
```

This has just the same effect as i++.

(*j)++ is also, quite notably, entirely different from j++. j++ changes the address held in j from 5000 (our example's address) to (5000 + sizeof(int) =) 5004.

Figure 11-1 depicts the memory layout with i (value 24) residing at memory address 5000 and j holding the address of i (and no increments carried out).

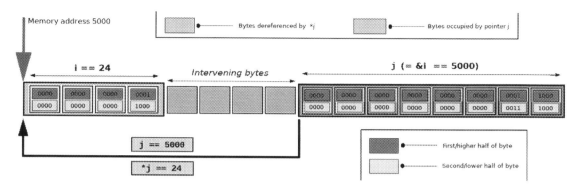

Figure 11-1. *An int pointer (embodied by the bold black arrow)*

Be sure you understand—and agree with—Figure 11-1. If not, things will get difficult. In C, one must always be willing to visualize memory layout.

There are a couple of points to deliberate on for the declaration: `int * j = &i;`

- Most problems with understanding basic usage of pointers are a direct result of falling into the trap of forgetting that this declaration revolves around two numbers, not just the one number i (which occupies four bytes in memory). The address at which i is stored is saved as the second number j (which occupies eight bytes in memory under the AMD64 architecture).

  The declaration `int * k = 0;` gets just one number k spanning eight bytes.

- As far as the compiler is concerned, spaces on either side of the asterisk in a pointer declaration are optional. But code is eminently more readable and comprehensible (particularly for someone getting acquainted with pointer usage) with the space before the asterisk discarded and the one after retained—although this runs contrary to standard, recommended coding guidelines for C, which, quite often as well as quite incorrectly, suggest the opposite.

  The preceding declarations thus become:

```
int* j = &i;
// (The style above stresses j as a separate number)
// The 'standard' style: int *j = &i;
```

```
    // (This form suggests &i is being assigned to *j: Not true)

    int* k = 0;
    // (k is what is called a null pointer: all 64 bits off)
```

The standard pointer declaration style becomes even more misleading when we bring in strings and functions. So, we'll just stick with removal of the space before the asterisk and retention of the one after. The one thing you must not do with this pointer declaration style is declare a pointer among a bunch of declarations in a single statement. This is the reason C+ forbids multiple declarations in one statement.

Pointers can, when needed, be subclassed. At times, you will need to be sure that the pointer cannot alter the variable it holds the address of (pointer-to-const) or that the address a pointer holds does not change (const pointer):

```
const int* j = &i; // makes (*j)++ impossible
int* const j = &i; // makes j++ impossible
```

The const modifier can be used to declare normal variables too, not just pointers:

```
const int n = 1024; // n can never change
```

Another special type of pointer is one that points to an unspecified type:

```
int n = 99;
void* pn = &n;
printf("%p\n", pn); // prints the address of n
```

void* pointers are used heavily in programming interfaces as they accommodate all pointer types. Runtime casting determines the further behavior of a void* pointer.

Another pointer type is the null pointer, which holds the hypothetical address 0. If a pointer has been assigned 0, the program promises not to use the pointer any further before assigning a valid memory address to it—otherwise, the program will crash.

A good safeguard against null pointers is the rudimentary if:

```
if (ptr)
{
    // do something with ptr

}
else
```

```
{
    // first make ptr point to a valid memory address
    // now do something with ptr

}
```

It is a good, sound practice to initialize a pointer with the value 0 until you get some valid memory address to assign to it.

11.1.7 Arrays

The original C term for array is "vector," but we will use the term array because the term vector could cause confusion with the C++ type `std::vector`.

When declaring an array in C, you can specify the array length yourself or let the compiler compute it (at compile-time). Since the array size (and therefore the array length) must be known at compile-time, you must use a numeric literal for the length or leave out the length input for the compiler to determine on its own.

Here is an array of three integers:

```
int iarray[] = { 2, 5, 9 };
```

–or–

```
int iarray[3] = { 2, 5, 9 };
```

The elements of the array can be denoted with `iarray[0]`, `iarray[1]`, and `iarray[2]`.

Arrays in C are closely tied to pointers. So next we need to tackle the relationship between pointers and arrays.

When you declare an array, C automatically generates a pointer to the first element in the array. The name of the pointer is the same as the name of the array.

```
int iarray[] = { 2, 5, 9 };
```

You declared an array. Backstage, the compiler also generated an implicit pointer:

```
int* iarray = <address where the first integer (2) got stored>;
```

If you print out *iarray (in effect dereferencing iarray as a pointer), you will see 2 in the output. The iarray pointer generated by the compiler is a const pointer: it will always point to the first element in the array. It is also an implicit pointer because no separate memory is allocated for the pointer.

Elements in an array occupy contiguous (i.e., no-gap-between) memory. Printing *(iarray + 1) is therefore guaranteed to output the array's second element. The second element of iarray can thus be accessed with either of two equivalent ways:

```
iarray[1]
-OR-
*(iarray  +  1)
```

Let's put some illustrative code around the iarray[] array:

```c
#include <stdio.h>

int main()
{
    int iarray[] = { 2, 5, 9 };

    // The following operation is known as casting, i.e. type-change
    // We  are changing (int* const) to (int*)
    int* ptr = (int*) iarray; // iarray is const; ptr is non-const
    ptr++;                    // step INC

    // The standard way to find the gap (in bytes) between pointers:
    printf("A: %ld\n", (char*) ptr - (char*) iarray);

    printf("B:  sizeof(ptr)  =  %d\n",  sizeof(ptr));
    printf("C: sizeof(iarray) =  %d\n", sizeof(iarray));
    return 0;
}
```

The preceding code prints the following:

```
A: 4
B: sizeof(ptr) = 8
C: sizeof(iarray) = 12
```

Here are notes for the output:

- A: We added 1 to the pointer `ptr` at step INC (pointer increment). But inside memory, `ptr` is pushed (1 * `sizeof(int)` =) 4 bytes ahead of `iarray`.

- B: You cannot compute the array length or size via the explicit pointer `ptr` because `sizeof(ptr)` just returns the size of a pointer (8 bytes). You can, though, compute the array size with the implicit pointer `iarray`. If you need the array length instead, use `sizeof(iarray)/si zeof(iarray[0])`.

Note   Incrementing a pointer by 1 increments the address it holds by the number of bytes corresponding to (the size of the data type pointed to).

An explicit pointer can never be used to compute an array's length or size.

11.1.8 Differentiating Between Stack and Heap

The preceding section opens a gateway to one fundamental concept in C: the difference between stack memory and heap memory.

It also opens a gully to squeeze in operator `new`—which actually is a C++ facility, but can be used in C when using `c++` as the compiler. (C itself uses `malloc()`, declared in the header file `stdlib.h`.)

Whenever the C compiler steps into a function (including `main()`), it initializes a special memory management pointer informally known as top-of-stack (TOS), which for simplicity we can assume to start at the value 0 at the beginning of a function.

If the function declares a variable, such as `int d1 = 1;`, the compiler allocates four bytes for `d1` and pushes TOS up by four.

Let's say your code then has:

```
if (d1)
{
    int d2 = 2;
    int d3 = 3;
}
```

Stepping into the if, the compiler will save the original TOS pointer (which is 4). Then d2 and d3 get pushed onto the stack, and TOS gets pushed up another (4 * 2 =) eight bytes.

The if block then ends and the compiler rewinds the stack. This means TOS is restored to the original value, 4. Similarly, when the function itself comes to an end, TOS falls all the way back to 0.

Since stack memory is precious (typically just a few MB), you should attempt to keep big variables (like an array of length 10000) out of the stack. Instead, such variables should go into the heap, which you can think of as a vast ocean of memory available at runtime, and not at compile-time. Heap is a more efficient representation of memory, allowing faster traversals and a wider range of operations (not just push and pop, the only operations available in the stack).

We can now return to the example of the previous subsection:

```
int iarray[] = { 2, 5, 9 };
```

The preceding declaration creates a stacked array, the size of which as reported by operator sizeof is 12.

The heap option is known as dynamic allocation (vis-a-vis stack allocation we used previously). Heap (or dynamic) allocation is done with operator new:

```
int* parray = new int[3]; // parray itself resides in the stack
```

You can then fill up the elements, which lie in the heap:

```
parray[0] = 2;
parray[1] = 5;
parray[2] = 9;
```

The total memory consumption of the array is 8 bytes (stack) plus 12 bytes (heap). With heap allocation, all that the compiler knows upfront about memory is that a pointer needs to be allocated (on the stack). The rest of the memory is obtained at runtime as per the programmer's needs (on the heap). It is worth stressing that compile-time memory allocation occurs entirely on the stack.

Note   You cannot obtain the number of elements in the heaped array via its pointer: sizeof will simply report the size of the pointer, which is always 8 in the AMD64 architecture.

While stack memory is entirely managed by the compiler, memory obtained on the heap has to be released manually. Or else you would create a memory leak.

Heap memory release is done with operator `delete`:

```
delete[]   parray;
parray = 0;
```

If the pointer points not to an array but to a variable, the square brackets should be omitted:

```
delete pvariable;
pvariable = 0;
```

When you call operator `delete` on a pointer, you must assign 0 to it. If you don't zero out the pointer, you create a dangerous kind of pointer known as *wild pointer*—a pointer that's neither null nor points to a valid memory location. It will remain wild until you assign a fresh, valid memory address to it with the `new` operator. If you try to use the pointer while it is wild for normal operation, your application will crash. While source code can guard itself against null pointers with an elementary `if` check, there is no safeguard against a wild pointer.

One final point that fits in this section is that C compilers never check for array boundaries. If you create an array of size 3, and then write to `element[3]` (which actually means element number 4 because array indexing starts at 0), you will be writing to overflowed memory—with the unhappy, possible fallout of crashing the application.

11.1.9 Strings in C

Having got the hang of pointers, it is time to look at a widely used application of pointers: C-style strings.

C-style strings are pointer paradigms with a twist. Here is an introduction:

```
char* ptr = "Hello"; // statement A
```

It seems an impossible statement. At RHS, you have a string literal (bunch of ASCII symbols in double quotes) to be assigned to LHS, which is a numeric entity (pointer).

When developing the C language, Dennis Ritchie decided that a string literal would be placed in memory and the address of the first symbol in the string literal would be returned to serve as a placeholder for the string literal in the remaining expression.

So what happens with the previous statement is that "Hello" is stored in memory and the address of H gets assigned to ptr. An elegant facility that makes up for C's lack of a separate string type and permits highly efficient string operations.

Beware of the difference between ptr and *ptr. ptr is a pointer to the start to the string literal "Hello", while *ptr is the starting char itself. In other words, H. Just as dereferencing an int pointer dereferences four bytes, dereferencing a char pointer dereferences just one byte.

There's one point to note about string literals. Before the compiler stores them in memory, it automatically appends a null byte.

Note   A null byte is 0 assigned to each of eight contiguous bits; the set of which can also be denoted as \0. A "null byte" is also called a "null char".

\0 can be also assigned to a long (64 bits). Remember, 0 is the same as \0.

A null byte serves as end-of-string marker. Any C library function that deals with a string processes the string only up to the position of the first byte that has a value of 0. If the string has no null byte, the function will overshoot the string's boundary and quite likely crash the application.

Statement A is thus perfectly equivalent to: char* ptr = "Hello\0";

Figure 11-2 depicts the memory layout with the string "Hello" residing at memory address 5000, and the pointer ptr pointing to the string.

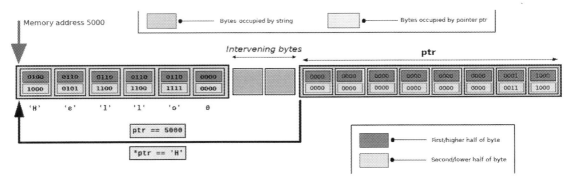

Figure 11-2. *A char pointer (embodied by the bold black arrow)*

Neither `ptr` nor `*ptr` is equal to "Hello": `ptr` evaluates as 5000, and `*ptr` evaluates as 72, the ASCII code for H. When referenced by code at runtime though, `ptr` gets replaced by the string residing at 5000, the address it evaluates as.

There are a few useful string-manipulation functions you need to know.

- `strlen(p)` determines the length of the string (pointed to by) `p`.

- `strcpy(p1, p2)` copies the data of `p2` into the buffer for `p1`.

- `strcat(p1, p2)` appends the data of `p2` to the buffer pointed to by `p1`.

- `strcmp(p1, p2)` compares the buffers of `p1` and `p2`, returning 0 if they are same.

C string functions are declared in `<string.h>`, which you can `#include` as usual. `strcpy()`/`strcat()`/`strcmp()` have size-wise counterparts that mandate the maximum buffer offset to be operated on: `strlcpy()`/`strlcat()`/`strncmp()`

It is not the best idea to use `strlen()` to find out whether or not a string is empty.

```
if (strlen(p) > 0)
{
    // do something with pointer p
}
```

is better written as:

```
if (*p)
{
    // do something with pointer p
}
```

Similarly, copying an empty string into a buffer with `strcpy()` is better done with:

```
*p = 0;
```

Of course, you have to ensure that `p` already points to a valid memory location before you can start reading from or writing to `*p`.

Statement A is also roughly—albeit not exactly—equivalent to:

```
char ptr2[] = { 'H', 'e', 'l', 'l', 'o', 0 };
```

which is nothing but a long-hand way of writing:

```
char ptr2[] = "Hello"; // statement B
```

So what is the difference between statement A and statement B?

They seem so similar that, between them, there seems to be a redundancy.

Here they are again, juxtaposed for clear comparison:

```
char* ptr   = "Hello"; // statement A
char ptr2[] = "Hello"; // statement B
```

ptr2, an implicit pointer auto-generated by the compiler, is a const pointer. But what is pointed to by ptr2 is variable. So you cannot alter the address ptr2 holds, but you can alter its buffer:

```
ptr2[0] = 'C'; // Hello becomes Cello
```

Essentially this means that you cannot do ptr2 = <>;, but you can always do *ptr2 = <>;.

Now let's return to statement A. With ptr, the reverse becomes true: ptr is a non-const pointer. So these are permissible:

```
ptr++; // ptr now points to 'e'
ptr = "Something else"; // ptr now points to 'S'
```

But what ptr points to is const—*even though this has not been declared*. Strings declared via the explicit pointer arrangement and initialized with a string literal have their contents stored in memory as read-only. So while you can do ptr = <>;, you can never do *ptr = <>;.

The funny thing is, because of the way ptr has been declared, the compiler will allow you to write *ptr = <something>; in your code. It will compile successfully and then—at runtime—it will crash your application.

Therefore, for safety, always prefix const when declaring a string pointer initialized with a literal:

```
const char* ptr = "Hello"; // statement A modified for good
```

The string pointed to by ptr is deemed an immutable string: it can never change. The array pointed to by ptr2 is mutable at runtime.

11.1.10 Signature of `main()`

C permits you to prototype `main()` in three different ways, each of which can return `void`, but should preferably always return an `int`:

- `int main(void)`: This form disables any startup parameters.

- `int main()`: This declares `main()` with an empty argument list, but `main()` will accept any number of parameters, including zero.

- `int main(int argc, char* argv[])`: If you need to process startup arguments, you can use the `main()` declaration, which utilizes a pointer to an array of strings. `argc` is the number of startup arguments (minimum 1), while the `argv` array holds each of the command-line arguments to the application (the first being the name of the executable itself). The `v` at the end of `argv` stands for vector, the original C term for array. The argument names `argc` and `argv` are not standard and can be anything of the user's choice.

Since `argv` is both an array and a pointer, the declaration can also be stated as:

```
int main(int argc, char** argv)
```

C under Unix permits yet another signature, which is prohibited by POSIX:

```
int main(int argc, char* argv[], char* envp[])
```

The `envp` array holds the program's environment.

POSIX mandates instead that you use one of the three standard signatures, and when you need to explore the environment, use the global variable `environ`:

```
extern char**  environ;
// The location of environ's definition is implementation-specific

int e = 0;

while (environ[e])
{
    puts(environ[e++]);
}
```

11.1.11 Branching and Looping

if-else and switch-case statements are largely self-illustrative. So I will leave them to self-enlightenment.

A special—and very useful—form of if-else is the ternary operator ? (which can be used for assignment as well as execution control):

```
int i = 101;
int i2 = (i > 100) ? i :  100;
(i2 > 200) ? puts("Big") : puts("Not  so  big");
```

Looping is done with for and while, just as in shell scripting.

A for loop in C resembles:

```
for (int n = 0; n < 100; n++)
{
    printf("n = %d\n", n);
}
```

The for condition is actually a composite of three parts (all optional).

- int n = 0;   : Executed once when the loop begins

- n < 100;   : Evaluated at the start of each iteration

- n++   : Performed at the end of each iteration

Since all three components are optional, an infinitely-looping for is for(;;){}.

A while loop resembles:

```
int n = 128;

while (n > 100)
{
    printf("n = %d\n", n);
    n--;
}
```

11.1.12 Arithmetic and Logical Operations

Mathematical operations are carried out with the well-known operators, like +, ++, *, and /. You can readily use them as you are wont to. One operator that bears a mention is %, the modulus operator. It returns the remainder of a division. For example, 7%3 returns 1.

Bit-wise operations need to be understood well—C code tends to use those quite heavily. We'll focus on five bit-wise operators: LSHIFT, RSHIFT, AND, OR, and XOR.

For our illustration, we'll take two decimal numbers (one-byte-wide each, corresponding to the data type char):

- 3, which corresponds to binary (0 0 0 0 0 0 1 1)

- 6, which corresponds to binary (0 0 0 0 0 1 1 0)

Bit shifting is done with << (left shift) and >> (right shift), both of which take a numeric operand (which we will call n).

Left-shifting moves all the bits in a number n spots to the left, with the vacancies on the right getting filled with 0:

```
char j = 6 << 4; // yields binary 0 1 1 0 0 0 0 0 = 96
```

Right-shifting moves all the bits in a number n spots to the right, with the vacancies on the left getting filled with 0:

```
char k = 3 >> 1; // yields binary 0 0 0 0 0 0 0 1 = 1
```

The other three bit-wise operators compare bits at the same locations in two numbers. For each pair of bits compared:

- AND (&) returns 1 if both bits are 1, otherwise it returns 0.

- OR (|) returns 0 if both bits are 0, otherwise it returns 1.

- XOR (^) returns 0 if both bits are 0 or both bits are 1. Otherwise it returns 1.

The following computation table should now be readily comprehensible:

```
3 AND 6:                3 OR 6:                 3 XOR 6:

  0 0 0 0 0 0 1 1 (3)      0 0 0 0 0 0 1 1 (3)      0 0 0 0 0 0 1 1 (3)
& 0 0 0 0 0 1 1 0 (6)    | 0 0 0 0 0 1 1 0 (6)    ^ 0 0 0 0 0 1 1 0 (6)
-----------------       -----------------       -----------------
= 0 0 0 0 0 0 1 0 (2)    = 0 0 0 0 0 1 1 1 (7)    = 0 0 0 0 0 1 0 1 (5)
```

XOR, short for Exclusive OR and pronounced "zor," is a pretty interesting operator. Note that, as computed, (3 ^ 6) returns 5. Further, (5 ^ 3) returns 6, and (5 ^ 6) returns 3. In other words, the three numbers 3, 5, and 6 form a XOR ring in which the third number can always be "guessed" by XOR'ing the other two numbers.

In general, the following assertion will succeed for any two integers n and m:

```
assert(n == ((n ^ m) ^ m));
```

(To use assertions in your code, you need to #include <assert.h>.)

This characteristic is utilized in many encryption algorithms. You can yourself encrypt the contents of a file by XOR'ing each of its bytes with a magic number (denoted by m in the previous assertion). The encrypted file can only be decrypted by someone who knows that magic number: XOR'ing each byte in the encrypted file with that magic number will yield the original unencrypted file.

Bit-wise AND and OR have logical counterparts: && (which I will cheekily call *LAND*) and || (which I'll call *LOR*).

Both logical operators treat numbers as booleans: non-zero numbers evaluate as true, while 0 evaluates as false.

LAND returns true if both booleans are true. Else it returns false.

(1 && 2) thus returns true. Quite noticeably, (1 & 2) returns 0 (equivalent to false) because 1 is binary 01, and 2 is binary 10. (01 AND 10) finds no bit that is on in both representations, yielding 0 as the return value.

LOR returns false if both booleans are false. Else it returns true.

It helps to know that LAND and LOR will evaluate the second entity only if needed: (0 && <expression2>) will return false, and (1 || <expression2>) will return true, without <expression2> being evaluated at all at runtime.

11.1.13 Functions

Every C function must return something. If a function has nothing suitable to return, its declaration should use the return type void. In this context, void means "nothing," which is different from null (zero). This is also different from what void means in the declaration void* p;: the declared void type means "anything".

Functions in C need to be declared before first usage. If a function is implemented before first usage, no separate declaration is necessary, but is usually advisable for ease of reference. Function implementation is also known as function definition.

Both the following are technically acceptable:

```
int fx(int y);

int main()
{
    fx(5);
    return 0;
}

int fx(int y)
{
    printf("%d\n", y);
    return 0;
}
```

```
int fx(int y)
{
    printf("%d\n", y);
    return 0;
}

int main()
{
    fx(5);
    return 0;
}
```

Either way, the function fx() is said to have the prototype:

```
int fx(int);
```

As you can deduce, a function's prototype is just the declaration without argument variables' names.

Just like variables, functions have addresses too. From a programmer's perspective, a function's address is envisaged most easily as its opening brace.

A function's prototype can therefore be used to generate a pointer to the function. For our example function fx(), we can generate and use the pointer as follows:

```
int main()
{
    int (*pfx)(int) = &fx;

    (*pfx)(9);
    return 0;
}
```

This code prints 9 on standard output.

If a function's declaration is in some other header file, you need to #include that header (before first use). If the function's implementation is in a library other than the standard C library (libc), your sources must link to that library when you build your sources' binary—otherwise, the compiler will succeed and then the linker will gripe.

One final point in the context of functions is the static keyword. A variable declared in a function as static will be initialized just once and will have its value preserved for the next run:

```
int fs()
{
    static int s = 0; // initialization will occur only at first run
    s++;

    printf("%d\n", s);
    return s;
}
```

Each time fs() is invoked, it will print one more than during the previous run.

11.1.14 Declarations and Definitions

In C, declaration is telling the compiler a variable's type (or a function's signature).

Definition means acquisition of memory—whether for a variable or for a function. Once something has been defined, it has a valid address inside memory, and therefore you can generate a pointer to it.

This statement is noteworthy:

```
int i;
```

Obviously, this qualifies as a declaration. But since nothing has been assigned to i, the value of i is undefined and you will get garbage if you print i as such. But i itself is defined: the compiler automatically acquires stack memory for variable declarations. The foregoing declaration is thus both a declaration as well as a definition.

The situation gets trickier with a pointer that is intended to point into the heap:

```
char* p; // You intend to later do: p = new char[1000];
```

Is p defined? You can argue that the eight bytes p needs in the stack would be secured, so it is defined. The counterpoint, of course, is that—until operator new is invoked—p points to garbage and should therefore be considered undefined. The way I see it, the body is defined; the spirit is not.

The following statement at the global level (i.e., outside any function) in file source1.c is a pure declaration (i.e., no definition):

```
extern int x;
```

What this statement tells the compiler is: this source code file would like to use a variable x, which is defined in some other source code file. The compiler will then proceed to compile the source code file, generating its object code, which has a placeholder for x. The linker must be able to fully resolve the placeholder.

Let's say the other source code file is `source2.c`. That file must have a statement such as:

```
int x = 0; // The definition of x
```

If the writer who wrote `source2.c` wants x to not be visible to any other source code file (compilation unit), it can declare and define x as follows:

```
static int x = 0; // Invisible to all other compilation units
```

If `source2.c` declares x as `static`, linking will now fail owing to an unresolvable placeholder in the object code for `source1.c`.

A variable declared as `static` thus means entirely different things depending on whether the declaration is within a function ("preserve value across runs") or outside of any function ("hide from other compilation units").

11.1.15 Structs

The C programming language allows you to create data structures, each identified by the keyword `struct`. A `struct` is a conglomerate type:

```
struct student
{
    char name[64];
    int roll_number;
    double gpa;
};
```

struct instances are almost never passed as such to functions. Instead, when passing a `struct` instance to a function, you pass in a pointer: `void fx(student* ptr);`. If you pass in the instance itself, the compiler will copy the whole instance into the function. This is inefficient and prevents the function from acting on the original instance.

Note   C uses call-by-value only when passing arguments to functions. If you pass
in a `struct` instance, the instance gets copied. If you pass in a pointer, the pointer
gets copied. If you need to pass in the original pointer itself, you can't—but you
can pass in a pointer to the pointer (and then dereference, or double-dereference,
inside the function).

If `fx` wants to process an array of `student` instances, it can accept two arguments.
The first argument is a pointer to the first element, and the second argument is for the
number of elements in the array:

```
void fx(student* ptr, int max);
```

A C `struct` is not permitted member functions, which is a key difference with object-
oriented programming. Note that since we are using c++ as the compiler, the compiler
will allow you to use member functions in a `struct`. But we will not utilize that facility
and stick to C semantics (until we hit the land of Vala).

Inside `main()`, you can create a `student` variable and use it as follows—quite notably,
with . or -> needed when accessing its members:

```
student stud;                           student* pstud = new student;

stud.roll_number = 1234;                pstud->roll_number = 1234;
strcpy(stud.name, "Chuck");             strcpy(pstud->name, "Chuck");
stud.gpa = 2.0;                         pstud->gpa = 2.0;
```

`(sizeof(student))` should report:

```
sizeof(roll_number) + sizeof(name) + sizeof(gpa) = 4 + 64 + 8 = 76.
```

But it doesn't—it reports 80. This is the number of bytes any `student` variable
occupies on the stack.

There's nothing foul here. For reasons related to efficiency, C compilers inflate the
size of a `struct` so that its stack consumption falls along word boundaries. A word in
computation is the equivalent of the size of a pointer under the architecture concerned.
Since AMD64 uses 8 bytes for a pointer, `struct` sizes will always be multiples of 8
(unless you use special pre-processor directives that force the compiler to squeeze every
possible extra byte out of the `struct`).

If you want to reduce the size of a struct, reduce its stack consumption. student. name occupies 64 bytes on the stack. You can cut it down to 8 by declaring name not as a statically-allocated array but as a pointer:

```
struct student
{
    char* pname;
    int roll_number;
    double gpa;
};
```

Our struct's size falls from 80 to 24, but now it needs you to initialize the pname pointer with memory allocation:

```
student stud;                           student* pstud = new student;

stud.roll_number = 1234;                pstud->roll_number = 1234;
stud.pname = new char[64];              pstud->pname = new char[64];
strcpy(stud.pname, "Chuck");            strcpy(pstud->pname, "Chuck");
stud.gpa = 2.0;                         pstud->gpa = 2.0;
```

If you declare the student variable via the pointer mechanism (pstud) as RHS in the preceding code snippet, you create a memory leak by cleaning up with the very clean-looking code:

```
delete pstud;
pstud = 0;
```

The reason the memory leak occurs is that pstud itself holds a handle to dynamically allocated memory (courtesy pname).

When you are done with pstud, the right way to release all heap memory is:

```
delete[] pstud->pname;
pstud->pname = 0;
delete  pstud;
pstud = 0;
```

The memory leak occurs with the statically-allocated stud object too if you let it get popped off the stack without releasing memory first with: delete[] stud.pname;

As a side-note, it is perfectly safe to call operator delete on a null pointer, which is another reason to zero out a pointer after releasing its memory.

There is another way to `create` student with a low stack size and with greater flexibility. You can declare name as the C++ type `std::string`, which you can use if you `#include <string>` (and then use c++, not cc as the compiler).

Here is the revised declaration for the `struct`:

```
#include <string>

struct student
{
    std::string name;
    int roll_number;
    double gpa;
};
```

The following client code in `main()` shows sample usage:

```
student* pstud = new student;

pstud->name = "";
pstud->name   +=  "Chuck";

printf("%d\n", sizeof(*pstud)); // Size is 24 this time around too
puts(pstud->name.c_str());      // c_str() yields a read-only C-string

delete pstud;
pstud = 0;

return 0;
```

`std::string` has a member function `c_str()`, which creates a copy of the C++ string variable as a read-only, traditional C-style string.

The reverse—conversion of a C-style string to `std::string`—is possible too:

```
const char* p = "Hello";
std::string ss;
ss.assign(p);                    // Or: ss = p;
printf("%d\n", ss.length());     // prints 5
```

11.1.16 Preprocessor

A significant agency in the build process is the preprocessor (cpp under Unix), which gets to look at your sources before the compiler does. It is not often that the preprocessor (or the linker) gets invoked independently: invoking the compiler itself is the usual way of invoking the preprocessor.

The preprocessor's primary tasks are:

- Text substitution

- Enabling conditional compilation, i.e., determining what portions of the sources are to be revealed to or hidden from the compiler

All directives to the preprocessor begin with a # sign. When the preprocessor looks at the following lines

```
#include <some_header1>
#include "some_header2"
```

it just inputs the contents of the files some_header1 and some_header2 to replace the directives. In effect, what the compiler gets to see is the contents of the headers in place of the #include directives.

The convention for headers in angular brackets is to fulfill any -I command-line switches (each of which can specify a directory path), and then search in system-default directories. A typical example of the latter is /usr/include.

The convention for headers in double quotes is to search in the current directory, although compilers are free to search system directories as well.

Another common directive to the preprocessor is:

```
#define SOME_CONSTANT 1024
```

When the preprocessor sees the preceding directive, it searches to the end of the file for the token SOME_CONSTANT and replaces it with 1024 (unless SOME_CONSTANT gets redefined/undefined).

Just in case you are not familiar with the term "token," it is just a sequence of symbols that must be treated together when parsing source code.

`while(counter>100)` is the same as:

```
while (
counter
> 100
)
```

That's a total of six tokens.

If you need to parse some text yourself for its tokens, C has a very useful routine called `strtok()`, which does that job (read `man 3 strtok` for its usage). A couple of other parsing-related functions are `strstr(p1, p2)` (search string p1 for substring p2) and `strchr(p, <ch>)` (search string p for `char <ch>`).

What if your sources had the following code:

```
#include <some_header>
#include <some_header>
```

Would the preprocessor pull in the same header twice?

It depends on whether `some_header` incorporates a header guard. A header guard is simply the concept of enclosing your header's contents in a section enabled by a unique preprocessor constant:

```
#ifndef __SOME__HEADER__
#define __SOME__HEADER
// contents of header
#endif
```

If there is no header guard in `some_header`, header input would indeed occur twice—possibly leading to build failure. That's why well-written headers use header guards.

11.1.17 Variable Argument Lists

The pre-processor's text substitution services are not restricted to just global constants. The pre-processor can also create macros, which are functions expanded inline:

```
#define SUM(a, b) ((a) + (b))
```

The use of macros is deprecated because they deprive you of the compiler's type-checking routines. But compilers use macros internally for a variety of tasks.

One such task is the powerful feature of variable argument lists for functions.

Let's say you've been asked to write strcombine()—a combination of strcpy() and strcat() that can copy the first string and then append not just one string to the destination buffer but any number (zero included) of them.

The most common way of implementing variable argument lists is to pass in pointers for each of the variables you want to be processed by the function. The final argument is 0 (signifying a null pointer), which stands for end-of-arguments.

```
#include <stdarg.h>
#include <assert.h>
#include <string.h>

char* strcombine(char* dest, const char* src, ...)
{
    assert(dest);
    assert(src);

    const char* p = 0;
    va_list   vl;

    va_start(vl, src);
    strcpy(dest, src);

    while (p = va_arg(vl, const char*))
    {
        strcat(dest, p);
    }

    va_end(vl);
    return dest;
}
// main() can now use: strcombine(ptr, "Hello", "World1", "World2", 0);
// Note: main() must pre-allocate sufficient memory for ptr
```

va_list is a type that is implemented in different ways by different compilers. Whatever the implementation, it can hold multiple and variable number of pointers.

va_start(), va_arg(), and va_end() are usually implemented as macros by compilers. va_start() retrieves the first argument and initializes va_list with it. All further arguments are popped off with va_arg(). When va_arg() returns something that denotes end-of-arguments (a null pointer in the preceding code snippet), we stop looking for further arguments and call va_end(), which gracefully finalizes the va_list and lets our function return normally.

11.1.18 Input/Output

To read from standard input, the C library functions getchar() and scanf() should serve you in good stead. Similarly, for writing to standard output, puts() and printf() are usually enough.

To format a buffer in memory and output formatted text to the buffer, you can use memset() and sprintf():

```
char buffer[32];
memset(buffer, 0, sizeof(buffer));  // nulls all the chars in buffer
// anything else //
sprintf(buffer, "%d", 1234);        // prints "1234\0" to buffer
```

When you need to read from or write to a disk file (or write to standard error), you'll have to use the stream-based file I/O functions of C, of which there is a handsome army. The stream written-to/read-from is a FILE* pointer. The type FILE as well as all I/O routines are declared in <stdio.h>

The principal I/O routines are:

- fopen(): Opens a new stream and returns FILE*; null upon failure
- fseek(): Sets the file position indicator for stream
- fread(): Reads bytes from stream
- fscanf(): Reads a field from stream
- fwrite(): Writes bytes to stream
- fprintf(): Prints formatted text to stream
- feof(): Checks for end-of-file condition for stream
- fflush(): Commits all pending I/O operations on stream
- fclose(): Closes the stream

You can read more about the I/O routines from the respective man pages.

11.1.19 Using System Calls for I/O

One excellent option to keep in mind for I/O under Unix is using system calls—service requests made directly to the Unix kernel using low-level, native functions (and not the standard C library functions). While the system call approach does not necessarily lead to any performance advantage over C library routines, it allows for more fine-grained control. Low-level facilities (e.g., file locking) are available only when using system call-based I/O.

If you decide to use system calls for I/O, the primary calls to use are `read()` and `write()`. But you have to be prepared for one hiccup: `read()` does not guarantee to read all data in a single shot, and `write()` does not guarantee to write all data in a single shot. So you have to restart them until all data has been processed.

Here is a sample utility that copies a file using system calls.

```c
#include <string.h>
#include <assert.h>

// Unix system headers
#include <sys/stat.h>
#include <sys/file.h>
#include <unistd.h>

int copyfile(const char* infile, const char* outfile)
{
    struct stat filestat;
    int result =  stat(infile, &filestat);

    assert(result  ==  0);
    assert(S_ISREG(filestat.st_mode));
    // In production code, replace assertions with error handling

    const int len = filestat.st_size;

    // For huge files, you'll want to implement a proper data structure.
    // The following approach is fine for illustration though. char*
    buffer = new char[len + 1];
    memset(buffer, 0, len + 1);

    int infd = open(infile, O_RDONLY); // need no mode for O_RDONLY
```

```
int outfd = open(outfile, O_RDWR | O_CREAT, 0644);
assert(infd  > 2); // 0 = stdin; 1 = stdout; 2 = stderr;
assert(outfd > 2);

int inpos = 0;
int outpos = 0;

while (inpos < len)
{
    i += read(infd, (char*) (buffer + inpos), len - inpos);
}

while (outpos < len)
{
    j += write(outfd, (char*) (buffer + outpos), len - outpos);
}

close(infd);
close(outfd);

delete[]   buffer;
buffer = 0;

// Return error code if needed. The C standard for success is 0:
return  0;
}
```

Very little error handling is done in this code, except for a few assertions, which work only in debug mode and are likely to be treated as comments by the compiler when building for optimized release mode.

This utility is equivalent to cp file1 file2. More instructive is the equivalent of cat file1 > file2: we send file1 over a pipe created with the pipe() call.

Communication over a pipe can take place only between two processes forked via fork(), another system call. fork() splits the invoking process into two copies— one deemed parent and the other child. So a call to pipe() is invariably followed immediately by a call to fork().

The parent and the child forked off are both exact copies (except for the child's new process ID) of the original process, which now becomes the parent. The child's PID (process ID) is determined at runtime by the kernel, and cannot be known in advance.

The fork() call has two distinct return values—the child's PID to the parent, and 0 to the child. The forked parent process thus gets to learn the child's PID, but the child remains blissfully unaware of the parent's PID.

Figure 11-3 depicts a process being split with a call to fork().

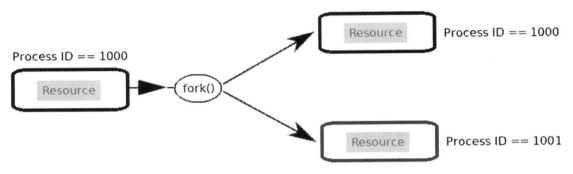

Figure 11-3. *Forking under Unix*

The resource depicted in Figure 11-3 becomes directly relevant to pipe communication as a set of two file descriptors—one for input, one for output—which the original process creates. Communication over those file descriptors by convention is taken as one-way: either the parent process writes and the child process reads, or the other way round. This is akin to the shell when you pipe a command's output to another command's standard input.

The sources that follow add an interesting twist: the sender (parent) process sleeps for a millisecond after sending every block of 4096 bytes. The writer (child) process must read the pipe (and write to the disk file) until the parent sends data across.

```
#include <string.h>
#include <assert.h>
#include <sys/stat.h>
#include <sys/file.h>
#include <unistd.h>

#include <time.h>                // Copy          *
                                 // these         |
                                 // lines         |
void millisleep()                // wherever      |
{                                // millisleep()  |
    struct timespec request
```

```
                                                    // is          |
    request.tv_sec = 0;                             // invoked     |
                                                    // in          |
    request.tv_nsec = 1000 * 1000;                  // the         |
    // 1 = nano; 1000 = micro; 1000 * 1000 = milli  // remainder   |
                                                    // of          |
    nanosleep(&request, 0);                         // this        |
}                                                   // chapter     *

int pipefile(const char* infile, const char* outfile)
{
    const int bs = 4096;

    int fd[2];
    pipe(fd);

    if (fork())
    {
        close(fd[0]); // parent just writes to the pipe using its fd[1]

        struct stat filestat;
        int result = stat(infile, &filestat);

        assert(result == 0);
        assert(S_ISREG(filestat.st_mode));

        const int len = filestat.st_size;

        char* buffer = new char[len + 1];
        memset(buffer, 0, len + 1);

        int infd = open(infile, O_RDONLY);
        assert(infd > 2);

        int iread = 0;

        while (iread < len)
        {
            iread += read(infd, (char*) (buffer + iread), len - iread);
        }
```

```
    close(infd);
    int written = 0;

    while (written < len)
    {
        int iwrite = 0;
        int to_write = ((len - written) >= bs) ? bs : len - written;

        while (iwrite < to_write)
        {
            iwrite += write
            (
                fd[1],
                (char*) (buffer + written + iwrite),
                to_write - iwrite
            );
        }

        written += to_write;
        millisleep();
    }

    delete[] buffer;
    buffer = 0;

    close(fd[1]);
}
else
{
    close(fd[1]); // child just needs to read the pipe using its fd[0]

    int outfd = open(outfile, O_RDWR | O_CREAT, 0644);
    assert(outfd > 2);

    char* buffer = new char[bs + 1];

    while (1)
    {
        memset(buffer, 0, bs + 1);
```

```
        int oread = read(fd[0], (char*) buffer, bs);

        if (oread <= 0)
        {
            break;
        }

        int owrite = 0;

        while (owrite < oread)
        {
            owrite += write
            (
                outfd,
                (char*) (buffer + owrite),
                oread - owrite
            );
        }
    }

    close(outfd);
    close(fd[0]);

    delete[] buffer;
    buffer = 0;
    }

    return 0;
}
```

It might be worthwhile to explicitly note that the parent and child have their own file descriptors for the pipe: fd[0] and fd[1] in the parent are independent of fd[0] and fd[1] in the child. So pipe() followed by fork() leads to four file descriptors.

Also note that the child process can get its parent's PID if it needs to—all it needs to do is use the getppid() system call. If the parent has already exited by that time, getppid() returns 1—the PID of init, the very first process created by the kernel. A related call is getpid(), which returns the process's own PID.

11.1.20 Multithreading with pthreads

The original Unix created at AT&T was a single-threaded operating system, in which any application serially fed operations to the CPU in a single channel of execution. Figure 11-4 shows three sets of operations lining up for the CPU to act on.

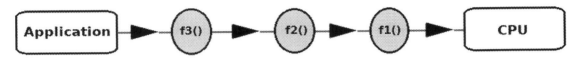

Figure 11-4. *The single thread way of operating*

The red-marked feeder line, along which the packets of operations are fed into the CPU, is the channel formally called a thread. With just one thread at the kernel's disposal, f2() cannot start as long as f1() runs, and then f3() has to wait its turn while f2() is being executed.

Until roughly 1990, this was all that was possible. Your application would be allotted a thread along which you could communicate operations to be executed to the CPU.

Under Unix, if the process needed to open another execution channel, it had to fork off a new process, which too had a single thread.

The 90s changed the game. Since creating a whole new process is an expensive operation demanding a lot of work and resources, the multi-threading idea surfaced: creating a new channel in the scope of the current process. This required a lot less work from the CPU and the OS. A process now still starts with only one thread, called the main thread. But the main thread can create more threads when needed.

Figure 11-5 shows the three sets of operations now running in parallel in the same process, each set hosted on a different thread.

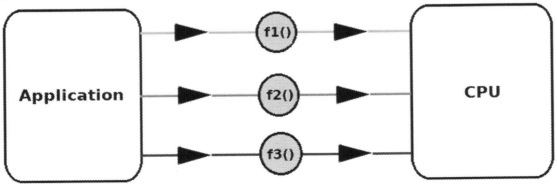

Figure 11-5. *The multiple thread way of operating*

Let's say f1() corresponds to main(), which means the top, red line in the preceding diagram represents the main thread. The top line—and therefore main()—must stay in business to give the other threads the chance to operate and finish off gracefully before returning. If main() returns, the whole process comes to an end.

The assignment the CPU has to undertake is to divide time between the threads so that each of them gets time—ranging from seconds to nanoseconds—to execute its operations. This assignment goes under the formal name of *context-switching.* Note that the CPU has to perform context-switching at two levels: context-switching among processes, and context-switching among threads in each process.

Under GNU systems, creating a new thread is done with pthread_create(). Before you call pthread_create(), you'll need a function that accepts an argument of type void* and has a return type of void*. The operations listed in that function will run on the new thread. To wait for the thread to finish, the creator can call pthread_join().

Here is a small utility to print the English alphabet on a new thread, starting with the letter passed in by main(). Build this with -lpthread to link to the pthread library.

```c
#include <pthread.h>
#include <stdio.h>

void* print_alphabet_lowercase(void* pv)
{
    char* pc = (char*) pv;

    for (char ch = *pc; ch <= 'z'; ch++)
    {
        printf("%c\n", ch);
        millisleep();
    }

    return 0;
}

int main()
{
    char starting = 'm';
    pthread_t pth;
```

```
    pthread_create(&pth, 0, &print_alphabet_lowercase, &starting);
    pthread_join(pth,  0);
    return 0;
}
```

All applications that want to use POSIX multithreading need the programmer to #include <pthread.h> in the sources and then link to libpthread with the command-line argument -lpthread to cc or c++ when compiling.

If the creator thread does not want to wait on the child thread, it should invoke the function pthread_detach() on the new thread so that any resources allocated for it by the kernel are automatically freed upon its exit. Further, if a thread needs to retrieve a handle to itself, it can call the pthread_self() function.

Soon after you start spawning threads in your code, you will run into synchronization problems. The following code shows the mess when the main thread tries to print to standard output too—the child thread's code, the same as before, continues to print the English alphabet in lowercase.

```
#include <pthread.h>
#include <stdio.h>

void* print_alphabet_lowercase(void* pv)
{
    for (char ch = (*((char*) pv)); ch <= 'z'; ch++)
    {
        printf("%c\n", ch);
        millisleep();
    }

    return 0;
}

int main()
{
    char starting = 'm';
    pthread_t pth;

    pthread_create(&pth, 0, &print_alphabet_lowercase, &starting);
```

```
    for (char ch = 'A'; ch <= 'Z'; ch++)
    {
        printf("%c\n", ch);
        millisleep();
    }

    pthread_join(pth, 0);
    return 0;
}
```

If you run the preceding code, you will find the output a garbled-up mixture of uppercase and lowercase letters. This happens because the main thread and the child thread are competing for a shared resource—standard output. The calls to `millisleep()` make the garble easier to notice.

The right way to write the preceding code is to synchronize with a mutex. The pthread library has a built-in type called `pthread_mutex_t`, a handy macro to initialize a mutex `PTHREAD_MUTEX_INITIALIZER`, and mutex locking/unlocking functions. If thread A locks the mutex, thread B will block trying to acquire the lock too, as long as thread A does not give up the lock.

```
#include <stdio.h>
#include <pthread.h>

pthread_mutex_t pmt = PTHREAD_MUTEX_INITIALIZER;

void* print_alphabet_lowercase(void*      pv)
{
    pthread_mutex_lock(&pmt); // mutex lock

    for (char ch = (*((char*) pv)); ch <= 'z'; ch++)
    {
        printf("%c\n", ch);
        millisleep();
    }

    pthread_mutex_unlock(&pmt);                    // mutex unlock
    return 0;
}
```

```
int main()
{
    char starting = 'm';
    pthread_t pth;

    pthread_create(&pth, 0, &print_alphabet_lowercase, &starting);
    pthread_mutex_lock(&pmt);                   // mutex lock

    for (char ch = 'A'; ch <= 'Z'; ch++)
    {
        printf("%c\n", ch);
        millisleep();
    }

    pthread_mutex_unlock(&pmt);                     // mutex unlock

    pthread_join(pth, 0);
    return 0;
}
```

In more complicated scenarios, using a mutex alone may not be enough. For such cases, the pthread library provides another data type—pthread_cond_t—which has to be used in conjunction with pthread_mutex_t. An interesting variation of the condition idea is the barrier: pthread_barrier_t.

I will leave research of pthread_cond_t and pthread_barrier_t to your own devices.

11.1.21 Socket Programming

For communication between processes on different machines, the standard methodology is *sockets*, which form the heart of TCP/IP networking. The original concept of communication via sockets was developed by the Berkeley Software Distribution (BSD) group at the University of California, Berkeley. Windows' implementation of sockets called Winsock is derived from—and bears a fair bit of resemblance to—Berkeley sockets. Most of the API names are the same in both GNU-based systems and Windows.

Application programming with sockets does not generally require detailed understanding of the layers involved, or how packets are routed from source to destination. The socket API calls are generally what you need to be concerned with. All socket-related functions are implemented under Unix as system calls.

One end of the communication channel in socket programming serves as a daemon (or server), while the other end serves as a client. The server keeps listening to the network, accepting connections from clients. Multiple clients can be simultaneously connected to a single server. When a client is done with all the communication it needed with server, it closes the socket at its end.

To communicate with a client, the server actually uses two sockets: one network-wide socket for accepting connections, and one socket (per client) for the actual communication with the client. The socket that accepts connections uses a fixed port number that the client must know in advance. The other socket uses a random, unique port number assigned by the operating system. So if there are n clients communicating with a server, the server has n+1 active sockets.

Establishing (and communicating over) a socket on the client side requires three steps:

1. Create a socket with the socket() call.

2. Connect the socket to the address of the server using the connect() call.

3. Send data using the write() call and receive data using read().

Establishing the server end is a five-step process:

1. Create a socket with the socket() call.

2. Bind the socket to a particular port using the bind() call.

3. Establish a willingness to accept incoming connections and specify the maximum queue length of incoming connections with the listen() call. If you set the maximum queue length to 0, the operating system will set the queue length to an implementation-defined reasonable value.

4. Accept a connection with the accept() call. This call will typically block until a client connects. The accept() call returns the descriptor of a new socket.

5. Send and receive data on the file descriptor returned by accept().

The last step is usually done on a new thread obtained via a call to pthread_create(). (You can though, if you want, instead use fork() to create a new process for communicating with the client.) The main thread just runs a loop to block on accept() and creates a client-specific thread each time accept() returns.

Also, like accept(), the read() call will block until data is available on the socket. Nonblocking socket I/O is possible, but is beyond the scope of this book.

Figure 11-6 is the communication schema for the server and the client when using Berkeley sockets. The diagram uses the symbol ▶◀ to depict a socket.

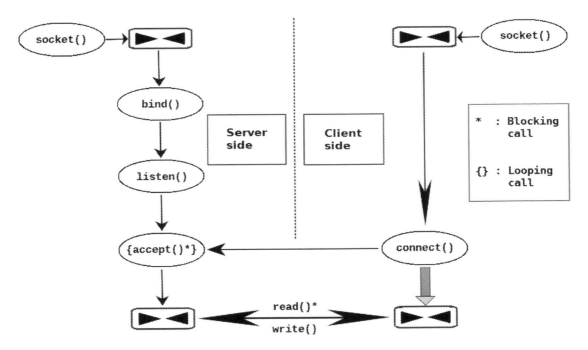

Figure 11-6. *Establishing and communicating over TCP/IP sockets*

Although still too early for the reader to feel well-versed, I find it best for the field of sockets to take the plunge straightaway into coding, and then plug the gaps in socket literacy as the need arises. We'll club all our knowledge of C with the introductory discourse on sockets to write a nifty pair of utilities:

- A very simple, non-secure FTP server ezftpd that supports file exchanges (but not interactive logins)

- A client `ezftp` that can download files from and upload files to the server with:

```
ezftp 192.168.1.3 get <file> // downloads <file> from ezftpd@192.168.1.3
ezftp 192.168.1.3 put <file> // uploads <file> to ezftpd@192.168.1.3
```

ezftpd needs one startup argument: the path of the directory that serves as its root. Any files uploaded show up here. Any files for which a download is requested must be available here (in the root of the directory). The port number the server listens on is 6666, with no restrictions on file sizes.

The sources that follow are broken into three parts—a header file that declares and defines common code, the server, and the client. Each part has introductory comments.

The first part contains the common sources. This part uses the `nothrow` option for operator `new`. This disables exceptions and ensures that a null pointer is returned upon failure.

Here are the common sources placed in a header file `ezftp.h`:

```
#ifndef EZFTP_H
#define EZFTP_H

#include <stdio.h>
#include <stdlib.h>
#include <string.h>
#include <ctype.h>
#include <new>
#include <unistd.h>
#include <sys/stat.h>
#include <sys/file.h>
#include <netinet/in.h>
#include <sys/socket.h>
#include <arpa/inet.h>

const int PORT = 6666;
const long MB = 1024*1024;

const char* CMDGET = "get";
const char* CMDPUT = "put";

int assert_zero(long n)
```

```
{
    if (n != 0)
    {
        fprintf(stderr, "Runtime check (n == 0) failed\n");
        exit(-1);
    }

    return 0;
}

int assert_greater(long n, long floor)
{
    if (n <= floor)
    {
        fprintf(stderr, "Runtime check (n > floor) failed\n");
        exit(-1);
    }

    return 0;
}

int f_receive(int datasocket, const char* infile)
{
    int fd = open(infile, O_RDWR | O_CREAT, 0644);
    assert_greater(fd, 2);

    int written = 0;

    while (1)
    {
        char* pbuffer = new(std::nothrow) char[MB];
        assert_greater((long)  pbuffer,  0);

        memset(pbuffer, 0, MB);

        int result  =  0;
        int iwritten = 0;              // written during this iteration

        int iread = read(datasocket, pbuffer, MB);
```

```
        if (iread <= 0)
        {
            delete[] pbuffer;
            pbuffer = 0;

            break;
        }

        while (iwritten < iread)
        {
            result = write
            (
                fd,
                (char*) (pbuffer + iwritten),
                iread - iwritten
            );

            assert_greater(result,   0);
            iwritten  +=  result;
        }

        written += iwritten;
        delete[] pbuffer;
        pbuffer = 0;
    }

    close(fd);
    return written;
}

int f_send(int datasocket, const char* infile)
{
    struct stat filestat;
    int result = lstat(infile, &filestat);

    if ((result != 0) || (! S_ISREG(filestat.st_mode)))
    {
        fprintf(stderr, "Bad filename: %s\n", infile);
        return -1;
```

```
}

const int len = filestat.st_size;
int fd = open(infile, O_RDONLY);
assert_greater(fd, 2);

int written = 0;

while (written < len)
{
    char* pbuffer = new(std::nothrow) char[MB];
    assert_greater((long)  pbuffer,  0);

    memset(pbuffer, 0, MB);
    result = 0;

    int iread = 0;          // read during this iteration
    int iwritten = 0;       // written during this iteration

    const int to_read = (len - written >= MB) ? MB : len - written;
    const int to_write = to_read;

    while (iread < to_read)
    {
        result = read
        (
            fd,
            (char*)  (pbuffer  + iread),
            to_read - iread
        );

        assert_greater(result,  0);
        iread += result;
    }

    while (iwritten < to_write)
    {
        result = write
        (
```

```
                datasocket,
                (char*) (pbuffer + iwritten),
                to_write - iwritten
            );

            if (result <= 0)
            {
                delete[] pbuffer;
                pbuffer = 0;
                close(fd);
                return -1;
            }

            iwritten +=  result;
        }

        written += to_write;
        delete[] pbuffer;
        pbuffer = 0;
    }

    close(fd);
    return written;
}

#endif
```

The ezftpd daemon needs one startup argument: the path of the directory that serves as its root FTP directory.

The server does not consider sub-directories for any get/put requests from the client. So anything the client wants to download must be available in the root of the directory. When uploading a file, the client can provide the full path of the file (/a/b/c/d.txt) or just the base name d.txt—the server just considers the base name as relevant for uploads and downloads.

The server uses a pthread to communicate with the client.

One important safeguard the server utilizes at startup is signal(SIGPIPE, SIG_IGN); ignore the broken pipe syndrome. This shields the daemon code from an unclean peer socket closure, which could result from a runtime exception in the client code.

Here are the sources for the server, which you can save as the source code file
ezftpd.c:

```c
#include "ezftp.h"

#include <pthread.h>
#include <signal.h>

void* send_or_recieve(void* pv)
{
    int datasocket = *((int*) pv);

    char cmd[8];
    char filename[256];
    char buffer[1024];

    memset(cmd, 0, sizeof(cmd));
    memset(filename, 0, sizeof(filename));
    memset(buffer, 0, sizeof(buffer));

    int rcv = read(datasocket, buffer, sizeof(buffer) - 1);

    if (rcv <= 0) // peer closed its socket, perhaps
    {
        return (void*) 1;
    }

    buffer[sizeof(buffer) - 1] = 0;
    buffer[rcv]   =   0;
    char* ptr = buffer;
    strncpy(cmd, ptr, 3);           // should be "get" or "put"

    ptr += 3;                       // the next byte must be whitespace

    if (! isspace(*ptr))
    {
        fprintf(stderr, "Bad command: %s\n", cmd);
        return   (void*)  1;
    }

    while(isspace(*ptr) || strchr(ptr, '/'))
```

```
    {
        ptr++;
    }

    strcpy(filename,  ptr);
    filename[sizeof(filename) - 1] = 0;

    if (! (*filename))
    {
        fprintf(stderr, "Missing file name\n");
        close(datasocket);

        return (void*) 1;
    }

    if (strcmp(cmd, CMDGET) == 0)
    {
        f_send(datasocket,  filename);
    }
    else if (strcmp(cmd, CMDPUT) == 0)
    {
         f_receive(datasocket, filename);
    }
    else
    {
        fprintf(stderr, "Bad command: %s\n", cmd);
        close(datasocket);

        return (void*) 1;
    }

    close(datasocket);
    return (void*) 0;           // return a null pointer on success
}

int main(int argc, char** argv)
{
    int result = 0;
```

```
if (argc == 2)
{
    result = chdir(argv[1]);

    if (result != 0)
    {
        fprintf(stderr, "Unable to chdir into %s\n", argv[1]);
        return 1;
    }
}
else
{
    fprintf(stderr, "Need root directory path\n");
    return 1;
}

signal(SIGPIPE, SIG_IGN);
// Guard server from broken pipe resulting from client-side exceptions

sockaddr_in sv_addr;
memset((char*) &sv_addr, 0, sizeof(sv_addr));

sv_addr.sin_family = AF_INET;
sv_addr.sin_addr.s_addr = INADDR_ANY;
sv_addr.sin_port = htons(PORT);

int fd = socket(AF_INET, SOCK_STREAM, 0);
assert_greater(fd, 2);

result = bind(fd, (sockaddr*) &sv_addr, sizeof(sv_addr));
assert_zero(result);

result = listen(fd, 0);
assert_zero(result);

fprintf(stderr, "Accepting connections on port %d\n", PORT);
fprintf(stderr, "Press Ctrl-C to stop the server\n");

while (1)
{
```

```
      pthread_t pth;
      sockaddr_in cli_addr;

      socklen_t len = sizeof(cli_addr);
      memset((char*) &cli_addr, 0, len);

      int datasocket = accept(fd, (sockaddr*) &cli_addr, &len);
      assert_greater(datasocket, 2);

      fprintf
      (
          stdout,
          "Received connection from %s:%d\n",
          inet_ntoa(cli_addr.sin_addr),
          ntohs(cli_addr.sin_port)
      );

      pthread_create(&pth, 0, &send_or_recieve, &datasocket);
   }

   close(fd);
   return 0;
}
```

You can compile the server with c++ -lpthread -o ezftpd ezftpd.c.

You can then create a dedicated directory for ezftpd, perhaps $HOME/ezftproot. Launching the server can then be done with:

```
/path/to/ezftpd $HOME/ezftproot
```

Just to be absolutely sure you don't forget, you will need to launch the server before you try to issue any get/put requests from the client side.

The client always sends "get" or "put" as the first four bytes, followed by the name of the file to get/put.

Here are the sources for the client, which you can save as ezftp.c:

```
#include "ezftp.h"

int handshake(int datasocket, const char* protocol, const char* infile)
{
```

```
    int i = 0;
    int result = 0;
    char cmd[1024];

    strcpy(cmd, protocol);    // protocol can be "get" or "put"
    strcat(cmd, " ");
    strcat(cmd, infile);

    cmd[sizeof(cmd) - 1] = 0;
    const int cmdlen = strlen(cmd);

    while (i < cmdlen)
    {
        result = write(datasocket, (char*) (cmd + i), cmdlen - i);
        assert_greater(result,    0);
        i += result;
    }

    return 0;
}

int main(int argc, char** argv)
{
    bool failed = false;

    if (argc == 4)
    {
        // First ensure that server IP/command/filename are not empty:
        for (int i = 1; i < argc; i++)
        {
            if (! *(argv[i]))
            {
                failed = true;
                break;
            }
        }

        if ((strcmp(argv[2], CMDGET) != 0) && (strcmp(argv[2], CMDPUT) != 0))
        {
```

```
        failed = true;
    }
}
else
{
        failed = true;
}

if (failed)
{
    fprintf(stderr, "Usage: ezftp <server IP> <command> <filename>\n");
    fprintf(stderr, "<command> can be get or put\n");
    return 1;
}

sockaddr_in  addr;

memset((char*)  &addr,  0,  sizeof(addr));
addr.sin_family = AF_INET;
addr.sin_addr.s_addr = inet_addr(argv[1]);
addr.sin_port = htons(PORT);

int datasocket = socket(AF_INET, SOCK_STREAM, 0);
assert_greater(datasocket, 2);

int result = connect(datasocket, (sockaddr*) &addr, sizeof(addr));
assert_zero(result);

if (strcmp(argv[2], CMDGET) == 0)
{
    result = handshake(datasocket, CMDGET, argv[3]);
    assert_zero(result);

    f_receive(datasocket,  argv[3]);
}
else if (strcmp(argv[2], CMDPUT) == 0)
{
    result = handshake(datasocket, CMDPUT, argv[3]);
    assert_zero(result);
```

```
        f_send(datasocket, argv[3]);
    }
    else
    {
        fprintf(stderr, "Bad command: %s %s %s\n", argv[1], argv[2],
        argv[3]);
        close(datasocket);
        return 1;
    }

    close(datasocket);
    return 0;
}
```

You can compile the client with c++ -o ezftp ezftp.c.

11.1.22 Addressing the Makefile

GNU's make (gmake under FreeBSD) is a powerful and flexible source code compilation
and build system. Makefiles that exploit GNU make features and syntax are more
intelligent than traditional makefiles. In fact, the GNU make world is so much richer that
GNU grants it a new, optional name: *GNUmakefile*.

Naming your makefile a GNUmakefile ensures that you accidentally don't invoke the
traditional make, which only looks for a file named makefile. Of course, GNU make can
also handle traditional makefiles (but not makefiles under FreeBSD's ports, which only
the native FreeBSD make understands).

The appendix has a small GNUmakefile that you can use to build your small projects
for creating an executable binary.

11.2 Graphical Application Development with Vala

While we are now familiar with C—which underpins the Vala programming language—
there is one more frontier to conquer before we can realistically hope to work fluently
with Vala: the principles of object-oriented programming, often called OOP.

We won't enter into a full-bodied OOP discourse. Rather, we will just focus on the
basic concepts that can facilitate transition from C (not object-oriented) to Vala (entirely
object-oriented).

11.2.1 The Bare Essentials of OOP

We start by looking at why OO programming is needed—i.e., when it is needed at all (which is not always, by any means). A few pages down the line, I will point out advantages and disadvantages of OOP just before starting the Vala essay.

We return to our `struct student` for illustration, using two compilers `cc` and `c++` to show what OOP is and a broad picture of how it is implemented. Once the OOP picture becomes clear, switching over to the Vala language—and `valac` as the compiler—should be a cinch.

For our illustration, we will also use the term "client code" to refer to `main()`, although a client can be any code that uses our `struct`.

```
struct student
{
    char name[64];
    int roll_number;
    double gpa;
};
```

If I need to print a `student` object's members, I could create a function like this:

```
void print(student* ptr)
{
    puts(ptr->name);
}
```

The foregoing function is fine in itself. The problem begins when I create another `struct` that's a special type of `student`:

```
struct research_fellow
{
    double stipend;
    char name[64];
    int roll_number;
    double gpa;
};
```

Essentially, the idea is that `research_fellow` is a `student` who gets a stipend (fellowship) for her research.

Two problems pop up here:

- We can't pass a research_fellow* pointer to print() without first type-casting it as a student* pointer.

- If we type-cast, the results will be strange, if not disastrous: puts(ptr->name) inside print() will access the bytes for stipend as a char* pointer.

The multi-pronged OOP solution begins by putting print() into the struct itself. And then we use a very special identifier in place of the ptr pointer argument: this.

Our student now effectively becomes:

```
struct student
{
    char name[64];
    int roll_number;
    double gpa;

    void print(student* this)
    {
        puts(this->name);
    }
};
// C (and therefore the C compiler cc) will not permit the code above
```

c++ will compile the code in the preceding snippet—with the rider that this is implicitly passed in, and not declared explicitly. Effectively, the C++ struct declaration becomes:

```
struct student
{
    char name[64];
    int roll_number;
    double gpa;

    void print()
    {
        puts(this->name);
    }
};
```

What c++ does is generate the C-compatible code that uses a pointer-to-function (and not a member function) for print() inside student. We look at the translation scheme along with the client code:

```
/* C++ code */                        /* equivalent C code */

struct student                        struct student
{                                     {
    char name[64];                        char name[64];
    int roll_number;                      int roll_number;
    double gpa;                           double gpa;

    void print()                          void (*p_print)(student*);
    {                                 };
        puts(this->name);
    }                                 void print(student* this)
};                                    {
                                          puts(this->name);
                                      }

int main()                            int main()
{                                     {
    student stud;                         struct student stud;
                                          stud.p_print = &print;
    strcpy(stud.name, "Chuck");           strcpy(stud.name, "Chuck");
    stud.print();                         (*(stud.p_print))(&stud);
    return 0;                             return 0;
}                                     }
```

Of course, the translation, as depicted in the foregoing scheme, is a drastic simplification of what happens under the hood, but it still is true in its spirit to what happens for you in the background. We can forget about the under-the-hood details because: a) we are not into creating compilers ourselves, and b) those details are fairly unpleasant to look at.

The next OOP prong is inheritance: derive research_fellow from student, putting into research_fellow only the pieces not already available in student.

Since C itself does not (and never will) support inheritance, the C++ compiler has to do all the work to generate the equivalent C code for our struct as well as any client code. This work, quite naturally, is highly implementation-specific: c++ implementation would be entirely different from Microsoft's Visual C++ implementation.

Whatever the implementation, the translated C code becomes even uglier—and hence can be ignored for our simple purpose of OOP illustration.

Our research_fellow now becomes:

```
struct research_fellow : student   // cc will not permit this; c++ will
{
double stipend;                         // Rest everything is same
};
```

The comment "Rest everything is same" is heartening for those who like things to remain simple, and disheartening for those always aspire for greater complexity.

On the one hand, the client code can continue to do this:

```
struct research_fellow rf;
// initialize rf's members;

rf.print();
```

On the other hand, research_fellow::print() is still tied to the definition inside student. This naturally would invite criticism from fellowship supervisors, who would like research_fellow::print() to print not just the name, but the value of the stipend too.

This is where the final OOP prong comes in: runtime polymorphism, aka virtual functions. If student declares print() prefixed with the keyword virtual, the programmer is allowed to plant a special version of print() inside research_fellow.

```
struct student
{
    char name[64];
    int roll_number;
    double gpa;

    virtual void print()            // cc will not permit this; c++ will
    {
        puts(this->name);
    }
};

struct research_fellow : student
```

```
{
    double stipend;

    void print()
    {
        puts(this->name);
        printf("stipend = %.2f\n", this->stipend);
    }
};

int main()
{
    student stud;
    strcpy(stud.name, "Chuck");
    stud.print();                       // uses student::print()

    research_fellow rf;
    rf.stipend = 1000;
    strcpy(rf.name, "RF");
    rf.print();                         // uses research_fellow::print()

    return 0;
}
```

It is important to understand that if research_fellow does not have a special version of print(), the definition inside student will get used. I won't repeat the code to prove this, but you can try this on your own—just to convince yourself.

Once you understand the preceding point, it is a fairly logical and natural deduction that the compiler has to accommodate print() as a function the runtime address of which might vary. With a virtual function declared inside student, the instance declaration research_fellow rf; forces the compiler to build a special pointer-to-function into the rf instance as per the following pseudo-coded algorithm that goes into action at runtime:

```
rf.ptr_print = address-of-{student::print()}

if [ research_fellow defines its own print() ]; then
    rf.ptr_print =  address-of-{research_fellow::print()}
fi
```

Read the next couple of pages to understand why this algorithm can't work at compile-time.

Our structs might declare not just print(), but any number of virtual functions—let's pick virtual void play() as another virtual function packed into student, and virtual bool is_phd() packed into research_fellow. Notably, is_phd() is not declared in the student struct.

The only way the compiler can scalably accommodate multiple virtual functions is by using a pointer to an array of pointers:

```
rf.vptr[0] = address-of-{student::print()}
rf.vptr[1] = address-of-{student::play()}
rf.vptr[2] = address-of-{research_fellow::is_phd()}    // Note this

if [ research_fellow defines its own print() ]; then
    rf.vptr[0] = address-of-{research_fellow::print()}
fi

if [ research_fellow defines its own play() ]; then
    rf.vptr[1] = address-of-{research_fellow::play()}
fi
```

Even though it's still pseudo-code, this code is a good representation of what OO compilers do. Note that the compiler has to hard-wire the address of is_phd() to the definition inside research_fellow because student does not declare this function.

Planting a special definition for a virtual function inside a subclass is called *overriding*. (Under Vala, you have to use the keyword override when supplying the special definition in the subclass.)

The vptr pointer (which is pointer-to-[array-of-{pointers-to-functions}]) is a pretty famous pointer. In OO chatter-and-banter, its name is instantly recognized the world over as it is—vptr, the virtual function pointer.

Although all the OO prongs have now been dealt with, there are two final points not clear from the foregoing discussion that we must discuss before laying out an OO terminology charter and moving over to Vala.

A student pointer can be assigned the address of a research_fellow object:

```
student* psr = new research_fellow;    // LEGITIMATE
```

The psr pointer has been declared as student* but actually receives research_fellow* at runtime. This is why vptr addresses cannot be populated at compile-time. At compile-time, the compiler can legitimately neither answer the question nor ignore the skull-and-bones in Figure 11-7, while populating the virtual function table (vtbl). Keep in mind the modified psr declaration (top rectangle) used to amplify the compiler's problems.

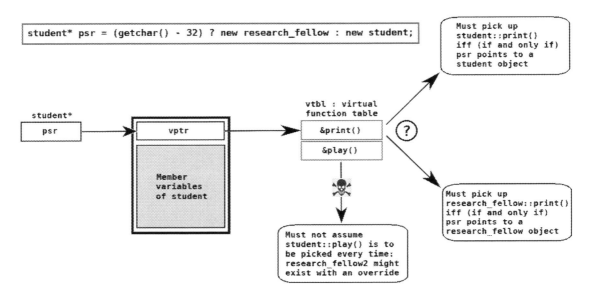

Figure 11-7. *vtbl is Very Truly Beyond Liberties*

The following operation is not permitted with psr:

```
bool b_phd = psr->is_phd();                // NOT LEGITIMATE
```

In other words, when you invoke a function f() on psr (which was declared as student*):

- The compiler will first check whether f() has been declared in student. If not, the compiler will throw a compile-time error. (The only way to invoke is_phd() with psr is to declare psr as research_fellow*, not student*.) If you see Figure 11-7 again, you will find that is_phd() is missing from the virtual function table.

- If research_fellow defines f(), the compiler will have research_fellow::f() executed at runtime.

- If research_fellow does not define f(), the compiler will make provisions for student::f() to be executed at runtime.

11.2.2 Charter of OO Terminology

Consider these tidbits:

- A struct is now termed a class. student is referred to as a base class (or superclass, when it is being derived from), while research_fellow is referred to as a derived class (or subclass).

- A superclass can be used to derive any number of subclasses, and each subclass can act as a superclass for classes derived from it (e.g., derived from research_fellow, not from student directly). Each such class still is a subclass of student.

- Every class has a few implicit functions. Two such functions are *constructor* (runs automatically on instance initialization) and *destructor* (runs automatically on instance destruction), both of which can be manually coded (or else the compiler will insert do-nothing versions).

- A constructor can never be declared as virtual (because object construction must always start with base class initialization), but the destructor can be declared as virtual (allowing the most specialized destructor to run).

- The constructor is the name of the class with an argument list (e.g., student() or research_fellow(char* _name, double _stipend)), while the name of the destructor is ~ prefixed to the class name and with an empty argument list (e.g., ~student() or ~research_fellow()).

- Members in a class can be of at least three types: private, which can be accessed by code in the class itself; protected, which can be accessed by code in the class itself as well as subclasses; and public, which can be accessed anywhere, including client code in main(). C++ restricts itself to those three types, while Vala introduces a fourth type: internal, which caters to the package-based nature of Vala. An internal member can be accessed from within its package, but not globally.

There is one point on which Vala notably differs from C++: overloading. C++ permits any number of functions with the same name fx() to occur in a single class as long as each version has a unique parameter list. Vala prohibits overloading. If you want to overload under Vala, you have to put in a period after fx and then supply a suffix as well as the argument list:

```
fx()                    // no argument
fx.with_int(int i)      // with an int argument
```

The two preceding declarations mean the following declarations are no longer permitted in the class:

```
fx(int)
fx.with_int()
```

11.2.3 Benefits and Drawbacks of OO Programming

The benefits of object-oriented programming are often overstated, and—even more significantly—the disadvantages understated. There is a serious cost to be paid when you make your code object-oriented—its working is no longer transparent and easy to comprehend, both to the writer as well as to the reader.

In many ways, it would be ideal to be able to write a single-line code to bring up a Hello World message such as this:

```
object.msg("Hello  World");
```

The client code looks very clean and is just one line long. Those are the primary benefits of OO programming.

But when things start going wrong, the number of layers to investigate is too high. Which is why OO is never used for anything that bears resemblance to systems programming, a job entirely reserved for C.

For graphical application development, though, OO is an ideal playground. All graphical widgets and windows are inter-related, allowing for hierarchies that propagate base code down into increasingly special types: Object, for instance, could serve as a base for Widget, which could serve as a base for TextBox, which could serve as a base for SingleLineTextBox and ScrolledTextBox. Using derived types thus permits reuse of code that's available higher up the hierarchy.

11.2.4 The World of Vala

Vala brings many high-level programming abstractions to Unix: namespaces, objects, interfaces, signals, strong type checking, and assisted memory management. At a lower level, Vala generates C as its intermediate code. This enables Vala to easily use libraries with a C Application Binary Interface (ABI). Vala's syntax, while similar to C, is even more reminiscent of C#.

I will greet you to the world of Vala programming with a Hello World program, and then put in the relevant notes.

```
public class hwWindow : Gtk.ApplicationWindow
{
    public hwWindow(hwApplication app)
    {
        Object(application: app, title: "Hello World");

        var button = new Gtk.Button.with_label("Click Here");
        button.clicked.connect(this.button_clicked);

        this.window_position = Gtk.WindowPosition.CENTER;
        this.set_default_size(300, 60);
        this.add(button);

        this.show_all();
    }

    void button_clicked(Gtk.Button  button)
    {
        string msg = "Hello  World!".reverse();

        var dialog = new Gtk.MessageDialog
        (
            this,
            Gtk.DialogFlags.MODAL,
            Gtk.MessageType.INFO,
            Gtk.ButtonsType.OK,
            msg
        );
```

```
        dialog.response.connect(() =>
        {
            dialog.destroy();
        });

        dialog.show();
    }
}

public class hwApplication : Gtk.Application
{
    public hwApplication()
    {
        Object(application_id:   "org.example.HelloWorld");
    }

    protected override void activate()
    {
        (new hwWindow(this)).show();
    }
}

int main()
{
    return (new hwApplication()).run();
}
```

Save this code as a text file named hello.vala, and then compile it with valac, the Vala compiler. Our standard compilation command will be:

```
valac --pkg gtk+-3.0 --debug <file>
```

--pkg gtk+-3.0 pulls in the files to interface with the GTK+ (version 3) package. The GTK+ package is a graphical toolkit library written in C. Behind the scenes, the first interface file is a Vala Application Programming Interface (VAPI) file. This specifies how Vala code should be translated to the relevant C code for the GTK+ library. The second file is a pkg-config file that contains the relevant C compiler and linker flags. The VAPI and pkg-config files will have the same name, but different file extensions.

The --debug switch (optional) pulls source file and line number references into the compiled executable for runtime debugging (with gdb).

If you run the executable and click the Click Here button, it will display the message Hello World! (in reverse), as shown in Figure 11-8.

Figure 11-8. *Making the world go the other way round with Vala*

Although this is just a simple Hello World application, our first Vala venture has many points of interest that need to be elaborated on:

- In Vala, the keyword this denotes a reference (i.e., another name) for the invoking object, and not a pointer, although Vala does support pointers too. The this reference is internally implemented as a pointer itself.

- The root of GTK's class hierarchy is a class named Object. All windows and widgets are thus certain to be subtypes of Object.

- The two entry-point classes in a graphical Vala application are Application and ApplicationWindow. There are shortcut ways to create Vala GUIs with a bit less code, but the method we used suits all occasions and purposes.

- Vala widgets usually have one or more signals (events), which get triggered at runtime as per user interaction. Application, for instance, has an activate signal (which we have used in the code snippet to create a window), and MessageDialog has a response signal (which we have used in the snippet to destroy the dialog itself).

- A signal handler can be a normal function, or furnished as a *here-function*—a nifty Vala feature that technically goes under the name lambda expression or anonymous function. Like the shell's here-doc, a here-function has no name—just a definition. The prototype of the here-function is already known: the prototype is what would have been had the lambda expression been written as a normal function instead. Signal handlers are called synchronously (one after the other), never simultaneously with another signal handler already active). They typically use a separate handler thread in order to avoid UI freezes.

- Vala implements a variant of the garbage collection mechanism known technically as "deterministic reference counting," which releases memory for objects no longer being referenced. So you can freely use operator new and forget about heap memory management.

- When you use operator new, you can assign the reference returned to a variable declared with the keyword var. The compiler will automatically deduce its type from the statement's RHS.

- Vala has a built-in string type named string.

One thing that's not apparent from this Hello World code is probably the most important point: Vala code is pure C wrapped in Vala language constructs.

If you compile the hello.vala file with --ccode, the Vala compiler will generate the C file for you to, lo and behold, be grateful for what Vala does. That C file would be something like 260 lines (vis-a-vis our .vala's 53 lines)—and most of it abstruse stuff that we would usually prefer to leave somebody else to work with.

For ease of reference, here is the C code generation command:

```
valac --ccode --pkg gtk+-3.0 <filename>
```

It's now time for you to play with Vala on your own for a while. I suggest you carry out the following exercise:

Create a Vala application with one widget of type Gtk.Entry (which is a kind of textbox). At runtime, when the user types some text in the textbox and presses `Enter`, the text is echoed to standard output.

The text that follows includes a few tips to help you out.

- *Tip 1:* Entry has a signal named activate that gets triggered when `Enter` is pressed in the textbox.

- *Tip 2:* Entry has a property named text that gets/sets the text in the widget.

- *Tip 3:* stdout.printf(mystring) prints the string named mystring to standard output if mystring has a trailing newline.

You can refer to the following URL for developing your mini-application:

https://developer.gnome.org/gnome-devel-demos/stable/entry.vala.html.en

When you return from the exercise (hopefully with success), we will launch into a full-fledged Vala GUI application—a Body Mass Index tool. If you don't know what BMI is, it is your weight divided by your height squared. Weight is in kg, while height is in cm, and a healthy BMI score is in the range of 18.5 to 25.

11.2.5 Vala Documentation

Consider these three URLs for Vala documentation:

- `https://developer.gnome.org/gnome-devel-demos/stable/beginner.vala.html.en`—The perfect place to start learning about Vala's widgets and sample usage code.

- `https://valadoc.org/gtk+-3.0/Gtk.html`—API reference for Vala widgets and other types. Read the next paragraph for more.

- `https://wiki.gnome.org/Projects/Vala/Documentation`—The Vala language reference site.

It is natural that as a Vala newbie, you will initially visit the first site for snippets that demonstrate the use of widgets in Vala. As you pick up flair, you will find the Valadoc site to be a gold mine: brilliantly, exhaustively documented, and catering to both newbies and experts. The first time you visit Valadoc, just type `Gtk.Entry` into the Search box at the top-left in your browser, and everything you need to know about `Gtk.Entry` will be dished out.

Before I close out the section, there is one important point that I must expressly mention: A GTK window can have just one widget. If you need multiple widgets in your application (almost always true), that widget must be a container: `Gtk.Box` or `Gtk.Grid`. The container can have any number of widgets added to it. The `ApplicationWindow` instance just has the container.

11.2.6 The BMI Tool Written in Vala

All that we are doing here is create a GUI for calculating/displaying/saving the Body Mass Index score of a user aged 20+ years. The BMI formula is weight/(height*height), with weight in kg and height in cm. A healthy BMI is in the range 18.5 to 25.

There are two ways you can use this section.

- Try to write the BMI tool yourself and then compare your tool with mine.

- Run my tool to see what it does, and then create your BMI tool to mimic mine.

Either approach is as good as the other.

If you decide to use the first route, here are the broad specs for the tool as implemented in my code (which uses a `Grid` container):

- The user's name is captured in an `Entry` widget (read as `Gtk.Entry`).

- A `CheckButton` widget is used to verify that the user's age is at least 20 years.

- If the name is blank, or the age verification switch is not toggled on, all command (push) buttons in the `ApplicationWindow` are disabled.

- The user's weight is captured in a `Scale` widget (horizontally oriented).

- The user's height is captured in a `SpinButton` widget.

- The BMI score is shown in a `TextView` widget, which prints the user's name, weight, height, BMI, and a summary result based on the BMI score (i.e., whether healthy/underweight/overweight).

- The user can save the BMI report as a text file (created as `GLib.File`).

The only part that is tricky is the last step: saving the contents to a file. The following code shows you how to do that with a `TextView` widget named `view`:

```
Gtk.TextIter iter_start, iter_end;
view.buffer.get_bounds(out iter_start, out iter_end);
string contents = view.buffer.get_text(iter_start, iter_end, false);
```

You can then pass in `contents.data` as the first argument to the `replace_contents` member function of the `GLib.File`.

The application that I developed has a wacky feature: "Powered by Vala" watermarks along the bottom edge of the window, which have slanted text labels. Of course, you don't need to implement the slanted labels in your own tool, which is why I have left them out of the specs.

Figure 11-9 is a preview of the application yielded by the sources that follow.

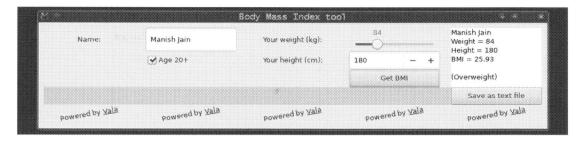

Figure 11-9. *A body mass index tool written in Vala*

Here are the sources for the BMI tool that I created:

```
public class bmiWindow : Gtk.ApplicationWindow
{
    Gtk.Grid grid;
    Gtk.ScrolledWindow scrolled;
    Gtk.TextView view;
    GLib.File?  file;

    Gtk.Entry entry_name;
    Gtk.CheckButton check_age;
    Gtk.SpinButton spin_height;
    Gtk.Scale scale_weight;
    Gtk.Button button_getbmi;
    Gtk.Button button_savebmi;

    Gtk.Label label_name;
    Gtk.Label label_height;
    Gtk.Label label_weight;
    Gtk.Label  label_vala[5];

    public bmiWindow(bmiApplication app)
    {
        Object (application: app, title: "BMI tool");

        this.title = "Body Mass Index tool";
        this.set_default_size(600,  200);
        this.set_border_width(10);
```

```vala
grid = new  Gtk.Grid();
grid.set_column_spacing(20);
grid.set_column_homogeneous(true);

label_name = new Gtk.Label ("Name:");
grid.attach(label_name,  0,  0,  1,  1);

entry_name = new Gtk.Entry ();
entry_name.changed.connect(entry_name_changed);
grid.attach_next_to(entry_name,  label_name,  Gtk.Position
Type.RIGHT);

check_age = new Gtk.CheckButton.with_label ("Age 20+");
check_age.set_active(false);
check_age.toggled.connect(this.check_age_toggled);
grid.attach_next_to
(
    check_age, entry_name, Gtk.PositionType.BOTTOM, 1, 1
);

label_weight = new Gtk.Label ("Your weight (kg):");
grid.attach(label_weight,  2,  0,  1,  1);

scale_weight = new Gtk.Scale.with_range
(
    Gtk.Orientation.HORIZONTAL, 40, 200, 1.0
);

scale_weight.set_hexpand(true);
scale_weight.value_changed.connect(scale_weight_changed);
grid.attach_next_to
(
    scale_weight, label_weight, Gtk.PositionType.RIGHT, 1, 1
);

label_height = new Gtk.Label ("Your height (cm):");
grid.attach(label_height,  2,  1,  1,  1);
```

```vala
spin_height  =  new  Gtk.SpinButton.with_range  (140,  200,  1);
spin_height.set_hexpand(true);
spin_height.value_changed.connect(spin_height_changed);
grid.attach_next_to
(
    spin_height, label_height, Gtk.PositionType.RIGHT, 1, 1
);

button_getbmi = new Gtk.Button.with_label("Get BMI");
button_getbmi.set_sensitive(false);
button_getbmi.clicked.connect(getbmi_clicked);
grid.attach(button_getbmi,  3,  3,  1,  1);

scrolled =  new Gtk.ScrolledWindow(null,  null);
scrolled.set_policy(Gtk.PolicyType.AUTOMATIC, Gtk.Policy
Type.AUTOMATIC);

view = new Gtk.TextView();
view.set_wrap_mode(Gtk.WrapMode.NONE);
view.buffer.text = "";
scrolled.add(view);

grid.attach(scrolled, 4, 0, 1, 4);
button_savebmi = new Gtk.Button.with_label("Save as text file");
button_savebmi.set_sensitive(false);
button_savebmi.clicked.connect(savebmi_clicked);
grid.attach(button_savebmi,  4,  4,  1,  1);

var hseparator = new Gtk.Separator (Gtk.Orientation.HORIZONTAL);
grid.attach (hseparator,  0,  4,  label_vala.length,  1);

for (int i = 0; i < label_vala.length; i++)
{
    label_vala[i]  =  new  Gtk.Label("Powered  by  Vala");
    label_vala[i].angle  =  10;
    label_vala[i].set_pattern("  ___ ");
    grid.attach(label_vala[i], i, 5, 1, 1);
}

this.add(grid);
```

```vala
        this.show_all();
    }

    void entry_name_changed(Gtk.Editable e)
    {
        check_age.set_active(false);
    }

    void check_age_toggled(Gtk.ToggleButton cb)
    {
        button_savebmi.set_sensitive(false);
        view.buffer.text  =  "";

        button_getbmi.set_sensitive
        (
            (entry_name.text.length  > 0)  &&
            (cb.get_active())
        );
    }

    void scale_weight_changed(Gtk.Range range)
    {
        view.buffer.text  =  "";
        button_savebmi.set_sensitive(false);
    }

    void spin_height_changed(Gtk.SpinButton  spin)
    {
        view.buffer.text = "";
        button_savebmi.set_sensitive(false);
    }

    void getbmi_clicked(Gtk.Button b)
    {
        double wt = scale_weight.get_value();
        double ht = spin_height.get_value()/100;
        double bmi = wt / (ht * ht);
```

```vala
    string sz = entry_name.text;
    sz += "\n";
    sz += "Weight  =  %d\n".printf((int) scale_weight.get_value());
    sz += "Height  =  %d\n".printf((int) spin_height.get_value());
    sz += "BMI  =  %.2f\n\n".printf(bmi);

    if (bmi > 35) sz += "(Severely obese)";
    if (30   < bmi   <= 35) sz += "(Obese)";
    if (25   < bmi   <= 30) sz += "(Overweight)";
    if (18.5 < bmi   <= 25) sz += "(Healthy weight)";
    if (16   < bmi   <= 18.5) sz += "(Underweight)";
    if (bmi      <= 16) sz += "(Severely underweight)";

    view.buffer.text  =  sz;
    button_savebmi.set_sensitive(true);
}

void savebmi_clicked(Gtk.Button b)
{
    var save_dialog = new Gtk.FileChooserDialog
    (
        "Save BMI report",
        this as Gtk.Window,
        Gtk.FileChooserAction.SAVE,
        Gtk.Stock.CANCEL,
        Gtk.ResponseType.CANCEL,
        Gtk.Stock.SAVE,
        Gtk.ResponseType.ACCEPT
    );

    save_dialog.set_do_overwrite_confirmation(true);
    save_dialog.set_modal(true);

    if (file != null)
    {
        (save_dialog as Gtk.FileChooser).set_file(file);
    }

    save_dialog.response.connect(save_response);
```

```vala
        save_dialog.show();
    }

    void save_response(Gtk.Dialog dialog, int response_id)
    {
        var save_dialog = dialog as Gtk.FileChooserDialog;

        switch(response_id)
        {
            case Gtk.ResponseType.ACCEPT:
                Gtk.TextIter iter_start;
                Gtk.TextIter    iter_end;

                view.buffer.get_bounds(out iter_start, out iter_end);
                file = save_dialog.get_file();

                string contents = view.buffer.get_text
                (
                    iter_start, iter_end, false
                );

                file.replace_contents
                (
                    contents.data,
                    null,
                    false,
                    GLib.FileCreateFlags.NONE,
                    null,
                    null
                );

                break;

            case Gtk.ResponseType.CANCEL:
                break;
        }
        dialog.destroy();
    }
```

```
}
public class bmiApplication : Gtk.Application
{
    public bmiApplication()
    {
        Object(application_id: "org.example.bmiApplication");
    }

    protected override void activate()
    {
        bmiWindow wnd = new bmiWindow(this);
        wnd.show();
    }
}

int main(string[] args)
{
    return new bmiApplication().run(args);
}
```

11.2.7 Vala Is Not Just GUI Development!

Vala is a complete programming language—what you can do with plain C can be done
with Vala (and whatever cannot be done with plain C can never be done with Vala).
Note, though, that you cannot (easily) use Vala for systems programming—the language
was not designed for that.

Here is a snippet that shows usage of pointers (deprecated) in Vala:

```
int* ptr = new int[8];

for (int i = 0; i < 8; i++)
{
    ptr[i] = i;
    stdout.printf("i = %d\n", ptr[i]);
}

delete ptr;
```

The preceding code is pretty much the same as in C++, except that the delete operator is not permitted the square brackets even when deleting a pointer to an array. Note that the call to the delete operator is mandatory if you allocate a pointer. Using a pointer directly means you have opted out of Vala's assisted memory management.

You can do multi-threading with Vala. As in the last snippet, the following sample counts up from 0 to 8—with the counting done this time on a spawned thread, and with a small sleep (duration: 0.1 seconds, or 100000 microseconds) thrown in between successive outputs.

```
class MyThread
{
    private int maxcount;

    public MyThread(int _maxcount)
    {
        this.maxcount = _maxcount;
    }

    public void* run()
    {
        int counter = 0;

        while (counter < this.maxcount)
        {
            stdout.printf("%d\n", counter);
            counter++;

            Thread.usleep(100000);
        }

        return (void*) Thread.self;
    }
}

int main()
{
    if (! Thread.supported())
    {
        stderr.printf("Cannot run without thread support\n");
```

```
        return 1;
    }

    message("MAIN THREAD: %p", (void*) Thread.self);

    try
    {
        var mythr = new MyThread(8);

        Thread<void*>  thr  =  new  Thread<void*>.try
        (
            "Spawned thread", mythr.run
        );

        thr.join();
    }
    catch(Error e)
    {
        stderr.printf("%s\n", e.message);
        return 1;
    }
    return 0;
}
```

You can also easily do network programming with Vala. The major classes to work with (all in the GLib package) are:

```
Resolver
```

```
SocketClient
```

```
SocketListener
```

```
SocketConnection
```

```
DataInputStream
```

```
DataOutputStream
```

Here is a small Vala client that can download from ezftpd.

```
using GLib;
```

```vala
int main(string[] args)
{
    if (args.length != 3)
    {
        stderr.printf("Need 2 args: <server name or IP> <downfile>\n");
        return  1;
    }

    Resolver  resolver  =  Resolver.get_default();
    List<InetAddress> addresses = resolver.lookup_by_name(args[1], null);

    InetSocketAddress inetsock = new InetSocketAddress
    (
        addresses.nth_data(0),
        6666
    );

    SocketClient client = new  SocketClient();
    SocketConnection conn = client.connect(inetsock);
    DataInputStream response = new DataInputStream(conn.input_stream);

    var file = File.new_for_path(args[2]);

    string message = "get ";
    message += args[2];
    conn.output_stream.write(message.data);

    var dos = new DataOutputStream
    (
        file.create(FileCreateFlags.REPLACE_DESTINATION)
    );
    while (! conn.is_closed())
    {
        uint8 byte = 0;

        try
        {
            byte = response.read_byte();
```

```
        }
        catch(IOError e)
        {
            break;
        }

        dos.put_byte(byte);
    }
    dos.close();
    return 0;
}
```

I would also like to refer you to a very nice version of `wget` written in Vala available for ready use at `http://www.jezra.net/blog/File_downloader_in_Vala_with_a_GIO_socket`.

11.3 Summary

This is the end of the chapter, and hopefully the beginning of a new one in your Unix programming essay.

Both C and Vala are excellent skills to have in your armor.

C is the rock-solid, rock-stable language that has been the engine of systems programming for decades. And that won't change.

The C+ language proposed in this chapter is essentially C with a few improvements (available as of now only via C++). Once you are at ease with C+, you can continue using it as such. Or you can try to move into pure C, which should not be difficult. But trying to migrate to C++ is pointless: C++ does not add anything useful for the programmer beyond what is already available as C+.

Vala represents the logical evolution of C. Vala does not take anything away from C— it just provides a fantastic high-level programming environment that delivers C code for you, while you code in Vala's eminently friendlier language constructs.

If this chapter shapes your programming skills and career in the times to come, we can all happily say `return 0;`.

APPENDIX

The Last Frontier

This appendix lumps together all the extra fragments referred to in the book. The topics covered in this appendix are as follows:

- Solution to the difficult `step` in Chapter 1

- Sources for the shell script `tcase` from Chapter 3

- Sources for the shell script `extract.sh` from Chapter 3

- Setting up a swap partition shared by FreeBSD and Linux from Chapter 5

- Sources for `halt.c` from Chapter 8

- GNUmakefile for creating an executable from Chapter 11

A.1 Solution to the Difficult **Step** in Chapter 1

```
:%s/\<\([[:alpha:]]\)[[:alpha:]]*\([[:alpha:]]\)\>/\1\2/g
```

Explanation: The first back-reference `\<\([[:alpha:]]\)` homes in on the first letter of any word. The second back-reference `\([[:alpha:]]\)` matches the last letter of that word. Anything between the two references (matched by `[[:alpha:]]*`) is omitted during substitution.

© Manish Jain 2018
M. Jain, *Beginning Modern Unix*, https://doi.org/10.1007/978-1-4842-3528-7

A.2 Sources for the Shell Script **tcase** from Chapter 3

```
#!/bin/sh

out="

_tcase_()
{
    while [ -n "$1" ]; do
        first='echo $1 | cut -c1 | tr [:lower:] [:upper:]'
        rem='echo $1 | cut -c 2-'
        lrem='echo $rem | tr [:upper:] [:lower:]'

        [ -z "$out" ] && \
        out="${first}${lrem}" || \
        out="${out}  ${first}${lrem}"

        shift
    done
}

if [ $# -gt 0 ]; then
    for v in $*; do
        _tcase_ $v

    done
else
    read v
    _tcase_ $v
fi

echo $out
exit 0
```

A.3 Sources for the Shell Script `extract.sh` from Chapter 3

```
#!/bin/sh

casemode=""

die()
{
    [ $# -eq 0 ] && exit 1

    [ $# -gt 1 ] && \
    echo "error initiated at line $1 :
    $2" 1>&2 || \
    echo "$1" 1>&2

    exit 1
}
while echo "$1" | grep '^-' > /dev/null; do
    case "$1" in
        -i)
            casemode="-i"
            shift
        ;;

        *)
            die "$LINENO" "Invalid optional arg: $1"
        ;;
    esac
done
[ $# -ge 1 -a $# -le 2 ] || \
die "$LINENO" "Usage: 'basename $0' [-i] <file> [<string>]"

f=""

[ -e "$1" ] && \
f='realpath "$1"' || \
die "$LINENO" "Usage: 'basename $0' [-i] <file> [<string>]"
```

```
[ -f "$f" ] || \
die "$LINENO" "Usage: 'basename $0' [-i] <file> [<string>]"

sz="unix"
# $sz is string to search for as a word; can be overridden with $2

[ $# -eq 2 ] && sz="$2"

instances='grep -c -w $casemode "$sz" "$f"'
[ $instances -gt 1 ] || exit 0

first='grep -w -n $casemode "$sz" "$f" | head -n 1 | sed 's|:.*||''
firstplus='expr $first + 1'

last='grep -w -n $casemode "$sz" "$f" | tail -n 1 | sed 's|:.*||''
lastminus='expr $last - 1'

mid=""

if [ $lastminus -gt $firstplus ]; then
    mid='cat "$f" | head -n $lastminus'
    lines='echo "$mid" | wc -l'
    to_tail='expr $lines - $first'
    mid='echo "$mid" | tail -n $to_tail'
fi

echo "$mid"
exit  0
```

A.4 Setting Up a Swap Partition Shared by FreeBSD and Linux from Chapter 5

You can easily set up a logical drive in your disk's extended partition as swap space shared by your FreeBSD and Linux installations. If your box has multiple hard disks with one of them an SSD, it's best to set up the swap partition in the SSD. That will make your system's swaps work at 3x speed.

Let's say your extended partition is sda4 (ada0s4 under FreeBSD), with an existing logical drive sda5 (ada0s5 under FreeBSD), and 5GB spare space at the end. You can use the spare space to host a shared swap partition sda6 (ada0s6 under FreeBSD), created as a partition of type 0x82 (linux-swap).

There are three ways you can create /dev/sda6 as a swap partition:

- Using the Linux installer (i.e., at the time of Linux installation)

- With the Linux command fdisk /dev/sda (using 0x82 as the partition ID)

- With the FreeBSD command gpart (using linux-swap as the partition type)

The Linux approach is interactive and thus not easy to document. I'll document the gpart approach, assuming a 500GB disk with three primary partitions already in place and no extended partition yet. There is 100GB at the end of the disk that can be used for setting up ada0s4, an extended partition (aka, EBR slice) with two nested (aka, logical) drives: ada0s5 (95GB, type linux-data) and ada0s6 (5GB, type linux-swap).

```
gpart add -t EBR ada0                      # ada0s4
gpart create -s MBR ada0s4
gpart add -t -s 95G linux-data ada0s4      # ada0s4s1, 95 GB
gpart add -t linux-swap ada0s4             # ada0s4s2, spans remainder
```

Reboot. Upon reboot, the device names /dev/ada0s4s1 and /dev/ada0s4s2 will change to /dev/ada0s5 and /dev/ada0s6, respectively. Note also that the scheme created (MBR) on ada0s4 is a workaround: the right scheme actually is EBR, but trying to create that scheme often fails (owing to a bug in gpart), with the result you might not be able to add any partitions to the EBR slice.

If you want, you can now create an Ext2/Ext3/Ext4 filesystem on ada0s5 (use mkfs.ext2 /dev/ada0s5). Then, continue with the following steps to share the swap partition ada0s6.

No matter which way you create the swap partition, Linux needs a special signature in that partition to start swapping to it. FreeBSD does not and it will overwrite the Linux swap signature when using the partition for swap space. This means that you have to get your Linux installation to reinsert the signature each time you boot into Linux (after previously having booted FreeBSD). Reinserting the signature requires you to run the command mkswap on the swap partition (sda6 in our example).

With the swap partition sda6 (ada0s6 under FreeBSD) already created, carry out these steps:

1. Boot into Linux and determine (conveniently done with grep -IR swapon *) the script under /etc that runs the swapon –a command at boot time. Under Linux Mint, that script is /etc/init.d/checkroot.sh.

   Add the following line to that file just before the first occurrence of swapon:

   mkswap /dev/sda6

   If Linux's /etc/fstab does not have an entry for sda6, add the following therein:

   /dev/sda6 none swap sw 0 0

2. Then boot into FreeBSD and add the following line to FreeBSD's /etc/fstab:

   /dev/ada0s6 none swap sw 0 0

   Next, run the command swapon -a to activate /dev/ada0s6 as a swap partition immediately under FreeBSD. If you want explicit confirmation, run the swapinfo command.

3. Boot into Linux again and make sure everything works normally with the command free, which will show swap usage.

   You can also set up the swap partition in the FreeBSD slice. For that, refer to the following URL:

   http://www.tldp.org/HOWTO/Linux+FreeBSD-3.html

A.5 Sources for **halt.c** from Chapter 8

```c
#include <stdio.h>
#include <time.h>
#include <stdlib.h>
#include <string.h>
```

```c
#include <assert.h>
#include <windows.h>
#include <psapi.h>

void errexit()
{
    fprintf(stderr, "\aUsage : halt.exe <n>\n");

    fprintf
    (
        stderr,
        "If 1 <= n <= 24: halt at [0]n:00 hrs (24-hour format)\n"
    );

    fprintf
    (
        stderr,
        "If n > 24: halt when process with pid n exits\n"
    );

    exit(-1);
}

void PrintLastErrorMessage(int err)
{
    char msg[256];

    FormatMessage
    (
        FORMAT_MESSAGE_FROM_SYSTEM,
        0,
        err, 0,
        (char*) msg,
        sizeof(msg)/sizeof(msg[0]),
        0
    );
```

```c
    msg[(sizeof(msg)/sizeof(msg[0])) - 1] = 0;
    fprintf(stderr,  msg);
    fprintf(stderr, "\n");
}

int wait_hrs(int hr)
{
    assert((hr > 0) && (hr <= 24));
    hr = (24 - hr) ? hr : 0;

    char msg[256];
    time_t  tt;
    time_t* lptt = &tt;

    sprintf
    (
        msg,
        "This system will auto-shutdown at %2d:00 hrs\n",
        hr
    );

    fprintf(stderr,  msg);

    while (1)
    {
        time(lptt);

        if ((localtime(lptt))->tm_hour  ==  hr)
        {
            break;
        }

        Sleep(60000);
    }

    return 0;
}
```

```c
int wait_pid(int pid)
{
    assert(pid > 24);

    char msg[256];
    HANDLE hnd = OpenProcess(SYNCHRONIZE, 0, pid);

    if (hnd <= 0)
    {
        fprintf
        (
            stderr, "\aCould not get handle to process %d\n", pid
        );

        PrintLastErrorMessage(GetLastError());
        return  -1;
    }

    Sprintf
    (
        msg,
        "This system will auto-shutdown once process id %d exits\n",
        pid
    );

    fprintf(stderr,  msg);
    int result = WaitForSingleObject(hnd, INFINITE);
    assert(result == WAIT_OBJECT_0);

    CloseHandle(hnd);
    return 0;
}

int halt()
{
    HANDLE hToken;
    TOKEN_PRIVILEGES tkp;

    int result = OpenProcessToken
```

```
    (
        GetCurrentProcess(),
        TOKEN_ADJUST_PRIVILEGES | TOKEN_QUERY,
        &hToken
    );
    assert(result);

    result = LookupPrivilegeValue
    (
        0, SE_SHUTDOWN_NAME, &tkp.Privileges[0].Luid
    );
    assert(result);

    tkp.PrivilegeCount = 1;
    tkp.Privileges[0].Attributes = SE_PRIVILEGE_ENABLED;

    result = AdjustTokenPrivileges
    (
        hToken, 0, &tkp, 0, (PTOKEN_PRIVILEGES) 0, 0
    );
    assert(result);

    result = InitiateSystemShutdown(0, 0, 0, 1, 0);
    assert(result);

    return 0;
}

int main(int argc, char* argv[])
{
    switch (argc)
    {
        case (2)    : break;
        default     : errexit();
    }

    int val = atoi(argv[1]);
```

```
    if (! (val > 0))
    {
        errexit();
    }

    int (*pfx_wait)(int) = ((val <= 24) ? &wait_hrs : &wait_pid);
    int result = (*pfx_wait)(val);

    if (result != NO_ERROR)
    {
        fprintf
        (
            stderr,
            "\aWait routine failed. Check argument validity\n"
        );

        exit(-1);
    }

    return halt();
}
```

A.6 GNUmakefile for Creating an Executable from Chapter 11

Here is a directory-based generic GNUmakefile for creating an executable from C (or C+) sources, using c++ as the compiler:

```
EXECUTABLE :=        $(shell basename  $(shell realpath .))
SOURCES :=           $(wildcard *.c)
OBJECTS :=           $(patsubst %.c, %.o, $(SOURCES))
CC :=        c++
CFLAGS :=        -Wall
LDFLAGS :=         -lpthread
```

```
all :           $(EXECUTABLE)

%.o :           %.c $(wildcard *.h)
        $(CC) $(CFLAGS) -c $< -o $@

$(EXECUTABLE) : $(OBJECTS)
        $(CC) $(OBJECTS) -o $@ $(LDFLAGS)

clean:
        rm -f *.o 2>/dev/null
        rm -f $(EXECUTABLE) 2>/dev/null
```

This GNUmakefile assumes that your project headers and source code files are located in the same directory, the base name of which is used for the executable generated.

The := operator used for assignments in the GNUmakefile requests values to be assessed just once, and not every time the variable is referenced, which is what would happen with the = operator.

The GNUmakefile also automatically pulls in threads support, which many applications need nowadays. If you do not want threads support, just delete the -lpthread setting for LDFLAGS. If you want additional dynamic library libXYZ.so to be linked to, append -lXYZ to the LDFLAGS assignment.

Index

© Manish Jain 2018
M. Jain, *Beginning Modern Unix*, https://doi.org/10.1007/978-1-4842-3528-7

V

Printed in the United States
By Bookmasters

3 1170 01071 8520